THE WINCHESTER POWERHOUSE

THE WINCHESTER POWERHOUSE

The Lives of the Bishops to the
Kingdom of Wessex

AD634 to 1070

Anthony Paice

The Book Guild Ltd

First published in Great Britain in 2024 by
The Book Guild Ltd
Unit E2 Airfield Business Park,
Harrison Road, Market Harborough,
Leicestershire. LE16 7UL
Tel: 0116 2792299
www.bookguild.co.uk
Email: info@bookguild.co.uk
Twitter: @bookguild

Copyright © 2024 Anthony Paice

The right of Anthony Paice to be identified as the author of this
work has been asserted by them in accordance with the
Copyright, Design and Patents Act 1988.

All rights reserved. No part of this publication may be
reproduced, transmitted, or stored in a retrieval system, in any form or by any means,
without permission in writing from the publisher, nor be otherwise circulated in
any form of binding or cover other than that in which it is published and without
a similar condition being imposed on the subsequent purchaser.

Typeset in 12pt Adobe Jenson Pro

Printed and bound by CPI Group (UK) Ltd, Croydon, CR0 4YY

ISBN 978 1835740 835

British Library Cataloguing in Publication Data.
A catalogue record for this book is available from the British Library.

To the largely Hampshire-born and unsung crew of the Royal Navy's 120-ton sloop, HMS Contest, who, in the 1840s, sent sixteen slaving vessels to the bottom and freed over a thousand slaves. Nobody put up a statue to commemorate their fortitude and service to humanity.

CONTENTS

Acknowledgements		ix
Foreword		xi
Introduction		xiii
St Berin	A Missionary Bishop from Rome	1
St Agilbert	The Diplomat from Paris	15
Wine and Lothair	The First Saxon and The Last Frankish Bishops to the West Saxon Kingdom	25
St Haeddi	A Holy Estate Agent	36
Daniel	Counsellor And Scholar	45
Over One Hundred Years of Obscurity		53
St Swithun	The People's Saint	67
Alfred's Bishops		78
The Bishops Of Expansionary Wessex		89
St Aethelwold	Monastic Reformer And Liturgist	100
St Aelfheah	Martyr	116
The Bishops On The Eve Of The Conquest		125
A Look Forward		152
Endnotes		159
Index		181

ACKNOWLEDGEMENTS

It has been a long haul since one lunchtime in the mid-1980s I relieved a moment of frustration at work by flicking idly through the list of Winchester bishops in Crockfords Clerical Directory. The names brought back memories of those spoken of with some reverence during my childhood.

During the long journey of research since there have been both encouragement and detraction, sometimes bordering on mockery. Those who obviously have no feel for the positive forces behind the early development of our liberal society – yawn; their eyes glaze over.

Others, however, have been intrigued and a few, some unknowingly, have provided that fillip every would-be author needs. And this volume might not have appeared but for Saddam Hussain who disturbed my life, as he did the lives of so many others. My persistence in researching the Anglo-Saxon Winchester bishops was my way of diluting his evil effect.

My specific thanks go to Canon Roland Riem, Vice-Dean of the Winchester Cathedral Chapter who listened to what I wanted to do and nodded in sympathy. Barbara Yorke, professor emeritus of Anglo-Saxon history at Winchester University, did the same; she read and commented on an early draft.

Substantial inspiration and support came from Dame Jinty Nelson, a fellow King's historian who sympathized with my argumentation and believed I had something worth publishing.

There is, however, one person who gave me timeless attention and detailed comment as I completed drafts of chapters. My old friend, Dr David Hill, put me right on many aspects ranging from grammar/spelling to a deeper understanding of the sometimes strange ways of the Christian Church.

I have to thank, too, the staff of the Hampshire Record Office, Winchester Cathedral Library, Lambeth Palace Library and the National Archives. They never yawned.

My sometimes singleminded study has tested the patience of two wives, neither of whom anticipated living with an ecclesiastical history nerd. To my late wife, Chris, and to my present wife, Anne, I owe a great deal of gratitude for their understanding, however much their patience might have been tried.

Anthony Paice
Ottershaw Park
20 June 2024

FOREWORD

As an amateur historian fascinated by church history, it gives me great pleasure to write this short foreword to my dear friend Tony Paice's scholarly work on the bishops of Winchester down to the Norman Conquest.

Although living in one of the dioceses recently carved out of Winchester, at heart Tony is a Wessex man with deep and long-standing roots in Winchester. Being a historian among his many other talents, it is natural that Tony should be drawn to and chronicle the lives of the Winchester bishops. This volume is a result of years of painstaking research.

But there is one thing this book is not. It is not a dry historical account based just on the scant verifiable knowledge that is available to the researcher. Tony has managed to bring each chapter to life so, as well as being a mine of information, each is eminently readable. The kingdom of Wessex was so influential in the development of Saxon Britain. The expansion of Wessex into the premier kingdom in what is now England was very much due to the close relationship of the Church to the secular rulers and their dependence on one other. Some might wish for the same today!

Tony's work provides an excellent counterbalance to the many volumes that have been written about the Celtic saints. I trust it will achieve a readership wider than those just interested in ecclesiastical history. It deserves so to do. I eagerly await the next volume.

Charles Gibson (Rev'd)

INTRODUCTION

Standing on top of the Westgate and looking down the length of Winchester High Street, a visitor might wonder how what looks like a modest eighteenth-century country town could ever have been the capital of England, let alone have earned the status of 'city'. True, the huge bulk of the cathedral dominates the skyline, as it does also from the motorway circling to the east, but then something similar could be said of neighbouring Salisbury and its outstanding spire. While gazing up at the Gothic architecture of the cathedral's medieval nave or passing the several chantries housing long-dead episcopal chancellors and treasurers of England, the same visitor will be told that the See of Winchester still ranks fifth in the Anglican hierarchy, well above much larger cities in the country. There is an anachronism here; the question has certainly been asked – why?

The answer is rooted in a history going back nearly fourteen hundred years to the great evangelical surges that brought Christianity back to post-Roman Britain. Of the three waves of conversion which arrived from the sixth century onwards, the last which established the Church in the south of England was, arguably, the most far-reaching and influential. And yet, it has received less recognition than the work of the great Celtic missionaries from Ireland and the late-sixth century thrust from Rome led by St Augustine. This first volume in a long-running study of the lives of the Winchester bishops to the present day traces the story from St Berin's arrival on the south coast in circa 634 to William the Conqueror's invasion; it describes how the Winchester bishops worked in partnership with the Wessex kings to entrench their spiritual and secular powers in parallel and, usually, in a happy and symbiotic relationship. They depended on the other for their advance, the king protecting and endowing the bishop; the latter giving moral and intellectual support emanating – in the eyes of many at the time – from divine providence. The prelates earned the gratitude of their royal hosts in the form of gifts of vast tracts of land in the south of England. This established the See of Winchester as the richest and the most desirable ecclesiastical fiefdom in the country, rivalling all others in Europe.

Bishops were more than stewards of a large estate in which they held the cure of souls. Their position and erudition made them respected counsellors in an expanding kingdom. This attracted even more endowment and the confirmation of earlier grants made in obscurity. By the end of the seventh century, the bishop had an impressive minster in Winchester; by the tenth, he had two standing side by side, now totally lost, except to the archaeologist. Within their walls lay centres of culture and scholarship which helped educate and civilise the king's court, while propagating the Christian message wherever Wessex held sway. Ideas and missionaries exported across the North Sea with the encouragement of the Winchester bishops played a major part in the conversion of the Low Countries and much of the Rhine Valley.

The spiritual authority of a bishop and his hold on the minds of the people were other important contributions, particularly in areas contested by other petty rulers. This explains why Winchester bishops came to hold estates in the west as far as Somerset and in the north as far as Oxfordshire. Possession of the Surrey Thames shore would keep them the closest of all their peers to the heart of government after London became the nation's capital. As the kingdom of Wessex consolidated, the secular and ecclesiastical courts cooperated closely with one another. In bad times, the patronage and spiritual requirements of the Church at parochial level provided the infrastructure which glued society together. Wessex would not have survived the Norse invasions of the ninth and late tenth centuries without it. This is in striking contrast with the collapse of all the other petty kingdoms.

The earlier bishops are wrapped in legend and, where accounts of their lives have survived, these are usually written centuries later. Moreover, the authors passed on headline miracles rather than empirical fact. Nevertheless, a towering figure like Bishop Aethelwold did not simply sit down in his cell and invent the cult of St Swithun; on the contrary, he could draw on an oral record and appreciation of the saint as a great man. Sadly, the documentation which would confirm the saint's reputation does not exist. And what the Vikings did not destroy in monastic libraries, the Normans censored out. A major drawback in this study has been the sheer lack of sources and the non-contemporaneous and unreliable aspects of those that have survived. We are left with a residue of incomplete and often biased accounts lacking in collateral. A prime example is Bede's much acclaimed history of the early English Church: it should not be taken at face value. Although without equal, it is one version of what happened through the eyes of a man hundreds of miles removed from the scene and with a mind presenting a strong political slant. Other chroniclers are few and far between. What they could not pin down, they guessed at. Apart, perhaps, from Aelfric of Eynsham writing at the turn of the tenth and eleventh centuries, who lamented the lack of recorded detail on Swithun, his fellows presented their tales of the past as if they were *gospel* truth. It is received, not researched, history. How the *Anglo-Saxon Chronicle*, first compiled during the reign of King Alfred in the later years of the ninth century, was able to identify dates from the arrival of Cerdic the Saxon over four hundred years earlier with any degree of accuracy is hard to imagine.

Legends and chronicles have to be placed in the context of their time but, unlike myth, there is usually more than an element of truth in them. In this account I have had to accept the paucity of facts available while considering what is most likely to have happened. It is, however, too easy to dismiss ancient historians; yes, they did not have the tools available to their modern counterparts, but it is sometimes forgotten that their monastic libraries held manuscripts that have disappeared since their time. There is very little in the Winchester Cathedral Cartulary that predates the Conquest, but in the eighth to tenth centuries there would have been a wealth of material in the scriptorium to consult and from which to work. Even in the fifteenth century, the chronicler of the day could refer to what might have been highly informative sources that were lost either during the Reformation or when the Parliamentarian soldiers sacked the cathedral, twice, during the Civil War.

In some respects, state records of the Anglo-Saxon period have fared better than the religious. Property law requires documentation which is rich in disputation and re-confirmation, in turn revealing the names of the parties and an insight into reasons why grants were made at the time. It also includes many uncertainties and, unsurprisingly where material wealth is at stake, a good deal of fraud. But the very fact that a fraudulent document exists raises the question why. Taking the bulk of charter evidence together, it is possible to assess the gratitude of the king to his bishop for counsel and support in successive campaigns in the field. Added to this was the extent to which episcopal administration of estates was considered by the ruler to be a secure form of tenure in areas still vulnerable to infiltration from rivals.

There is one more general observation that marks out the Anglo-Saxons from their Norman successors. Throughout the rise of Wessex, we hear little or nothing of prominent lay counsellors at the king's court, down to the eleventh century, at least. They must have existed, but perhaps such personalities were also censored out by the Church's monopoly of the record. Nevertheless, one might have expected rather more praise – or criticism – to have been accorded to secular figures; there was no lack of it after the Conquest. In Wessex, however, from the arrival of Berin onwards, it was the bishop who occupied the key advisory position due to his learning, eloquence and holy wisdom. Indeed, he sometimes became the very conscience of the king who, as his domain expanded, also found his need for men with administrative qualities increasing. With a monastic community producing a steady stream of literate clerks, it was only a matter of time before their skills were in demand. What subsequently developed into a royal chancellery and treasury at Winchester stemmed directly from this pool. By the end of the period the stature, sometimes charisma, of the 'royal' See of Winchester had been transformed into an institution – a powerhouse. It is no accident that the last bishop before the Conquest – Stigand – should have held on to both the Winchester and Canterbury Sees; as an embryonic chancellor, he was – beneath the king – head of state administration and, beneath the pope, head of the Church in England.

ST BERIN

A MISSIONARY BISHOP FROM ROME

Some time in the year 634,[1] after the winter storms had abated, a longboat – not unlike the one found buried at Sutton Hoo – slid out of the mouth of the River Seine and into the open sea dividing the Continent from Britannia. It remained within sight of land until it reached the tip of the Cotentin Peninsula, when it struck due north across the open sea for the southern tip of the Isle of Wight, then occupied by tribes originating from Jutland. Given a favourable wind, an experienced helmsman did not expect to be out of sight of land for more than an hour or so. Once off the island's south coast, the incoming tide washed his vessel into the sheltered waters of the Solent. It first touched land on a pebble beach to the west of Portsmouth Harbour, possibly Stokes Bay. Here, as was customary, the passengers jumped ashore and kissed the shingle in gratitude for their safe crossing of the Channel. On this occasion, they had additional cause for relief, for according to legend, the voyage had encountered exceptionally heavy seas. One account of their arrival suggests that the boat had actually foundered.[2]

Hugging the coast, the oarsmen would have taken the boat on to the already thriving Jutish port, later known as Hamwih or Hamtun, now Southampton. There is much room for speculation about what happened next. The boat's complement would surely have rested at the port and have made first contact with the elders of a local population curious about its business and onward destination. The people of Hamtun were used to 'foreigners' from the other side of the Channel, but these travellers were no ordinary traders. They had come to the right place, however, for the town was the centre of authority in the area and would later lend its name to the Saxon shire – Hampshire.[1] The Winchester tradition has it that the small party was in search of the petty king, Cynegils, for advice and support for their quest. Where was he? Some historians would argue that, if he regarded anywhere as his base, it would have been Hamtun.[3] This argument conflicts with the traditional connection between Cynegils[4] and Venta, present-day Winchester, some twelve miles inland. There is a problem with this linkage, however, which only dates from largely post-Conquest sources: no archaeological evidence for Saxon occupation of the old fortified Roman *civitas* (or local tribal capital) in the early seventh century has ever been discovered.[5] All we can reasonably contend, therefore, is that, following disembarkation, the passengers, as strangers, sought the whereabouts and eventually found the protection of Cynegils, the local Saxon tribal leader, whose influence seems then to have extended as far as the upper Thames Valley.[6]

The principal passenger on board was a missionary sent from Italy. Berin, whose name was subsequently Latinised as Birinus, came with a resolve to bring the Christian gospel to the fiercely pagan people known as the Angles who were thought to inhabit the British interior.[7] According to legend, Berin's reputation had gone before him with a story of his walking on water to retrieve an altar cloth he had left on the boat. Putting aside the miraculous, the story suggests that Berin, a devout man of God, held a service of thanksgiving shortly after reaching the shore, but had mislaid the cloth. Wading back to the boat to fetch it, his long white garb, floating on the surface, might easily have given rise to comparisons with Christ walking on the water.

What made Berin embark on such a mission? Was it some personal prayerful ambition or was it part of a wider evangelistic endeavour? Like St Augustine of Canterbury before him, we know very little of the man himself. Far less, in fact. There are no contemporary written accounts and any oral tradition that might have circulated at the time has long since

---

1   Down to the 1940s at least, birth, marriage and death certificates were issued with the heading "County of Southampton", the term also used throughout the Middle Ages.

been forgotten. Writing seventy years later, Bede, the principal chronicler of early English Church history, based at Jarrow, hundreds of miles to the north-east, was not closely informed of events in the south. In contrast, he did at least have second-hand access to the documents which illuminate Augustine's mission in Kent, and which were collated towards the end of the seventh century at Canterbury by the monk Albinus.

Who was Berin?

Berin's name suggests that he was of Germanic or Frankish stock. It is believed that he was born at the end of the sixth century, possibly in Lombardy. The Winchester tradition has it that he was a Benedictine monk at Pope Gregory the Great's St Andrew's monastery on the Caelian Hill in Rome,[8] where Augustine had been prior. It is said that he petitioned Pope Honorius I (625–638) to be sent to Britain as a missionary among those who had resisted Celtic evangelists from the north and Augustine's own endeavours from Kent. Berin's fervour contrasts with that of Augustine, who was instructed by Gregory to leave for Saxon shores and is understood to have been in some fear and trepidation on his way there. Unlike Augustine, too, Berin was consecrated bishop before his departure from Italy, by Asterius, Archbishop of Milan from 629 who died in 640 at Genoa. Berin was provided with a dispensation from Pope Honorius to find his own independent sphere of conversion work where he might establish a new bishopric in Britain. Intriguingly, we know nothing of what the dispensation might have said about the relationship he should have with Canterbury.

The political context

This fresh mission had come nearly forty years after St Augustine's conversion of Aethelbert, the Kentish sub-king, in 597. In the mind of the papacy at least, Augustine's success had already re-established the old Roman ecclesiastical provinces of Canterbury and York. At the turn of the seventh century, however, the Roman Church was becoming increasingly concerned at reports of Celtic missionaries working 'unsupervised' in a land which had earlier produced its fair share of schismatics.[9] Under

Pope Gregory the Great (590–604), therefore, the Church had sought to reassert its jurisdiction over those areas of the British Isles secured for Christianity during the fourth century, and which had sent bishops from London, York and Lincoln to the Council at Nicaea summoned nearly three hundred years earlier, in 325, by the Emperor Constantine.

Although history has been generally kind to Augustine's mission, he failed to push Christianity into southern and central Britain. Those followers who outlived him could not break out of Kent into the Thames Valley because pagan London, increasingly under the influence of the kingdom of Mercia, stood in their way. Indeed, London ejected its bishop within a few years of Augustine's death. Why was a fresh missionary impetus delayed? Given the lacklustre nature of the four short-reigning pontiffs that succeeded Gregory, there was little prospect of encouragement from the Vatican. On 29 October 625, however, a more decisive personality was appointed Bishop of Rome: Honorius I, a devout, if rich, aristocrat, sat in St Peter's chair. A reputed diplomat, he settled a number of tiresome disputes in the Italian peninsula. An admirer of Gregory and tonsured, he promoted monks over secular clergy. He recognised that evangelisation of Britannia had run out of steam and was also concerned at the way Celtic missionaries were veering away from the Roman tradition, notably on the dating of Easter.

Honorius was a man of action: he did not take pleasure in the abstruse debates raging in Rome about the nature of Christ's divinity, which featured a good deal of dogmatic obscurantism over so-called Monothelitism.[10] He sympathised with the Eastern Patriarch, Sergius I, who had written to Rome seeking to persuade Honorius that Church unity should not be compromised by disputes over Christ's status. Nor, Honorius would have argued, should it prejudice missionary efforts in northern Europe, particularly as the political and military turmoil which had raged during the first half of the seventh century in Frankish Gaul had abated. Old Roman roads across to the Channel were again passable for travellers, thanks to the ten-year reign of Dagobert I (629–639), ruler of Neustria, now the area of present-day Brittany and the Seine basin. From his base in Paris, Dagobert had managed to exert an ascendancy over much of the rest of Gaul, bringing with it a peaceful lull for safer travel conditions and some degree of judicial order. With Honorius' blessing, Berin's journey from Rome to the coast of Neustria, via Paris, took place right in the middle of this period. The return to strife-torn conditions, incidentally, goes some way to explaining why, if there was any attempt at discourse between Berin and Rome, no documentary record of it exists. This is in striking contrast to the significant number of earlier letters that have survived between St Augustine and Pope Gregory.

There is also no written evidence of contact between Berin and Canterbury. Two factors were at work. First and foremost, geo-political: the dense forests between Kent and the lands of the West Saxons, coupled with the persistent paganism of the lower Thames Valley, acted as a physical barrier to any dialogue. Secondly, there is more than a hint that Berin saw his mission to convert as no different from that of St Augustine; he was also commissioned by Rome and, therefore, had no reason to report through Canterbury. There is, furthermore, no documentation at this point to confirm whether or not Pope Honorius saw this missionary venture as falling under the authority of Canterbury. Indeed, for both political and geographical reasons, Paris would have been a more natural influence on the West Saxon coast at the time. Moreover, no cadre of literate scribes, secular or ecclesiastical, yet existed at the West Saxon court to write dispatches; there are no charters in the kingdom before the middle of the seventh century, at least amongst those that have survived. This is in striking contrast to the kingdom of Kent.

From the early sixth century, bishops on the Continent, once elected and confirmed in their sees by the local sub-king and his comites or advisers, were virtually irremovable. For a man with episcopal potential, not to mention ambitious missionary zeal, prospects in areas of unconverted Britain would have been doubly attractive. Whilst there is no evidence that Berin himself nursed metropolitan designs, the distinctly separate thrust of his work gave some additional credence to the ambitions of one or two medieval bishops who much later entertained the thought of becoming England's third archbishop.

What awaited Berin?

There is no record of any contact between Rome and the sub-king, Cynegils, before Berin's arrival at Hamtun. Neither do we know what papal guidance the evangelist had; there is nothing that replicates the careful briefing Augustine received from Pope Gregory. Some Christian influences, however, had already permeated Cynegils' court, brought in by trade and other intercourse with Neustria. As Berin passed through Paris, he would surely have sought out the latest intelligence on the situation in southern Britain as well as gifts and tokens of introduction and recommendation. Cynegils, of course, was not literate, but his long reign had established stability and a degree of sophistication in his still-pagan kingdom. According to Bede, however, Berin's goal was not the easier prospects of conversion around Hamtun, where the settlers had merged with pockets of Romano-Christian descendants living in the fertile and fish-rich Itchen and Test valleys[11]; rather, he was bent on the more difficult task of working among the reputedly savage and mysterious people further north, known as the Gewisse, over whom Cynegils' hold was far from secure.[12] The name suggests the progeny of some warrior ancestor, perhaps a sometime disaffected rival to the leaders of the 'soft south'; the debate on their origin is inconclusive. The wilder northern hills of Hampshire, however, would have been a more natural habitat for such a people who could have improved their subsistence economy by descending into the Thames Valley to raid commercial traffic or to exact 'protection money' from traders and travellers alike using the river as a highway.

Rivalries between petty kingships

Was there any other reason why Berin and a small band of Benedictine-inspired companions should choose a landing in present-day Hampshire rather than penetrate the British interior from the Thames estuary? Developments elsewhere suggest that there was. To the east, Christianity already had a tenuous hold on the little kingdom of Kent, despite its rejection by the East Saxons and then by the advancing Mercians in the Lower Thames around London. In East Anglia, another missionary bishop,

Felix, only just arrived there in the year 630 from Rome, was preaching the Christian message. Elsewhere, the picture was less encouraging: in 626 or 627, the petty kingship of Mercia, peopled by those Angles who had settled in the West as far as the Welsh border, passed to the infamous and rampantly pagan Penda. Within a few years, he had established hegemony over a vast area stretching from the Thames Valley to the Humber. True, in the north, Christianity had made a significant breakthrough when, in 627, the Italian-born bishop of York, Paulinus, baptised Edwin, King of Northumbria – but this was short-lived. By 633, the Northumbrians had been overwhelmed by Penda and the Welsh at the Battle of Hatfield Chase; Edwin had been killed and Paulinus had fled.

Almost miraculously, however, a new Christian champion, Oswald, rallied the Northumbrians in the following year, defeated the Welsh at Heavenfield in the north-west and secured an uneasy peace with Penda. Oswald now sought an alliance against Mercia by extending feelers towards the mercurial Gewisse, now loosely aligned with Cynegils in the south against Penda's expansionism. Berin's arrival in Hamtun on the eve of this new alliance was fortuitous, to say the least, rather than mere coincidence. He was presented with an opportunity to make himself useful to Cynegils and to offer counsel. Rome and Paris would have been delighted, since Berin was now treading the path that Augustine had followed in gaining influence with Aethelbert in Kent over thirty years previously. His clerical skills were doubtless put to good use during the preparations for the impending meeting with Oswald. He would have helped write dispatches – in Latin – and set up arrangements with Oswald's own clerical – and Christian – counsellors. So Berin acted as both diplomat and evangelist. As a Germanic speaker, he had sufficient grasp of the local patois to discuss important issues with Cynegils, perhaps assisted by an interpreter from Dagobert's court.

A baptism in the Thames

The two kings agreed to meet at Dorchester-on-Thames (Oxon), then very much a frontier town. Berin's journey north from Hamtun would have kept to the River Itchen, the trout-laden chalk-stream meandering across a wide and wooded flood plain. Here and there, signs of Romano-British cultivation and ruined farms were still evident. Given the deterioration in the road network, not to mention the feuding between Jutish and Saxon peoples, a river passage would have been more sensible and comfortable. At Venta, the Itchen divided into a number of swift-flowing, but shallow, streams which made further navigation impossible. Here still existed the ruins of Roman dwellings and fortifications of the abandoned tribal capital, which would have attracted myths and dubious history,[13] even Arthurian-type sagas: the patriarch, Cerdic, was said to have been buried within the ruins. Berin's onward journey was through more open country along the Roman road, via Silchester, to Dorchester[14] for the historic summit with Oswald. There, Cynegils not only swore allegiance to Oswald, the new Northumbrian king, and gave his reputedly beautiful daughter, Cyneburga, in marriage to him, but he was also baptised by Berin in the River Thames, close to where Dorchester Abbey stands today. Oswald looked on as godfather and raised his ally from the fontal waters. Following the example of Christ's baptism in the Jordan, Cynegils would have been totally immersed, arguing for a ceremony during the warmer months.

Berin's role must have impressed both kings, for he won their joint approval to continue his missionary work in and around Dorchester. Here Berin set down his bishop's stool,[15] as first pastor to the West Saxons. But why Dorchester? Although only a small village today, Dorchester was, until the end of the Roman period at least, a fortified town at an important crossing on the Upper Thames. Like Venta, it had enjoyed *civitas* status and, within its walls, some sub-Roman, even Christian, tradition would have survived. As the Gewisse had expanded their settlements as far north and west as Benson and Eynsham from the late sixth century onwards, Dorchester grew in importance as a centre of communications on the Thames frontier.

With the uncertainties posed by Penda's ascendancy, the value of the town as a key administrative and military base increased further. Had the ambitions of the two kings been realised and their common foe defeated, Dorchester rather than Winchester might have become the capital and centre of a larger confederation. Whether Dorchester could ever have vied with Winchester as a future royal capital is less certain, if only on racial grounds; the population in the surrounding country were largely Angles and a totally different tribal grouping from that of Cerdic's people. Their loyalty would have been less assured, particularly with the rise of Penda's Mercia.

Berin's conversion of the area to a gospel of peace, however, would have gone hand-in-hand with any policy of consolidation pursued by Cynegils and the containment of Penda by Oswald. Bede's wording is indicative: he records that the two kings conferred Dorchester on Berin "after many churches had been built and consecrated and many peoples called to the Lord by his pious behaviour". This suggests that after the royal baptism Berin was allowed to pursue his chosen mission among the local Angles for sound political reasons, but that formal recognition of his episcopal rights and status was delayed until he had proved his worth. According to Bede, the actual grant of land to Berin was made by King Oswald; this must have occurred before 5 August 642, the day that Oswald was slain by Penda.

Legacy and assessment

In geographical terms, Berin's achievement appears to have been quite modest. The tangible evidence of his success is slight, probably because the main resource around Dorchester for buildings was timber in contrast to ragstone-rich Kent where Augustine's mission had built more substantially. The village of Berinsfield, less than three miles along the Roman road from Dorchester to the strategically important Roman legionary fortress of Alcester (Warwickshire), has retained his name, although any surviving archaeological traces would likely have been destroyed by the construction of the Royal Air Force base there, or during redevelopment in the 1960s once it was abandoned. Nevertheless, the church of St Mary and St Berin, built by volunteers in 1961, stands as a testimony to the evangelist's memory and, aptly, is a symbol of ecumenical co-operation between the local Anglican and Roman Catholic congregations who share use of the building. All Saints' church at Wing in Buckinghamshire, some twenty miles north-east of Dorchester, may have been founded during Berin's lifetime or shortly afterwards. It claims great age and is probably built over a Roman edifice, as the use of many stray red tiles in the masonry suggests. Perhaps the missionary had been informed of or found an isolated Christian community there, still worshipping in a long since disappeared basilica. All Saints has a remarkably robust nave which could indicate its foundation on a much older and substantial building. Both examples tend to confirm that Berin continued to look to the pagans beyond the Thames for his new converts, leaving the people to the south to succumb to Christian influences now at work through royal patronage. However, many would have resisted the introduction of a new religion: oak worship persisted strongly in the New Forest which then stretched well to the north of Winchester. Further to the west, strong Celtic Christian influences would have proved too great a challenge for Berin's virtually lone mission – if he had been minded to look in that direction.

His main achievement, however, was the conversion of Cynegils and other important leaders of the peoples south of the Thames. He is supposed to have baptised two of Cynegils' sons: in 636, Cwichelm, his eldest and confederate-in-arms in fights with Penda and British tribes (who then promptly died), and Cutred in 639. Berin failed, at the outset, to win over Cenwealh, Cynegils' second son and successor in 643, who had previously married Penda's daughter in what was an ill-fated union. Cenwealh rejected his wife and was driven out of his kingdom by Penda as a result. It was not until 648 when, after three years' exile, Cenwealh was helped back on to his throne by his converted brother Cutred that conversion was consolidated in the royal household. In the same year, a grateful Cenwealh is recorded as having granted a large tract of land at Ashdown on the Berkshire Downs to his 'kinsman' Cutred. Stenton, the eminent Anglo-Saxon historian, argued that this represented more of an administrative area or province than a mere estate. If so, the king was delegating responsibility to his Christian brother for an area in the path of Penda's territorial ambitions. Having made a personal enemy of Penda when he put away his daughter, Cenwealh had been compelled to seek refuge with the East Angles, where he fell under the influence of the Christian king, Anna. History does not tell us why Cenwealh divorced his wife, but the act would have predated his conversion.

Thus, by 648 at least, from deep down in the much safer south, Cenwealh had recognised the advantages of the new religion and, as a token of his gratitude, caused work to start on the first Saxon church to be built at Venta on a site just to the north of the present cathedral. The association with Cerdic's legendary burial place must have been a factor. As Bishop to the West Saxon royal family, so the story goes, Berin was summoned from his area of mission to dedicate what was to become the 'Old Minster' to the Holy Trinity in honour of St Peter and St Paul. The choice of saints is indicative: it would certainly have met with the approval of Rome, since the papacy traced its doctrinal authority back to the two evangelists.

In a predominantly pagan land where men and women were all too aware of their mortality, Berin brought a message of faith in an afterlife linked to the pursuit of goodness in their lives. An existence after death was not, of course, a new concept, but the account of Christ's resurrection was unique; it was used as strong evidence that there could be surety beyond belief. To the Anglo-Saxons, who had their own gods to worship, it may have seemed more attractive than the Pelagian denial of Christ's divinity. Furthermore, the insistence that there was only one all-powerful and all-knowing God exerted a strong influence on the leaders of the time who came to fear that they might be answerable to such a higher authority. From now on, they could yet repeat the cruel actions of the past but, in the cold light of dawn, they might increasingly reflect on past misdeeds and seek the repentance and forgiveness Christianity offered – to save them from eternal damnation.

Although Cenwealh's personal motivation in causing a church to be built at Venta might be clear enough, Berin, based around Dorchester, was hardly in a position to direct its construction. Cerdic's burial place as a good candidate for the site was not the only consideration. The crowded and, potentially vulnerable, port of Hamtun would not have been an obvious choice for a holy project – not when there was a vacant, already revered and protected plot a few miles up the Itchen, undoubtedly evoking all sorts of venerated ghosts from the past. We cannot tell when Cenwealh first sent his foresters out into the surrounding woods to fetch timber for a prototype church. All we can say is that the building eventually erected was made – exceptionally – of stone and appears to have served as a cathedral, a bishop's church, from early on in its existence. The Old Minster – like Rome – was not built in a day. Rather, it was a project lasting for most if not all of Cenwealh's reign. And it is at this point that the archaeology shows that Venta was being re-populated,[16] undoubtedly by the families of artisans now being employed there.

Traditionally, and based on the *Anglo-Saxon Chronicle*, Berin is thought to have died on 3 December 650, and was buried at his church in Dorchester, not at Venta. However, his body was not to remain there long. Perhaps as early as 679, Bishop Haeddi (676–705) translated it to Venta. It was moved again by Bishop Aethelwold (963–984) on 4 September 980, this time to a shrine inside his 'New Minster'. Half a century later, in 1035, King Cnut is believed to have built another new shrine. Thereafter, there is some confusion over Berin's final resting place. It is known that Bishop Henry de Blois (1129–1174) built yet another new shrine in 1150, but it is also alleged that Berin's bier was returned to Dorchester Abbey. Given his ambitions to promote Winchester to an archdiocese, would Bishop Henry have lightly yielded up such saintly remains?

Nonetheless, twelfth-century stained glass installed shortly after its construction and depicting scenes from Berin's life survives at Dorchester Abbey and can be found behind the *sedilia*[2] below the south window of the sanctuary. Early in the thirteenth century, the Austin Canons at Dorchester claimed to possess his relics. This led to an inconclusive papal inquiry conducted in 1224 by Stephen Langton, the then Archbishop of Canterbury. Ironically, the pope at the time was the namesake – Honorius III – of Berin's original sponsor.

---

2   A bank of stone seats often set into the chancel wall on the south side of the altar and used by the priest or his assistant when not officiating during the Mass.

By the thirteenth century, miracles and visions were reported at Dorchester and the body of an unknown early bishop was discovered beneath the abbey, but these remains were too late to be those of Berin. This, however, did not deter the Dorchester claimants from adding more stained glass in the sanctuary's east window illustrating Berin's baptism of Cynegils. In 1320, at the end of a major rebuilding programme, a shrine was erected in the new and spacious south choir aisle. Sadly, the shrine was destroyed by the New Model Army during the Civil War. It was only in 1964 that a monument was erected by the then Bishop of Oxford, the right reverend Harry Carpenter, and was dedicated also to the memory of the first suffragan Bishop of Dorchester, Gerald Burton Allen (1939–1952).

The celebration of Berin's feast day, on 3 December, was eclipsed by those of later and more prominent Wessex prelates, and the influence of Dorchester loyalists could never have measured that of ascendant Winchester. The date of the feast day was still extant in the late ninth century Winchester Calendar, but by the eleventh century it had been omitted from the Old Sarum Calendar which was then being promoted throughout much of England. According to Goscelin, the eleventh century Benedictine biographer from northern France, the principal centres of Berin's cult were at Winchester, Dorchester and Abingdon Abbey, where sermons and lives of the saints which mentioned him survived until the Reformation. Berin's feast day was also included in a Roman martyrology from the late sixteenth century. Since Berin was not a martyr, it is tempting to see this as a post-Reformation political snub originating from the Vatican. Incidentally, the Roman Catholic chapel of St Birinus at Dorchester boasts a nineteenth-century figure of Berin with a prominent Roman nose!

Berin was a man imbued with a strong sense of purpose who delivered an effective message in the vernacular and with a conviction which stirred the minds of important political figures of his time. There is a story that he took his followers up Berin's Hill, over three hundred metres high, just to the south-east of Wallingford, where he had built a cell and preached from the summit. We know nothing of his companions, but one thing is certain: none of them was able to replace Berin on his death. This leads to the conclusion either that he was cut off from fresh and younger reinforcements from Rome, or that his organisational abilities did not match his oratory. Although Berin planted the Christian faith firmly in the West Saxon royal household, it would be some decades before the bishopric he founded settled down as a cohesive, administrative entity. Consequently, the Wessex See, though eventually falling under the sway of Rome and Canterbury, remained detached and uncertain in its ecclesiastical allegiance for much of the rest of the seventh century. But its star was firmly attached to the fortunes of the emerging house of Wessex, a factor which eventually gave the bishops of Winchester a national role and status few other diocesans could match until well after the Reformation.

Neither Berin nor his papal sponsor, Honorius I, have the reputations they deserve. In the latter's case, he was 'anathematised' (cursed) at the Third Council of Constantinople (Sixth Ecumenical Council) in 680/1. He was falsely accused, long after his death, of not accepting that Christ was both human and divine. A man like Honorius, however, took more notice of what Christ preached than of fruitless argumentation between pompous theorists. He was manifestly not a believer in Pelagianism, one who refuses to recognise Christ's divinity, but that is what he was condemned for.

ST AGILBERT

THE DIPLOMAT FROM PARIS

In the year 663,[17] just as the autumn weather was starting to threaten at sea, several large groups of mounted strangers passed through the settlement of a small fishing community and rode up to the craggy outcrop overlooking the bay. The local population were used to the holy men and women who had started to rebuild the old Roman settlement ruins on the clifftop, but these fresh arrivals were different. They included men whose rich clothing and ornaments proclaimed them to be of high birth, and who were accompanied by large retinues of warriors and counsellors.

The place was Streanaeshealh, an obscure name now identified with the port of Whitby on the then Northumbrian coast. The gathering in the Benedictine double monastery, founded only six years previously to accommodate both men and women, would become famously known as the Synod of Whitby, whose deliberations would settle the course of early English Church history, finally securing the dominance of Roman over Celtic Christianity in these islands. Among the more prominent visitors was Agilbert, the second Bishop to the West Saxons and a long way from his seat set down at Dorchester-on-Thames.

Schism

In the years after Berin's death there had been a deepening of the doctrinal division between those areas, mainly in the north, where the Celtic missionaries – inspiration for the Lindisfarne Gospels[18] – had been most active in evangelisation, and those in the south, where the influence of Rome had taken hold. In 633, Rome's foray into the north had been blocked when Bishop Paulinus was forced to flee from York following the defeat the previous year of his Northumbrian royal sponsor, King Edwin, at the hands of the Mercians. In the absence of Paulinus, the Celtic missionaries had continued to expand their work and spread their interpretations of Christian doctrine. Dialogue continued between the two camps, however, and in the end both sides agreed to meet at Whitby to thrash out their differences, which to the modern mind, at least, seem more to do with custom than fundamentals. The resulting Synod was attended by two rulers – Oswiu, King of Northumbria, and his son, Alhfrith, sub-king of Deira, based at York. The contending parties were led by Bishop Colmán of Lindisfarne, who supported the Celtic tradition and claimed precedence over Canterbury, and, on the Roman side, by their spokesman Wilfrid, a priest who was closely advised – and was fed his lines – by Bishop Agilbert.

The second Bishop to the West Saxons

Yet Agilbert was not from Rome; nor was he a West Saxon, although it has been suggested that his name in Old English – Aethelbert – could point to a Kentish connection.[19] He was, in fact, the son of a Neustrian noble of Frankish descent called Betto and the first cousin of St Audoin, born in 609 in the village of Sancy, now close to the Franco-Luxembourg border. Audoin, at the age of ten, and his younger brothers were considered mischievous, but their behaviour changed miraculously after their baptism by St Columbanus (540–615), the charismatic Irish monk and founder of several monastic houses in Gaul and in the Alps. At the age of only twenty-one, Audoin had helped the Abbess Theodechild to found the Benedictine double monastery at Jouarre in 630, and it was here that Agilbert began his religious life. Audoin went on to become Bishop of Rouen in 649 and the name of his diocese derives from the set of rules, or *Ruh Audoin*, he set down for his monks. He was also a prominent member of Dagobert I's court in Paris at the time of Berin's arrival. Audoin was known to have sent missionaries to pagan areas; he would have been a sponsor, perhaps even a role model, for his cousin, Agilbert.

Agilbert was too young to have remembered the momentous visit of Columbanus, but knowledge of it may have determined him to seek out the holy places in Ireland which had nurtured so great a religious mind. Like Berin before him, he took passage in an open boat from the Neustrian coast, but sailed west on a rather more perilous course which would have encountered contrary winds and currents. It is likely that, en route, his boat would have been forced to take shelter and re-provision on the Cornish coast where he may have made his first contact with Celtic Christians. Once in southern Ireland, he toured the religious centres which had been established there in the sixth century and was able to broaden the base of his earlier studies in Neustria. In contrast to its decline in pagan-invaded Britain, Christianity had flourished in Ireland. Those who had reached the island in the decades before Agilbert's voyage brought with them the monastic ideas and rule of the great Benedict, which were then re-exported to Frankish Gaul by men like Columbanus. Whatever Agilbert might have learnt from Audoin, about the importance of Christian discipline, had already been consolidated in Ireland. At the same time, he gained experience of the Celtic peoples and learnt about their nuanced interpretation of the Gospel story, particularly over the dating of the death and resurrection of Jesus which, so Bede contended, led to their conflict with Rome over when Easter should be celebrated.[20] After several years of study in a cradle of western Christianity, Agilbert returned to Neustria where he was consecrated as a missionary bishop, possibly by Audoin either at Rouen or Paris. He would retain strong connections with both cities.

It is not clear why Agilbert left Neustria again within a short space of time. One theory is that he was a member of a faction opposed to the mayor of Paris, Erchinoald,[21] and went into exile. The *Anglo-Saxon Chronicle* points to Agilbert receiving the West Saxon See in 649 shortly before Berin's death, which would suggest that he was already in the kingdom waiting in the wings. Confusingly, the Canterbury-written text of the *Chronicle* adds that he was ordained at the same time.[22] But a man of Agilbert's background and stature would hardly have arrived in the West Saxon court without confirmed pastoral and political credentials.

After the experience of his five-hundred-mile voyage to Ireland, there would have been little fear of repeating his predecessor's cross-Channel journey to the West Saxon court. Once there, his learned reputation, supported by messages of recommendation from Neustria, would have impressed King Cenwealh. During Berin's declining years, Agilbert was surely the man on the spot to succeed at Dorchester-on-Thames. That he was accepted as such is a further demonstration of the Neustrian or Francian influence rather than that of Canterbury in the early days of Wessex conversion.

The resurgence of Christianity in the North

Agilbert's appointment came at a time when the arrival of fresh ideas from Neustria and Ireland was turning the tide against the age-old paganism of the Anglo-Saxons, at least as far as their rulers were concerned. Contending petty kings were coming to realise that clever counsel which built alliances could reduce the need for strong-arm tactics and confrontation. The God that Berin and Agilbert talked about could also bring about victory when battle was unavoidable. In Northumbria, for example, the Christian beliefs of Oswiu were strengthened dramatically when, in 654, against all the odds, he defeated and slew pagan Penda, the same man who had slain his brother, Oswald, in 641 at Maserfelth. The night before the battle near present-day Leeds, Oswiu had prayed earnestly for victory and, miraculously, the next day, important Welsh allies failed to turn up to fulfil their undertaking to Penda. Having received a bloody nose, the Mercians, under Penda's son, Wulfhere, now turned their attentions to expansion into West Saxon territory; the heat was thereby off in the north and socio-religious issues that had lain dormant began to surface, principally a resurgence of the Celtic tradition.

A lobbyist for the Roman cause

While he would have been impressed by the charisma and achievements of Celtic saints like Columbanus, Agilbert's upbringing in Neustria, dominated by the Roman tradition, left him in full acceptance of prime obedience to papal authority. For even the Irish St Columbanus, founder of the famous Luxeuil monastery and a number of daughter communities on the Continent, had submitted to Pope Gregory I on the question of Easter – as far back as the beginning of the century. Indeed, the Church in Ireland had also submitted to Rome long before the Synod of Whitby. What the missionary bishops backed by Rome faced in northern Britain, therefore, was a determinedly independent, yet increasingly isolated, Celtic tradition that had kept the Gospel alive after rival efforts had faltered. Centred on the religious community of Iona founded late in the previous century by the famed St Columba, its main contentions concerned the date of Easter and the shape of the tonsure worn by monks. The dating of Easter also carried secular considerations: as the early English kings came to accept Christianity, they too had an interest in uniformity. How could a king celebrate Easter if his queen, brought up in a different tradition, was still days away from the most important Christian festival of the year – moreover, after having observed a Lenten fast?

How much time Agilbert actually spent in Dorchester is impossible to say; unlike Berin, he was said by Bede not to have understood the vernacular. Berin had remained in the mission field on the boundaries of West Saxon influence but had somehow got his message across at the itinerant court. By Agilbert's arrival, however, Mercian military pressure was increasing, which would have caused Cenwealh to retreat south, taking his bishop with him. If so, Agilbert would have had little missionary impact in the Thames Valley. Judging by the appointment in the mid-650s of the Francian-educated Deusdedit, a Saxon, as Archbishop of Canterbury, probably with King Cenwealh's support, local clerics of quality were already becoming available for Church posts. Agilbert, therefore, could have recommended one of these to act as his locum, either in Dorchester or Venta.

It is hard to escape the conclusion that an implicit reason for his arrival in Britain was to carry out a diplomatic offensive on Rome's behalf. We know that, at least two or three years before the gathering at Whitby, he left the West Saxons to their own devices and travelled north to argue for the Roman tradition and, logically, supremacy. Sometime in 661, he is believed to have convinced King Oswiu's son, Alhfrith of Deira, of the validity of the Roman case. In achieving this momentous coup – and like Augustine and Berin before him – he was helped by a senior royal female; in this case, the king's wife, Eanfled, who was already observing the Roman dating of Easter before Agilbert arrived at the Deiran court. This is hardly surprising since she was a daughter of King Edwin, the former King of Northumbria slain in 632, whose wife was, in turn, a daughter of King Aethelbert of Kent, St Augustine's first major convert. Faced with a family predicament and on advice from Agilbert, Oswiu and Alhfrith convened the Whitby Synod to decide whether it was Rome or Iona who had the stronger claim to legitimacy. Agilbert's influence was all the greater since, in the months leading up to the Synod, several of his colleagues, including Archbishop Deusdedit, had succumbed to the plague. Agilbert was, therefore, the most senior member of the Roman delegation present.

Agilbert's role at Whitby

Agilbert had already gained a reputation as a learned negotiator, but he also brought with him an understanding of the arguments adduced by both parties. His one disadvantage was that, as a diplomat, he was more used to one-to-one conversations, almost certainly with the aid of an interpreter. He probably found it more difficult to handle large gatherings of people speaking a variety of dialects than he would a dialogue with individual leaders in which his powers of persuasion were clearly formidable. Fortunately, he had with him the Abbot of Ripon and a future saint, Wilfrid, whom he had ordained in 661. Wilfrid had a breadth of experience and travel which, despite his Northumbrian upbringing, energised his opposition to the more introspective Celts – and he was a master of the vernacular, as Bede contends. He also had associations in south-east Hampshire where, during his mission to convert the Jutes in the Meon Valley, he would go on to found the original church at Warnford in 681.[23]

As chairman, King Oswiu called on Colmán, Bishop of Lindisfarne, supported by Cedd, Bishop to the East Saxons, to speak first.[24] Colmán sought to demolish the Roman argument which, he conceded, was based on St Peter's position as the first leader of the Christian Church and, after being handed down by the early Christian fathers, was issued ultimately as doctrine at the ecumenical Council of Nicaea. He drew, instead, on earlier calculations derived from Anatolius, a disciple of St John, whose eyewitness account of Christ's death (John 19:14) was the more authoritative. Peter, he might have added, had run away, unlike John who stayed to look after Christ's mother. With some justification, the Celtic party could claim that their stand was based on computations made much earlier than those accepted at Nicaea. And if there was ever any substance in the belief that would have prevailed at the time – that Joseph of Arimathea, if not present at the Crucifixion, then only hours afterwards, first brought Christianity to Celtic Britain – then Colmán's argumentation would have been doubly valid in the eyes of his supporters.[25]

Oswiu then invited Agilbert to introduce the Roman argument, but the bishop deferred to his 'disciple', Wilfrid, whose views he said were the same as his. And, Agilbert confessed, Wilfrid spoke the vernacular, which he had never mastered. Wilfrid's subsequent vigorous oration is well-documented and praised by Bede and it established him as a leading light in the English Church.[26] Be that as it may, primed by Agilbert, Oswiu's mind was already made up before the Synod convened, and it was his mentor who counselled him when to play the secular trump card. Who, Oswiu asked, held the keys to Heaven and was the rock on which Christ's Church was built? As the Northumbrian king made this point, he would have been aware that the religious house in which he stood was dedicated to St Peter. Moreover, its founder in 657, St Hilda, was hosting the synod. The king's intervention was probably staged: no one would deny that Heaven's keyholder was Peter, the man whom Christ had chosen to lead his disciples after the Ascension; faced with this argumentation, no secular leader would have wished to offend the saint who could bar them from Paradise. It was a foregone conclusion that the Roman case should be accepted and, bitterly disappointed, Colmán resigned his bishopric and later abandoned Northumbria for Ireland. The Celtic cause had lost its principal proponent and even St Cuthbert (circa 634–687), who became

Prior at Lindisfarne, submitted to Rome shortly afterwards. What took place at Whitby, therefore, was the culmination of a diplomatic process which Agilbert had orchestrated during the lead-up to the Synod. If Wilfrid was the actor, Agilbert was the director.

Agilbert's dismissal and subsequent career

Agilbert's authority in the Church remained undiminished and, in the absence of an archbishop in Canterbury, he consecrated several bishops the following year to replace those killed by the plague. They included Wilfrid, as Bishop of York, but this act was conducted "with great splendour at the royal estate (vicus) known as Compiegne",[27] since Agilbert had by then returned to Neustria. His decision to leave Britain was induced by developments in Wessex during his absence in the north. Bede writes that King Cenwealh, "after many years",[28] had grown tired of his bishop's foreign tongue and had looked for a replacement. That may have been the ostensible reason for Cenwealh's high-handedness, but it is more likely that he was frustrated by the prolonged absence of his peripatetic counsellor. He needed a ready adviser at his court, not a foreigner who seemed to be more interested in Church politics than in the affairs of Wessex. Accordingly, while Agilbert was still away in the north, Cenwealh introduced a new bishop at 'Wintancaster', thus in effect dividing the See. His choice of a Saxon gave substance to Bede's assertion about language, albeit this had not been a problem for Cenwealh in his relationship with Berin. Nor would it affect his choice of a Francian bishop in the future. Indeed, there may have been further political reason for the change: Dorchester was increasingly remote from the retreating West Saxon court and remained the centre of a different tribal grouping which was falling further under the influence of the by now ascendant Mercians. Indeed, when Chertsey Abbey on the Lower Thames was founded in 666 by Bishop Earconwold of London, it was King Wulfhere of Mercia, not Cenwealh, who issued the charter from his stronghold at Thame in Oxfordshire, less than twenty miles from Dorchester.

The king's decision offended Agilbert deeply, and he abandoned what was left of his See at Dorchester for a few months' stay with Alhfrith and

Wilfrid in Deira; he also visited the East Anglian court. But he was not a refugee since he was never in any physical danger from Cenwealh; he was simply too big a personality to continue as a bishop with a much-reduced area of authority. When he is next heard of, he is back in Francia – at Paris – where he succeeded Bishop Importunus whose last known attested charter is dated 666 or 667. Agilbert's reputation would have preceded him, and he was back, after all, in a country where he could be understood. There is the suggestion that the mayor of the Francian palace from 658, the notorious and paranoid Ebroin, had been instrumental in the preferment, but there is no evidence that Agilbert was closely aligned with him. It is more likely that he remained aloof from the cockpit of Neustrian politics which brought about Ebroin's deposition in 673, by which time Agilbert was dying or even dead. If he was involved in the mayor's removal, contemporary sources are remarkably silent about it.

Agilbert never returned to Britain. For several months during 668–9, he put his extensive experience and knowledge of the English Church at the disposal of the incoming Archbishop of Canterbury, Theodore of Tarsus, who passed through Francia on his way from Rome. Theodore was hand-picked by St Vitalian (the pope from 657 to 672) to bring administrative order and direction after a period of flux and disrupted tenure at Canterbury. Just as Berin had listened in Neustria to the latest stories about the situation in 'Angleland' before he embarked on his mission, so Theodore would have received a first-hand account from Agilbert of events surrounding Whitby and the personalities involved.

For all his unceremonious departure from the nascent kingdom of the West Saxons, Agilbert was commemorated in his own country. He died some time in or around 673, when he must by then have been in his sixties. In the same year, he had been recorded as a witness to Clotilde of Neustria's admittedly suspect foundation charter for the Abbey of Bruyères-le-Châtel.[29] He was laid to rest in the crypt of the Abbey of St Jouarre-sur-Seine and his brother, St Ebregisel, Bishop of Meaux, lies beside him. As abbess, his sister, Theodechild, was present at his funeral, making it a family occasion as well as a public one. Agilbert's fine late-seventh century sarcophagus, decorated with Celtic angels – a fitting reminder of his strong Irish associations – remains intact in the crypt. It remains the only firmly identifiable 'Winchester' episcopal tomb before the Conquest.

For the next thousand years there is no recorded veneration of Agilbert. No liturgical evidence for his early beatification or confirmation of any subsequent canonisation exists today. Nevertheless, some implicit approval of an earlier cult rests with the entry of St Agilbert's feast day of 1 April in a calendar compiled for English Catholics in 1686 during the reign of James II. The absence of recognition, however, does not diminish Agilbert's lasting achievement. He went far beyond Berin's limited success in influencing key figures in Wessex. Both before and at Whitby, Agilbert was able to persuade some of the most important political personalities in the north to accept the basis for a unified Church in Britain. King Cenwealh himself would come to regret losing him.

WINE AND LOTHAIR

THE FIRST SAXON AND THE LAST FRANKISH BISHOPS TO THE WEST SAXON KINGDOM

If Penda was the scourge of the Northumbrians, his son, Wulfhere, was rather more of a threat to the West Saxons, or 'Wessex'. This term is a comparatively late variation of *Westsaxeana rice* (kingdom of the West Saxons) which came into use in the seventh century; it was, of course, romanticised – and pushed west – by Thomas Hardy. The Wessex at the time of its first bishops was a petty kingdom centred on present-day Hampshire but thrusting west against the retreating Celtic peoples and north to defend itself from the Mercians pushing south. Hamtun was the link to the outside world, while Dorchester was an increasingly vulnerable stronghold on the Thames, a natural border. While it is still far too early to talk of Venta, or Wintancaster, as the capital of Wessex, the threat from Mercia caused King Cenwealh to consider establishing a more secure base in the south, and one not exposed to whatever might come from the sea. The natural protection Venta had received from the River Itchen and surrounding hills was complemented by a divine benediction – Cenwealh's rising Minster. The construction workers – masons, carpenters and other artisans – forming a growing settlement within the old Roman ramparts were also assured of plentiful supplies from the fertile Itchen/Test valleys; they would not go hungry. Thus, the very building of the Old Minster provided the foundation of an economic activity which transformed an empty ruin into a township. This new community would need a pastor.

The etymology of the name Winchester and the place's importance to the West Saxons are almost worthy of a thesis. There is no doubting the origin of *caster*, which derives from the Latin *castrum*, originally a camp and later a fortification, from which we get the modern 'castle'. In the early seventh century, when the name Wintancaster first appears, there was no stone-built Arthurian Camelot; rather, we should imagine a few hutments, or an encampment, taking advantage of the protection afforded by remains of the old Roman walled town, a construction not unlike Portchester, which survives to this day.[30] The term Winton, short for the genitive form Wintoniensis, and still used locally, not least by present-day bishops, is more difficult: some quote Nennius, a doubtful Welsh source who spoke of *Caergwintwg*, or 'white fortress'. Any traveller approaching the old *civitas* from the River Itchen and seeing the chalkstone outcrops in the surrounding hills might have appreciated the nomenclature. However, the Roman limestone and flint walls, weathered over the centuries, which skirted the riverbank would have looked distinctly grey rather than white – as the few remains still do today.

Another theory, much cited by Winchester primary schoolteachers in days gone by, was that the original title was really 'Witancaster', the camp where the Witan or council of wise men gathered to advise the ruler. This, however, ignores the fact that the Witan met in a number of places over the centuries and there is still that persistent first 'n' to explain. The truth is that we need look no further than a natural transition from Venta or Uenta (pronounced like 'went'). This later developed into Winton which could be translated as 'friendly town' (Old English *wine* and *tun*) – an early Saxon pun?! With its easy access to the sea and natural defensive position, allied with good sheep grazing on the overhanging Downs and a river teeming with trout, Wintancaster was surely an ideal place from which the West Saxons might eventually be governed, with the additional inspiration of the Old Minster. It followed that it should become the cultural or spiritual centre of the kingship, not the geographically insecure Dorchester.

Wine replaces Agilbert at a time of crisis

Wessex would have been considered one of the less significant kingdoms in Britain in the mid seventh century – and vulnerable. Cenwealh's behaviour towards his Mercian wife, Wulfhere's sister, was an enormous insult and sparked a quarrel little short of a blood feud. Fuelled by this and after his father's defeat in the north, Wulfhere pressed across the Thames into northern Hampshire shortly after he came to the Mercian throne in 657. Well before his death seventeen years later, he was hailed as the overlord of southern Britain. In the face of this threat from the Mercians, Cenwealh retrenched in southern Hampshire, where he had managed to retain his local authority and where his advisers were happier to assemble – in Hamtun or Wintancaster. Bereft of ecclesiastical advice at a particularly trying time, with Agilbert away in the north, the king cast around for another cleric whom he could trust or, perhaps as Bede would have us believe, was easier to understand. A man, too, who Cenwealh could expect to remain close by and who would continue to develop the site of the king's church, as much as anything intended as his mausoleum. He chose Wine (*friend* in Old English) as his new episcopal counsellor.

We do not know whether Cenwealh's choice was a personal whim or whether he received advice from outside. Given that the kingdom of Kent was also being menaced by Mercian encroachment along the Thames Valley, Cenwealh would have been looking for a defensive alliance with his eastern neighbour. It seems likely that he took advice from his Saxon compatriot,[31] Deusdedit (meaning 'God-gave' and named after the early seventh century saintly pope), who had been Archbishop of Canterbury since 655. It is unlikely, however, that Cenwealh had to gain the archbishop's sanction before he reordered Agilbert's diocese. But, as fellow Saxons, Deusdedit and Wine would not have been strangers to one another. Bede informs us[32] that Wine had also spent time in Neustria and was consecrated bishop there. From the little we know of him, it is conceivable that he made his own opportunities for preferment, perhaps as a re-export to Cenwealh's court from Francia. As a native speaker he would have been an improvement on Agilbert, both in the pulpit and as a presence in the council hall. When Wine arrived in Wintancaster is not known, but it is generally agreed that he was installed at Cenwealh's Minster between 660 and 662. Whether Agilbert was ever consulted while he was absent in the North is unlikely; as we have seen, he subsequently left the scene altogether.

Another political factor was at work. Although the Mercians were pressing southwards, the influence of Christianity was slowly moving north. Late in his reign, Penda had come to tolerate the new religion, although he was swift to despatch anyone he considered false or untrustworthy in their beliefs. By his death in 654, his elder son, Peada, had converted and, shortly afterwards, four bishoprics were created in Mercia. In this context, Cenwealh may have seen it politic to separate Dorchester – an area he could no longer control – from southern Hampshire and keep his own episcopal adviser close at hand. The Mercians had by now extended south of the Thames Valley.

Canterbury in disarray

The years that followed Wine's installation were visited by the plague, which carried off several senior clerics, including Archbishop Deusdedit in about 664. With Agilbert's departure to Neustria, accompanied or followed by Wilfrid, Wine was left as the only bishop in Britain consecrated in accordance with papal authority. Wine was not without initiative and, in Wilfrid's absence, consecrated the future St Chad[33] as Bishop to the Northumbrians at York. This he did with the assistance of two Celtic bishops – whose own consecration would naturally have been regarded questionable by Rome. With Deusdedit's successor also dying of the plague while on his first visit to Rome, and further delays in finding a replacement, the leadership of the Roman tradition in Britain was in disarray for several years. Wine was left to do more or less as he pleased.

According to Bede, the consecration of Chad attracted severe criticism from the Roman party; as such, it might also have been unwelcome to Cenwealh's pro-Canterbury, politically motivated sympathies. In 666, in the face of his king's unspecified displeasure, Wine was 'driven out' and sought refuge with Wulfhere of Mercia[34]; shortly afterwards, Bede continues, he purchased the See of London from the Mercian king.[35] If true, this would have deepened whatever offence he had already given Cenwealh. While such a case of simony seems to have been in stark contrast to the behaviour of his predecessors in Wessex and smacks of betrayal, the purchase of bishoprics was by no means rare, notably amongst Frankish clerics on the Continent. By the post-Conquest period, it had become part of the process of being confirmed in a See with a premium expected to be paid into the Vatican treasury, often to help finance crusades. After his accusation, Bede's account falls silent on the rest of Wine's life and the *Anglo-Saxon Chronicle* does not help either. We know that he did not attend the Synod of Hertford convened by Theodore, the reforming Archbishop of Canterbury, in 672. It is reasonable, moreover, to infer from the consecration in 675 of Earconwold, Wine's successor at London, that he had died some time before that date. After the death of Wulfhere, Earconwold would become known as Cenwealh's bishop, reflecting a change for the better in the fortunes of the West Saxons in the lower Thames Valley.

Although his association with Cenwealh's Mercian enemy would hardly have made him welcome back at court, the Winchester tradition claims that Wine returned there for the last three years of his life, living in penitence. According to Bede, Wine remained as Bishop of London until his death and, by then, a new Bishop to the West Saxons had been appointed.[36] Wine's name, however, was painted on one of the six mortuary chests in the cathedral, whose contents date from the seventh century. These include the bones of saints and princes scattered from the burial places desecrated by Cromwell's Parliamentarian soldiers during the sack of Winchester in both April 1644 and October 1645. Previously, the contents had been 'sorted out' by Bishop Fox in the early sixteenth century and it is certain that individual coffins had been moved a number of times before that! What survives today is a jumbled assortment of bones which present a huge challenge to forensic scientists. If the chests have indeed contained Wine's earthly remains, as Bishop Fox's cartularians would have insisted, some credence should be paid to the Winchester tradition.[37]

There is a further general consideration which points to Wine's interment at Winchester. Apart from the fact that no other site lays claim to him,[38] people in the Middle Ages were usually buried close to where they died, and quickly.[39] For obvious reasons, decomposing corpses were not traipsed across the land. Their coffins might be subsequently moved or, sometimes, even re-opened for the living to marvel at the uncorrupted body of a saint.[40] Whatever the pagan practices, scripture was now prescriptive enough: both the Old and New Testaments contain references to speedy burial, culminating in Christ's body being placed in Joseph of Arimathea's sepulchre the evening of his death. The Koran, originating, of course, from the desert, still sets down even more precisely that the deceased should be interred at the earliest opportunity. There is no reason to suppose, therefore, that an apparently penitent Wine back in Wintancaster should have been buried anywhere else. As far as Bede's account is concerned, we are faced with the conclusion that either he was unaware of the place of burial or that he excised it for being inconsistent with his essentially hostile attitude towards Wine.

Wine was an unimpressive 'first' bishop of Wintancaster. As a Saxon prelate, he was a poor representative of his people in the high Church office he sought, a point which would not have been missed by Bishop Agilbert in Francia. Nor, indeed, by the papacy, which was still seeking to expand the Christian frontier with missionary bishops well-grounded in theology and sound canonical practice. Wine has the dubious distinction of being the first bishop in Britain known to have been accused of simony, thereby setting an unfortunate precedent for countless prelates down to the Reformation to follow his example. With little or no detail about the man himself, other than Bede's sour commentary, it is hard to escape the conclusion that Wine failed to live up to the expectations either of his king, or of Rome. One cannot, however, ignore the politico-military see-saw between Mercia and Wessex which helps explain why Wine was persuaded to move on to advise the newly converted and more influential King Wulfhere. As a Northumbrian, and as a natural ally of Wessex, Bede would have seen Wine's apparent change of allegiance as the act of a 'trimmer' at best. But for his name to appear on a mortuary chest with others of distinction suggests that Wine was not without influential supporters – in Winchester, at least.

Lothair

Cenwealh's choice of the mercurial Wine deprived him of the consistent advice of an educated diplomat and counsellor. The absence of a strong literate presence, too, would have hindered the peaceful resolution of disputes along the Thames Valley. From 662 onwards there was, in practice, no bishop at Dorchester. Faced with continuing pressure from Wulfhere and without a man he could trust, the king appealed to Agilbert to return. Now well settled as a bishop in his native Francia, Agilbert declined, but instead recommended his nephew, Lothair (Latinised as Leutherius) and sent him to Cenwealh with Archbishop Theodore's blessing. Bede notes that the "people" also desired Lothair's appointment, which suggests that there was still a strong Frankish influence surrounding the king. Nevertheless, Cenwealh was obviously satisfied with the substitution and, at his request, Theodore consecrated Lothair as Bishop of Wintancaster in 670.

Lothair was one of four bishops who attended the Synod of Hertford in 672, the first gathering of the early English Church to put its new-found unity into practical expression. Nearly eighty years after St Augustine's mission, bishops were becoming pastoral administrators rather than pioneering evangelists. There were by now seven dioceses established – Canterbury, Rochester, London, Dunwich (on the East Anglian coast), York, Lichfield and Winchester – in effect forming a framework to consolidate the conversion of the still diverse ethnic groupings. Archbishop Theodore presided at the Synod and, as the pope's personal choice, established his authority over the other bishops. Episcopal precedence was agreed by date of consecration. There is no evidence, however, that Theodore sought to regulate the size of dioceses; indeed, the Synod ruled against change in the status quo. This left some dioceses, such as Rochester and Dunwich, dwarfed by Winchester, York and Lichfield which reflected the size of the kingdoms they served rather than any ecclesiastical consideration.

Little is known of Lothair's early life other than that he came from the Soissons area of Francia and was, like his uncle, a member of the Neustrian nobility. He would have received an education in theology and

Latin at one of the increasing number of monastic houses in Frankish Gaul. The obvious candidate is the Abbey of St Médard, founded by the Merovingian king, Clotaire I, on his estate at Crouy just outside Soissons. The abbey became a leading Benedictine house, but during his upbringing, Lothair would have absorbed a blend of monastic disciplines demanded by the two great patriarchs, St Benedict and St Columbanus.[41]

On his way to Canterbury in 668–9, Archbishop Theodore had spent some months with Agilbert in Paris familiarising himself with the religio-political situation across the Channel, and he surely would have met the priest Lothair there. The dating suggests that Cenwealh's appeal for a reliable bishop must have been made at about the same time. Interestingly, although the record is sparse, linguistic comprehension does not appear to have been an issue during Lothair's subsequent attendance at the Wessex court or travel round his diocese. Based in Wintancaster and generally better educated in Latin and canon law than Wine, he would have collected around him locally raised clerics who could, if necessary, act as interpreters.

Lothair arrived in Wintancaster during a period of a fluctuating balance of power. While Cenwealh had spent the previous decade fending off Wulfhere, he had also fought successfully against British tribes in the south-west, thus consolidating the influence of the West Saxons over present-day Dorset, Wiltshire and Somerset. According to a charter granted within a year of Lothair's consecration, but now considered to have been forged, a grateful Cenwealh is believed to have granted his Minster at Wintancaster a large tract of land at Downton, six miles south of Salisbury.[42] The land would stay within Winchester's estate long after the surrounding area came under the post-Conquest diocese of Salisbury. The revenue from this major centre of animal husbandry in the centuries to come would become a bone of contention between future bishops and the monks who worked and resided at the Minster and, later, at the Norman Cathedral. Latter-day monks would argue that the original grant of land had been gifted to the "Church of St Peter and St Paul", that is, to the institution and patently not to the bishop of the day, even though he might be their abbot. In the early centuries, however, the income helped to develop what was becoming essentially a religious community led by secular clergy, numbering acolytes and deacons through to fully ordained priests. It was not monastic, and it is unclear how many, if any, of those who served there were tonsured, even among the bishops appointed from within their number.

With the westward expansion, it is not surprising that, during his approximately six years as bishop, Lothair should have been closely associated with the founding of two abbeys in the West Country. He is recorded in a contemporary charter[43] as having granted land at Fontmell Magna in Dorset to Bectune, the abbot there. This is the first mention of a monastic-type settlement in the area, Shaftesbury being a ninth century foundation. The village boasts a memorial on the south side of the "Funtamel" stream running through it, indicating where the now long-extinct abbey once stood. Lothair was certainly associated with Fontmell, since a charter of Cointrid, son of King Ine, dated 704, mentioned Lothair as "of blessed memory". In this charter, Cointrid granted an additional thirty hides (3,600 acres) on the north side of the stream to the Bishop of Winchester. Such large grants of land contributed to the king's ability to control freshly accrued territory through the administrative capability and religious influence of the growing Church.

Lothair is also credited with having founded a monastery at Malmesbury and to have appointed Aldhelm as its first abbot. Records show[44] that Aldhelm, who was born at Sherborne in 639 of princely Saxon blood and was linguistically competent, had studied at Malmesbury for fourteen years under his tutor, Maeldulph, who died in around 675. This suggests, therefore, that until the traditional dating for the abbey's foundation, we should perhaps view Malmesbury as a former school and Aldhelm as its leading scholar. The existence of the founding charter, quoted by the early twelfth century historian William of Malmesbury, has been discredited by subsequent scholarship,[45] but it is known that Lothair was in regular correspondence with Aldhelm. On one occasion, Aldhelm apologised to his bishop that he would be unable to travel down to Malmesbury for Christmas because he was too busy with his studies at Canterbury. And, although monastic cells had appeared in Wessex two or three decades before Lothair's episcopate, it was during his time that the Benedictine Rule was introduced at Malmesbury under Aldhelm's direction. Moreover, William of Malmesbury's account of Lothair's grant of land to Aldhelm for monastic income is specific about time: "the eighth before the Kalends of September 672," and place: "done publicly near the river Bladon". This geographical detail is indicative since the river is identical with a stream running north of Oxford and close to present-day Blenheim, which would have been well inside Mercian territory.

Interestingly, Lothair is still described in the charter as Bishop to the Gewisse. This, in turn, might suggest that Dorchester had already been subsumed within an enlarged Winchester diocese. Another thought springs to mind: the monastic regimen at Malmesbury was more disciplined than any regimen being followed in 'soft south' Wintancaster, a point that the generally more militaristic Mercians would not have missed.

The discourse between two such learned men as Lothair and Aldhelm would also have stimulated thought on how the rule of law should be introduced and codified in the late-seventh century West Saxon kingdom. During his studies at the newly established school at Canterbury, Aldhelm is believed to have obtained a rare book on Roman law which formed the basis of his research.[46] When the two scholars met, this would have been fresh meat for dialogue and, as we shall see during the next episcopate, it found the ready appreciation of Ine, king, law-giver and Aldhelm's kinsman.

It is difficult to talk of an exact date when the bishop transferred his episcopal seat from Dorchester to Winchester. The founding of a major church at Wintancaster before Berin's death – with no similar edifice being established at Dorchester – indicates the way the wind was blowing. But the conflict over Agilbert and Wine's respective areas of responsibility seems to have put the transfer on hold; it certainly blurred the issue. By Lothair's episcopate, however, we can talk of one diocese which, for sound political reasons, was bound to centre on Wintancaster. From here, the West Saxon kings would foray westwards in concert with the evangelical impetus coming out of the Minster. And the further west they ventured, the more likely they were to come across Celtic Christian communities surviving from Roman times. This, together with more grants of land from a victorious king, would boost the wealth and influence of future bishops. By the time of Lothair's death in 676 – just over forty years since the arrival of Berin – his diocese stretched from Oxfordshire in southern Mercia to the Devon border.

ST HAEDDI

A HOLY ESTATE AGENT

The wily and long-reigning Cenwealh died in 672 and was succeeded by his widow, Seaxburh, an indication that, even in the absence of direct surviving heirs, the kingship was still very much a family affair. Seaxburh, though, lasted for little more than a year before she was succeeded by Aescwine, a distant relation, who ruled for only two years. It is from 676 that the diocese of Winchester is dated officially,[47] a convenient coincidence, therefore, that King Aescwine and Bishop Lothair should both die during the course of it and be succeeded by two substantial figures. The new ruler, Centwine, was described by his contemporary, Aldhelm, as a strong king who ruled his kingdom well and endowed many religious foundations. Aldhelm also describes the king as overlord of all the West Saxons, strongly indicating that he had thrown off Mercian encroachment and prevailed against its military dominance. He had also imposed his will over local warlords within his kingdom. It was against this more stable and cohesive background that Haeddi, the fifth Bishop to the West Saxons, consolidated his episcopate from Wintancaster and brought Berin's remains to the Minster there, further evidence that it was now regarded as the kingdom's mausoleum. From 679, Dorchester was formally made subordinate to Wintancaster and, not long after that, lost its bishop altogether. Thereafter, where the West Saxon king held sway, the See of Winchester – as I will now call it – extended without any suffragan until well after the Conquest.

Haeddi – also known as Hedda – was a Saxon and, although his actual birthplace has not been established, it has been suggested that he came from Headingly in Yorkshire, the name meaning 'clearing of the people of Haeddi'. If this were Haeddi's birthplace after all, it would imply that he was a scion of a senior Saxon family settled in the north. He would have been born shortly before Berin's arrival in Wessex and, of course, after the Paulinus mission had set itself up at York. We may, therefore, infer him to have been a second-generation Christian, his parents and household, perhaps, having been converted by Paulinus himself.

A northern upbringing does seem likely, however, since traditionally Haeddi is thought to have entered St Hilda's Abbey at Whitby as a young man.[48] If so, he would have been present at the 663 Synod. William of Malmesbury contends that Haeddi became abbot at Whitby,[49] which, if true, means he would have been placed in charge of the monks in the double monastic institution, firmly under the direction of St Hilda. There is a reference to Haeddi before he became bishop as "abbas et presbyter",[50] which confirms he had been both tonsured as a monk and ordained as a priest. To have been preferred to a major bishopric, however, he must have had a religious and administrative track record to impress. Critically, we are also told that he was on good terms with Archbishop Theodore, Rome's inspired choice for directing the entrenchment of the early English Church under the primacy of Canterbury. Yet, unlike his predecessor Lothair, Haeddi was not especially noted for his scholarship. Indeed, Bede wrote that Haeddi qualified for episcopal duties more through his love of goodness than by any book-learning.[51]

There is little doubt but that he was the personal choice of Archbishop Theodore and there are strong political factors to support this. With a lack of royal continuity since Cenwealh's death, a determined Centwine was in a position to make or influence the appointment. In addition, Theodore had a strong sense of his metropolitan authority and ensured that the Winchester bishop submitted to this. In Haeddi he would have a close ally when dealing with his own problems, not least the Mercian ravages of Kent in 676, including the destruction of Rochester. He would have valued an influential liaison at the West Saxon court in the common cause of constraining the expansionist Ethelred, the King of Mercia from 675, who sought to bring London and the south-east within his realm.

Although Haeddi's consecration took place in 676 in London, his attestation of a charter the year before suggests that he was already a member of the Wessex court in an administrative capacity. His first decade as bishop, however, was dominated by what was essentially tribal warfare: Centwine and his successor, Caedwalla, destroyed the tenacious South Saxon kingdom in Sussex and cleared the Mercians from territory south of the Thames stretching eastwards as far as London, all the while subduing the Jutes on the Isle of Wight and in the Meon Valley. At the conclusion of these campaigns, the heartland of the Wessex kingdom – the Itchen/Test basin – was no longer vulnerable to its neighbours. And, with every victory, the king thanked God for being on his side by granting yet more land to the Church. The effect on the diocese was to consolidate its hold on the south bank of the Thames, which would prove a vital asset for Haeddi's successors throughout the Middle Ages. From 676 to the end of the century, there are many charters inscribed by Haeddi which place him in a role resembling that of a royal estate agent. There is even an instance of his signing a charter without the king's counter signature.[52] For a man whose 'love of goodness' and lack of 'book-learning' had propelled him into the most influential bishopric at the time, Haeddi went on to gain a reputation for zeal and administrative ability which confirmed Theodore's faith in him. The See of Winchester was now a huge diocese and Haeddi, fortunately, possessed sound judgement in his selection of personal advisers and subordinates to whom he could delegate some of his numerous responsibilities.

For most of his episcopate there was little pressure to divide what could have been regarded as an unwieldy area of responsibility; in fact, Theodore's decree of 680 ruled that Winchester should remain untouched. In short, he had sufficient confidence in Haeddi to let him get on with it. In matters spiritual, too, there are indications that Theodore regarded his bishop as at least his equal: a short poem by the archbishop dated to 681 was addressed to his "friend Haeddi". Significantly, it appears to have been sent when Theodore issued his penitential, which directed how priests should hear confessions and accord penance; he commended himself to Haeddi's prayers.[53] This is a remarkable gesture and could even suggest that Theodore regarded Haeddi as his confessor.

Scholar or not, Haeddi could also turn his pen to a Latin epigram, as the following discovery by the antiquarian Leland, in the sixteenth century, shows:

> *"In honorem almissimi*
> *ac doctoris dulcissimi*
> *Sancti Pauli sollemniter*
> *ac vocato feliciter,*
> *Hedde, pontifex petitus*
> *ac cum amore accitus,*
> *dedicavit deicola*
> *atque clarus celicola".*

Unfortunately, it has been impossible to identify the church or altar that was being dedicated to Saint Paul,[54] but the epigram is considered among the oldest known examples of the genre in Northern Europe. Intriguingly, the text also refers to two other saints – St Deicola and Celicola, the latter almost certainly St Cecilia. Deicola, and his younger brother St Gallus, came from Leinster and accompanied St Columbanus to Gaul in circa 567. Variations of the historically suspect legend of Cecilia, a mysterious third-century virgin, claim that she was condemned to be suffocated in the Roman baths (which were heated for a night and a day) because she had converted hundreds of people, or because she had refused to make sacrifice to the Roman gods. Having survived this, she was finally – after three attempts – martyred by the sword. A follower of Columbanus would certainly have been revered in late-seventh century Wessex, but St Cecilia is more difficult to explain. She had become known as the patron of musicians for the angelic strains said to have been heard by her either at her marriage or in her visions, so the admittedly obscure reference in the epigram might suggest that the bishop was of a musical bent.[55]

As the secular power enlarged the West Saxon kingdom north and east, the Church under Haeddi continued to consolidate westwards with substantial endowments to the monastic houses at Glastonbury and

Malmesbury. The former had been a Christian sanctuary from well before the arrival of the Saxons and is, of course, associated with the legend of Joseph of Arimathea and the Holy Grail which many historians dismiss as medieval invention. William of Malmesbury, writing in the twelfth century, quoted from a document known to him: "No other hands than those of the Disciples of Christ erected the Church at Glastonbury".[56] His source was likely to have been the sixth century chronicler Gildas, who is considered by scholars to have been an unreliable historian. Gildas was the only major written source on late Celtic Britain and Haeddi would have been aware of his work, particularly his claim that Christianity arrived in Britain during the last years of the reign of Emperor Tiberius who died in AD37. The Glastonbury legend would have been well-known to Church leaders in the late seventh century and so it is not surprising that Haeddi's name should have been found inscribed on a stone – now lost – between two small pyramids once claimed to have marked the burial place of Arthur and Guinevere.[57] Haeddi would also have had access to the earliest charters concerning the abbey which refer to Glastonbury as the place where Christianity originated in Britain. With Somerset in the hands of the converted West Saxons, it was entirely natural for the bishop to act as a propagandist for the Glastonbury tradition – albeit without the Arthurian romance.

Propagandist or not, we have a charter illustrating Haeddi's approach to business that contrasts starkly with other, less authentic and rather more pretentiously worded charters. Dated 6 July 680, it granted five hundred acres of village land close by Glastonbury Abbey to the abbot, Haemgills, and is impressive for its brevity. The wording of the preamble also lays emphasis on the contrast between "change [in] the old order" and the changeless "reign of our Lord Jesus Christ". For Haeddi, good administration deserved to be entrenched by sound theology.

The other great benefaction was at Malmesbury where, as we have seen, Aldhelm was certainly active by the time of its generally accepted foundation, also in 676. As we have already noted, there had been a religious community at Malmesbury since the middle of the century when the Irish monk Maeldulph sought Bishop Agilbert's approval for the building of a monastic settlement near the Ingelbourne stream just outside the township. Aldhelm had received his early Christian instruction from Maeldulph, but his scholastic researches were spent at Canterbury and in Rome. His subsequent reputation as a teacher attracted would-be scholars from Neustria and elsewhere in Britain. In around 683, Haeddi appointed him as abbot of the new foundation. Interestingly, Aldhelm's abbey church was also dedicated to St Peter and St Paul, a further statement of intent to uphold Roman rather than Celtic doctrine concerning the dating of Easter, which would have remained a point of strong contention with British Christians in the west. Urged on by their archbishop, abbot and bishop would have worked hand-in-hand to maintain the Roman theological legitimacy.

Haeddi's influence on secular law

It was, however, in the development of secular law that Haeddi's influence behind the scenes was at its greatest. In 689, the impulsive Caedwalla was succeeded as King of Wessex by Ine. The years of expansion by military force were followed by a calmer period consolidating government of the kingdom. Four years after his accession, Ine summoned the *Witenagemot* (literally, 'meeting of wise men') which enacted what have become known as the 'Dooms' or Laws of Ine. The new king had Haeddi by his side and had also called on Earconwold, 'his bishop' of London, to attend. It is fair to assume that among the senior clerics and scholars, Aldhelm would also have been present. The deliberations of the Witenagemot – sometimes acclaimed as a synod – laid as much emphasis on 'the health of souls' as on the stability of the kingdom. In short, they bore Haeddi's stamp of approval.

Of the seventy-nine Laws of Ine, many concerned the life and practices of the Church as an integral part of society. What was considered right by the Church was encased in legal sanction. Thus, those who failed to have their children baptised within thirty days of birth were subjected to a fine; Sundays became 'holy-days' when work had to cease, and monastic bodies were required to observe 'right rule', that was, the Benedictine discipline. The tithe system was enshrined in law, whereby each Martinmas the householder contributed towards the sustenance of the local house of God, usually in corn.³ The frequent taking of Communion was encouraged, together with Confirmation, and any oath before a bishop was ascribed special solemnity. And the Laws of Ine also guaranteed the privilege of sanctuary, carrying with it immunity from arrest, even for capital offenders. In the decades that followed, the bishop and an ealdorman would sit side by side at the shire court to adjudicate on both the spiritual and the temporal laws. If an individual were required to "make deep satisfaction to God", it meant submission to severe penance imposed by the bishop. Ine's laws, therefore, promoted the office of bishop as an instrument of statecraft, and Haeddi's role in this was crucial.

Pressure to reduce the size of the diocese

Towards the end of his episcopate, pressure began to mount for division of the over-extended Winchester diocese, which by now stretched as far as the borders of the tiny Rochester diocese in Kent. The London diocese, on the northern side of the Thames, also presented a problem: it was a discrete entity, but its bishop, as we have seen, was recognising Ine rather than the Mercian Ethelred as king. Bishop Haeddi, despite having no suffragan bishops to assist him in his much larger diocese, appears to have continued to stand in the way of division. However, the death of Archbishop Theodore in 690, aged eighty-eight, removed support from Canterbury; indeed, the annual synod was already passing resolutions in favour of Winchester's borders being more narrowly defined. Haeddi's opposition continued, even down to 704 when the then Bishop of London, Waldhere, wrote to Archbishop Britwald to complain that synodic resolutions were not being adhered to. Waldhere even went so far as to argue that the Church should cease to communicate with the West Saxons if the archbishop's decree were not obeyed. The reaction of King Ine and his bishop to this demand can well be imagined. Whatever the rights and wrongs of the dispute, it seems clear that there were political factors at work: Waldhere was again becoming more beholden to the

---

3   The feast of St Martin of Tours, patron saint of France, celebrated on 11 November.

Mercian king, Ethelred, who, in sharp contrast to his military incursions, took a great deal of interest in Church affairs and is remembered for his generous endowments. He bore no brief for good relations with the court at Winchester. The Mercian rivalry with the West Saxons, in which the control of London was a touchstone, continued to wax and wane throughout the seventh and eighth centuries; it never went away. The belief that Bishop Haeddi was nearing the end of his life, however, provided a golden opportunity to cut the influence of the diocese down to size. Nevertheless, Winchester would not lose control of Southwark and London's South Bank until the late nineteenth century. This ensured that its bishop always had a presence – and a palace – in the emerging capital after the Conquest.

According to Bede and Florence of Worcester,[58] Haeddi died in 705; however, the *Anglo-Saxon Chronicle* records the death as 703 and adds that he had been bishop for twenty-seven years. He was buried outside the Winchester Minster, presumably, so that his shrine might be accessible to all the people. Whatever the reason, within a short time, miracles were reported at his tomb, and he came to be revered as a saint. Bede's account tells how people would carry away a little dust from the tomb to mix with water and give it to the sick to drink; both men and beasts, it was said, were cured as a result. The practice became so common that a wide ditch opened up around Haeddi's burial place. Bede's source would have been his regular correspondent, Bishop Daniel, Haeddi's successor. Daniel learnt of it from his close friend, Aldhelm, who in turn received the miraculous tales from a fellow monk called Pehthelm. How legends are born! Like Wine's, Haeddi's name also appears on one of the mortuary chests perched once again above the Chancel at Winchester Cathedral. As previously noted, we have Bishop Fox in the early sixteenth century to thank for the inscriptions. But which bones finally lay in which chest became impossible to say after the desecration by the Parliamentarian soldiers during the Civil War.

Like many early English and Celtic prelates, Haeddi was canonised at some point, although the date is not known, and Rome's sanction is not recorded. Strangely, however, his name was revered at Crowland, an early eighth century Benedictine foundation in Lincolnshire, dedicated to the memory of St Guthlac.[59] The abbey was destroyed by the Danes in 866 but refounded by King Edred in the tenth century – always an opportunity for re-writing history – and it is possibly then that Guthlac's ordination was credited to his near contemporary, Haeddi. In the sixteenth century, the bishop's name was also added to a Catholic 'martyrology' and his feast day given as 7 July; he was not, of course, a martyr! Whatever the truth of his canonisation, it is Haeddi rather than a man like Wine who deserves to be remembered, not only as the first substantive Bishop of Winchester, but also as a major contributor to the advancement of the power and influence of the Church in southern England. Although the See was reduced in size under his successor, the lands added to the episcopal estate under Haeddi remained as part of the Bishop of Winchester's temporalities down to the Reformation, even where they lay within a neighbouring diocese. This effectively maintained the bishop's influence in several counties long after the lands had been taken away.

DANIEL

COUNSELLOR AND SCHOLAR

The death of Bishop Haeddi cut the ground from under the feet of those in Wessex resisting the will of the archbishop and synods to reduce the size of the diocese. There were, however, other factors at work: the Winchester See could not keep growing indefinitely in parallel with the westward expansion of the kingdom of Wessex. By the early years of the eighth century, too, there was no longer any doubt about Canterbury's overriding authority in Church affairs, including in the choice of bishops. What Theodore had started in the creation of a diocesan structure across the petty kingdoms of Britannia, his successor, Britwald, would complete.[60] Within a year of Daniel's consecration as bishop, in 705, his diocese had been substantially reduced in size. In the West, it was now hedged by the creation of the diocese of Sherborne and, in the East, by the revival of the old Romano-British See of Selsey.[61] The latter was made easier by West Saxon military success against the South Saxons and progress in their conversion. Winchester, however, was given the Isle of Wight, where the Jutes had also been recently converted; the See continued to stretch northwards, retaining most, if not all, of present-day Surrey. The Thames would remain a natural diocesan boundary whether the West Saxon king ruled London or not.

Daniel's acceptance of the new order was made all the easier by the translation of his close friend Aldhelm from Malmesbury to the new See of Sherborne, a preferment, we are told, with which Aldhelm was not altogether happy.[62] The two prelates had been contemporaries as novices under the tutelage of Maelddulph, who we have already met as the founder of the religious school at Maelsburgh, which later became Malmesbury Abbey. From 676, under Aldhelm's direction, Malmesbury had emulated in the West the scholarship achieved at St Augustine's Benedictine monastery at Canterbury under Albinus, Bede's principal informant for his history of the early English Church. Both institutions were 'forcing houses' for clerics destined for future senior office. Besides scholarship, at Malmesbury at least, the emphasis was on asceticism. As a young man – and following an example set by Aldhelm and St David of Wales – Daniel would stand each night in the cold waters of the Inglebourne, the spot little more than a hundred metres from where the stream joins the Bristol Avon below Malmesbury. Here he is supposed to have purged himself of un-Godly thoughts. It is still called Daniel's 'spring' or 'well' by local people.

Daniel was born shortly after the middle of the seventh century and, given his Biblical name, almost certainly into an already converted family. It is also possible that he was of Romano-British descent, although unfortunately, there are no etymological clues to suggest where he might have been born. It is likely that he followed, even accompanied, Aldhelm to Canterbury and joined him in his researches. In this way he would have come to the attention of successive archbishops and may have stayed on some years after Aldhelm's appointment as Malmesbury's abbot. Without Canterbury's blessing, nevertheless, Daniel could not have succeeded Haeddi. That said, he would not have been totally unknown to the Wessex court and his long association with Nursling Abbey near present-day Southampton could suggest that he was from the West Saxon heartland.

A worthy successor to Bishop Haeddi

By the time of Daniel's succession, King Ine had reigned sixteen years and the legal codes he had promulgated were in force; in parallel, the first West Saxon synods were already a regular event. With these complimentary structures in place, the new bishop had to balance temporal and spiritual duties and priorities, a task his successors would find increasingly difficult to achieve, particularly after the Norman Conquest. At the time, the inherent conflicts do not seem to have been a major problem and, like his predecessor, Daniel gained a reputation for strong and wise administration. He played a leading role in the inspiration and interpretation of the judicial processes set in train by both Ine and Haeddi. Strikingly, he is described in Faris's *Life of St Aldhelm* as "vir in multis strenuissimus" – a man of enormous drive in many things.[63] He has also been considered one of the most learned and influential bishops of the great era of missionary endeavour that epitomised the Anglo-Saxon Church in the eighth century. Exemplary pastor that he was, Daniel was first and foremost a scholar. Dean Kitchin, for example, wrote that he should be credited with having founded "the Winchester school of learned men" at Cenwealh's Old Minster.[64] Certainly, he worked in partnership with his colleague, Aldhelm, to ensure that the religious houses, endowed in the wake of West Saxon expansion to the West, were made centres of learning as well as promoters of good works. During their respective periods of office, education and literacy increased and, despite its reduction in size, the See of Winchester gained in eminence and influence, with the Old Minster becoming a centre of scholastic excellence in its own right.

Without Daniel we would know little or nothing about either the origins or the early growth of Christianity amongst the West Saxons. It is thanks to him that details of their evangelisation made their way into Bede's history of the early English Church[65] – indeed, Bede acknowledged his assistance in the book's preface. Daniel wrote to his revered contemporary offering his knowledge on the spot of the conversion of present-day Hampshire, Berkshire, Sussex, the Isle of Wight and the West. Sadly, Daniel's letters to Bede are lost and the latter's editorial excision and natural preoccupation with events in the North seem to have reduced the amount of detail offered in his otherwise seminal work. In addition, of course, Bede was writing at the time of a cult which praised the work of Pope Gregory, Augustine's patron and, therefore, the original conversion and promotion of Christianity in Kent took priority in his eyes.

A mentor for missionaries on the Continent

Daniel was a good correspondent and, fortuitously, some of his writing has come down to us in the form of letters documenting the dialogue he had with the great Anglo-Saxon missionary St Boniface. Some commentators have concluded that the letters are twelfth or thirteenth century inventions, but Daniel and Boniface were contemporaries and, whatever the sourcing of the correspondence, there can be little doubt that the two – episcopal pastor and missionary – maintained contact over the years.

Despite an upbringing in Devon, Boniface's chosen home base was Nursling Abbey, originally Nhutscelle or Nutshalling, describing a water meadow where the (hazel) nuts grew.[66] It was but a day's horse-ride from Winchester, if that, or an open boat journey along the River Test into Southampton Water. In the early eighth century, this religious house became a major centre for would-be missionaries heading for the still pagan Rhine Valley and Frisia on the German coast. Daniel made it a priority to keep himself appraised of developments in the mission field.

Boniface set out from Nursling in 716, intent on converting the Frisians who would eventually murder him in 754. Within two years, however, he was back in Wessex suffering from despair at the difficulties he had encountered. One Frisian leader, Rathbod, is quoted as saying that he would "prefer to be with my ancestors in hell than with a few beggars in heaven".[67] It was Bishop Daniel who provided the pastoral counsel that was instrumental in turning a failed missionary into a saint renowned all over Germany. The Anglican Church in Bonn, the former capital of West Germany, is dedicated to St Boniface. It was Daniel who armed 'Wynfrith', Boniface's original title, with letters of commendation to "all Christian kings, dukes, bishops, abbots, priests and other spiritual sons" he might meet, in which he underlined the reward of the "eternal salvation" they would receive for extending hospitality and protection to the would-be evangelist. Such obedience to the will of God, he stressed, had saved "Abraham from doom in the flames of Sodom and Gomorrah".[68] As did other itinerant missionaries, Boniface travelled via Paris where the mayor, Charles Martel, "rendered invaluable assistance".[69] Martel – 'Hammer of the Franks' – is best remembered for his defeat of the Muslim armies at Poitiers in 732, but his forces also pushed into Frisia and the Rhineland where they offered protection to missionaries like Boniface.

Encouraged by Daniel, Boniface appears to have made early progress in Frisia since there is a reference in a letter to him from Bugga,[70] a fellow missionary, that Rathbod had been "laid low" sometime during the period 719–21. In defiance of local belief, Boniface is supposed to have cut down an oak dedicated to Woden, "adored as a god by all the peoples of Germania",[71] a rather insensitive act if seeking to win hearts and minds. He may have changed his tactics as a result of a letter he received from his bishop dated about 720. In this, Daniel advised Boniface to go easy on the idiosyncrasies of paganism and avoid giving unnecessary offence; he offered suggestions as to how a Christian alternative lifestyle might best be demonstrated through example. Daniel's emphasis on calmness and moderation has since been absorbed into missionary textbooks down to the modern age. In comparing the fruitful and warmer Christian lands favourably with frost-plagued pagan wastelands of the north, he was, perhaps, on less sure ground; the theme, however, recurs in subsequent missionary endeavours well into the twentieth century. Daniel also pointed out that the entire world had been polytheistic until "illuminated by the knowledge of the Omnipotent God, its creator and ruler, it was vivified through the grace of Christ and reconciled to God".[72] He would readily have seen the wisdom of using the old Roman festival of Sylvester and the parallel winter solstice as an appropriate opportunity for celebrating Christ's birth.

Another important letter, written between 732 and 744, in reply to Boniface's request for guidance on how to deal with bad priests, also reflects the bishop's moderating approach. In it Daniel exhorts the missionary not to cut himself off entirely from evil or to abandon the sinner. Drawing directly on Christ's parable of the weeds,[73] he advised that in this world the wheat and weeds should not be separated until the harvest, lest potentially good plants be destroyed prematurely. After all, he argued, good and evil had to live side by side until the Day of Judgement. For all his self-mortification, Daniel was no prig.

Mentor to King Ine

His understanding from his bishop of Christ's central message of repentance and rebirth was not lost on King Ine at the Saxon court, which could be a hotbed of internecine strife. Great law-giver that he undoubtedly was, even Ine had to fight battles, including against members of his own family. In 721 he had killed his kinsman, Cynewulf. The cause of the confrontation remains obscure, but it must have involved some dynastic dispute. Was it mere coincidence that in the same year, Daniel absented himself to visit Pope Gregory II,[74] who had given his blessing to Boniface's mission to Germany? It was a timely opportunity to give a personal report on progress in the mission field, but also to brief the pope on the political situation in southern Britannia. Since the departure of Berin ninety years before, this would have been a rare occasion for the Roman Curia to learn first-hand of the developing strategic importance of Wessex from their local and trusted representative. Sadly, Daniel's account of the visit and its subject matter are lost or buried in the Vatican archives, but it would have been meat for students of early English politics in Rome. Over subsequent centuries, pontiffs would regard a number of Winchester bishops as their valued informants at the English court and on the general political scene.

Alas, neither do we know how Gregory advised Bishop Daniel to handle internecine murder in Wessex. If it was to do with an affair of the heart, the dialogue would likely have been suppressed, given Rome's subsequent dogmas on celibacy and matrimony. Whatever, Ine's conscience was not assuaged, and he came to feel that kingship was incompatible with the health of his soul. He abdicated five years later and died in Rome in 727. The king would surely have turned to his bishop for intimate counsel that might have persuaded him to step aside for both the good of the realm and Ine's spiritual well-being.

A man facing increasing physical suffering

Towards the end of another long letter of guidance to Boniface on how best to "overcome promptly the obstinacy of ignorant minds", written by 725,[75] we learn that Daniel was already suffering from a long-standing affliction. In conveying his latest advice, he referred to his physical weakness through "bodily illness" and could "fitly say with the Psalmist – I know, O Lord, that Thy judgements are right, and that Thou in faithfulness has afflicted me". Although his admission refers scripturally to the Old Testament, it is also reminiscent of St Paul's remark to the Corinthians[76] that God had placed "a thorn in his flesh… to keep him from becoming conceited". For Daniel, an affliction was a test set by God, a belief that has persisted among religious ascetics for centuries.

That he was in great pain for the latter part of his life at least is attested by Florence of Worcester who wrote that, when he died some twenty years later in 745, it was "after extreme suffering on behalf of the heavenly army".[77] The early medieval chronicler's use of the Greek word 'agones', meaning constant and acute pain, is indicative, especially when we consider the long-term consequences of the bishop's determination to stand in cold water in all weathers. As already noted, the practice was not unique to Daniel; St David of Wales was called 'the waterman' for doing precisely the same thing. Early manuals sent out by Baden-Powell to his Scout movement included the advice of putting one's head in a bucket of water to allay unclean thoughts. In Daniel's case, it was his limbs that suffered, not his head.

Later correspondence with Boniface reveals that, in old age, Daniel was already blind: "Farewell, farewell, thou hundredfold, dearest one, though I write by the hand of another".[78] In return, the missionary wrote back in a larger hand out of consideration for his mentor's failing sight. One tradition has it that, as a result of his blindness and ill health, the bishop was unable to carry out his pastoral duties late in life. It was said that a generation of children remained un-baptised at a time when a network of parish priests had yet to be fully established. In 744, Daniel finally recognised his physical shortcomings and resigned the office of bishop. His last months were spent at his alma mater of Malmesbury where he died and was buried the following year. Having benefited so much from the work of both Aldhelm and his old companion, the monks of the house would surely have done all they could to make his last days as comfortable as possible. Perhaps they were inspired, too, by last conversations with a sage and learned counsellor steeped in religious and political experience from the world outside their community. And from one who showed no doubt in his expectation of an afterlife. Unfortunately, any memories scribbled down by his listeners have long since been lost and we are left with the second- or third-hand assertions of chroniclers writing centuries later about the bishop's tireless work in the diocese and personal austerity. There is enough evidence, however, to show that Daniel used his administrative and political acumen, laced with theological insight and conviction, to open up a new dimension in evangelisation. As a result, the Christian message was spread deep into the dark forests of Germania by a generation of Anglo-Saxon missionaries inspired by his leadership and encouragement.

OVER ONE HUNDRED YEARS OF OBSCURITY

With the passing of Bishop Daniel and in stark contrast to the vivid, if occasional, glimpses into his life, the See of Winchester fell into historical obscurity for over a hundred years. For the century or more post-Bede, sources are scarce and unreliable, while the annals of the *Anglo-Saxon Chronicle* are sketchy and non-contemporaneous. Yet it is a period of swaying power balances and momentous events which blind the casual observer to the steady advancement of Christian conversion in both Britain and on the Continent. Secular and ecclesiastical structures were built, helping to create the resilient and cohesive society that would eventually face down the Viking menace in the following century. Villagers in the countryside, preoccupied with eking out subsistence for their families, would not immediately have noticed this as progress, but they would surely have remembered the day their little wooden church was dedicated, and a priest came to live in the area. And if they were able to bring their excess produce into the Winchester market, especially on a feast day, they would have been impressed by the celebrations at the Minster, now the kingdom's last resting place for a growing number of dead saints and rulers.

Support for the mission field continues

Quietly, too, Winchester scholarship persisted at the Minster and, combined with the prominent religious houses in the diocese, notably

Malmesbury, Nursling and Wimborne, continued to reinforce Boniface's missionary drive in Frisia and along the Rhine Valley. Despite his martyrdom in 754, Franconia, Thuringia and Hesse had all been evangelised by the late eighth century. Like Boniface, many of the missionaries and luminaries of the early German Church were from what we must now call Wessex. Lull of Malmesbury, a West Saxon and, coincidentally, a cousin of Boniface, became Bishop of Mainz and eventually, in 781, its archbishop. His name suggests that he was small of stature, but he proved a great administrator. He was zealous in the development of the canon law of the Church, his inspiration being fed by books laboriously produced and lovingly illustrated in the Minster's scriptorium back in Winchester. He also founded Hersfeld Abbey in north-east Hesse as a Benedictine house where its ruins today are judged to be the most extensive for a Romanesque church in Europe. The archbishop died in 786 and was buried at his abbey beside St Wigbert, Abbot of Ohrdruf in Thuringia, who came from Glastonbury and founded a school for missionaries in Germania. In 852, Lull was also canonised; between them, they had gone a long way to ensuring that the German mission field was self-sufficient.

There were others who would have also derived comfort and support from their home diocese of Winchester: the brothers Willibald and Winnebald – who died respectively in 787 and 761, both from a now-forgotten abbey at Waltham in south-east Hampshire – who went on to become, respectively, Bishop of Eichstaett in Franconia and abbot at the double monastery of Heidenheim in Schwabia; and Burchard, who became Bishop of Wurzburg in 741. Most impressive, however, is the role of the many female missionaries, especially from the nunnery at Wimborne,[79] who left their house to take part in the evangelisation of Germany. For some fifty years during the eighth century, women were equal in their service to God in the mission field, a reflection of the respect with which they were held in Anglo-Saxon society. Lioba, who, with thirty other nuns, joined her kinsman Boniface in 748, was renowned for her physical beauty. This, however, was hardly the reason why, for twenty-eight years, she remained Abbess of Tauberbischofsheim in southern

Germany. Her intelligence and kindness exemplified the best that had been nurtured under the direction of the West Saxon See.

Bishop Daniel's last years witnessed a weakened hand on the administration of his diocese at a time when the authority of Canterbury was growing stronger. At Cenwealh's Minster in Winchester, now a thriving and prayerful monastic-like community, successive 'priors' entrenched their hold over endowments made since the foundation of the See. This sowed the seed for perennial post-Conquest disputes with the bishop of the day – who would pull rank – over the control of income their property generated. The eighth century, however, was a period when the growing number of religious houses acted as centres of discipline, serving their localities and representing to them the values of Christianity. In Winchester, the bishop was usually tonsured and doubled there as head of his increasingly conventual cathedral.[80] The emphasis remained on his spiritual, not secular, duties.

Mercian Ascendancy over Wessex

The period following the death of Ine of Wessex is one of Mercian ascendancy, with their king, Aethelbald (716–757), claiming the title of Rex Britannica in a charter of 736.[81] Wessex was reduced again to a sub-kingdom, a Mercian dependency even, and lost control of much of its recently won northern and western territory. No major personality, secular or spiritual, emerged in Wessex to threaten Mercian hegemony, which lasted through to the death of Offa in 796.[82] By the end of the eighth century, Winchester had waned in secular influence, while the Mercian See of Lichfield had waxed, even claiming in 787 an archbishop's pallium which it held for sixteen years, the only English diocese, apart from Canterbury and York, to do so. Indeed, on the death in 793 of Archbishop Jaenbert, Higebert, the so-called Archbishop of Lichfield was, exceptionally, able to claim that he was head of the southern province. It no doubt aided Higebert's status that successive Mercian kings had by that time expanded their influence into Kent.

Daniel's immediate successor was Hunfrith, who held the Winchester See for ten years until his death in 754. He was one of the eleven bishops –

of twelve by then appointed in the province of Canterbury – who attended the Council of Clofesho in September 746. The Synod of Hertford (672) had decreed that a council should be held annually on 1 August at Clofesho, possibly identical with Cliffe on the Isle of Grain in Kent. This latest synod had been convened in response to a fierce letter to Archbishop Cuthbert[83] from Saint Zachary, pope from 741 to 752, which demanded reform in the English Church and threatened excommunication in the event that this was not pursued. One interpretation of this parlous state of affairs is that, with so much talent moving on to the Continent, a degree of complacency and maladministration had set in amongst lesser personalities left behind. That assessment, however, ignores the fact that it was Boniface who set off papal alarm. As mentioned in the previous chapter, the missionary had already raised the issue of unrepentant sinners. Shortly after Daniel's death, Pope Zachary relayed Boniface's complaints about the widespread promiscuity amongst young priests in Germania. Some were spending their nights in bed with four or five women and then getting up in the morning to celebrate Mass.

By the time papal concern became an issue, pastoral leadership from Winchester had been diminished for several years. The generous endowments of the previous fifty years, moreover, had also dulled the early English Church's cutting edge at home. As a result, the synod drew up thirty canons, or directives, in response to the pope's command. They ranged from the first regulation of the behaviour, dress, tenure and appointment of parish priests to confirmation of Canterbury's leadership in the province. In addition, dioceses were directed to hold their own synods to help implement the decisions taken at provincial level. Also in attendance at Clofesho was King Aethelbald who had chosen Cuthbert as his archbishop, advancing him from his former remote, but still Mercian, Hereford diocese.

In 752, as his counsellor, Bishop Hunfrith would have witnessed a rebellious flurry from King Cuthred of Wessex who dared to challenge Aethelbald and, for the short period until his death four years later, regained a measure of independence. While there is no suggestion that Hunfrith encouraged his king's revolt, his view would have been canvassed, whatever other competing politico-religious priorities a Winchester bishop might have had. Cyneheard, Hunfrith's successor, who died in 770, continued to direct the diocesan gaze towards the German mission field in a series of letters, now lost, including to Archbishop Lull in Mainz.[84]

It is a sign of the Wessex decline – and with it the influence of the Winchester bishop – that we do not know exactly who Cyneheard's successor was. We have a name – Aethelheard – but he was demonstrably not the same man who became Archbishop of Canterbury in 793.[85] Offa of Mercia would never have allowed a Wessex bishop such pre-eminence. It is likely, however, that Aethelheard of Winchester came from a monastic house, probably Malmesbury, as previous commentators have suggested.[86] By the late eighth century, the religious members of the Minster were creating a leading centre of scholarship, which became more of an inward-looking ivory tower as the century wore on. Aethelheard's immediate successors – Egbald (778–780), whose name may have appeared on a charter given by Offa to Croyland monastery,[87] and Dudd (c780–785), should perhaps be seen as acting more like abbots at an influential 'monastic' school than partners in statecraft. They have warranted no more than brief mentions in the sparse and subsequently compiled written record of their day. But they were the men who directed the Winchester scriptorium: they sourced the gilding inks and parchment or vellum for the production of increasingly beautiful illuminated manuscripts, they encouraged the accomplishment of skills that created them, and they managed the supply line and distribution of books for the mission field. On a practical point, they also directed the farming of sheep and goats on the episcopal estate at Downton in Wiltshire, whose hides provided the parchment.

With the death of Offa at the end of the eighth century, the political balance began to change. Immediately after King Coenwulf succeeded Offa, he faced two years of Kentish rebellion. A major issue was the Mercian attempt to restrict Canterbury's authority to the dioceses south of the Thames – London, Rochester, Selsey, Sherborne and Winchester. Coenwulf sought to carve out a third ecclesiastical province by promoting his capital, Lichfield, to the control of dioceses in the Midlands. Kentish fury increased to a point when, in the face of probably unfair accusations of being a Mercian puppet, Aethelheard, the Archbishop of Canterbury, was forced to flee to the Continent. In response to the Kentish rebellion, Coenwulf mounted an audacious attempt to restore stability and, at the same time, to advance the Mercian standard. He petitioned Pope Leo III for the restoration of a united southern province of the English Church with the pallium moved from Canterbury to London, then a Mercian-dominated centre. Archbishop Aethelheard, however, was already lobbying Leo – also temporarily a refugee at the court of Charlemagne – for the full restitution of his rights and won papal assurance that "the Primacy of Canterbury should be venerated and honoured as the archiepiscopal See in all things".[88] With an uneasy calm restored in Kent, Aethelheard returned to Canterbury and the question of London becoming an archdiocese fell, never again to be revived.

In 801, having obtained letters of support from the Archbishop of York and accompanied by Bishop Cynebert (c785–c802) of 'Wessex', Aethelheard journeyed to Rome.[89] His object was to convince the pope that the southern province of England should be reunited under Canterbury and that the pallium extended to Lichfield should be withdrawn. Leo commissioned a close examination of the legal basis for the respective claims. Winchester's reputation for scholarship and record-keeping, combined with that of Canterbury, won the day. Indeed, while the Mercians had curtailed the activities and residential rights of the Canterbury school, Winchester, better protected by the Wessex king, remained inviolate.

The rebirth of Wessex under Ecgbert

Cynebert's successor – Eahlmund (c802–811) – attended the annual Council of Clofesho in 803 and the closeness of the two major southern Sees was marked again in 814 when Bishop Wigthegn (811–825) accompanied his archbishop to Rome.[90] Yet again, the cause of Archbishop Wulfred's journey was Mercian encroachment, including sequestration of Church land. Cuthred, the Kentish sub-king, who was the brother of the Mercian king, Coenwulf, would have done little to protect Canterbury's interests; a Winchester bishop at that time was in a far stronger position, at least in terms of scholastic research into constitutional rights. It was about to get stronger. In 802, the Wessex ruler and Mercian vassal Beorhtric died. For sixteen years since 786 he had reigned in Wessex as Offa's son-in-law and, with so powerful a patron, had been able to blunt those with a far more credible claim to the throne at Winchester. By far the most eligible claimant was Ecgbert, who could trace his ancestry back to Ine's brother and, therefore, to the royal line of Cerdic the Saxon, the founder of the West Saxon dynasty. For at least three years from 787, Ecgbert was forced into exile by Beorhtric, and he too had sought refuge with Charlemagne, who was no advocate for Offa's Mercian hegemony. At the time of Beorhtric's demise, the Mercian Coenwulf was too preoccupied with the continuing unrest in Kent to counter the universal acclamation in Winchester that Ecgbert should ascend the Wessex throne.

Ecgbert had bided his time in the years before his accession and, although no documentary proof exists, it is possible to see the minds of successive Winchester bishops at work – men of peace, counselling a waiting game. The circumstances did not change after Ecgbert became king. From Winchester, where he built a palace, he could watch while his bishop supported Canterbury against the overbearing Mercians – again, biding his time.

In a last major offensive to extend their borders westwards into North Wales, the Mercians bit off more than they could chew. Initially successful in having penetrated as far as Snowdonia but weakened in the effort of maintaining an army of occupation in mountainous terrain, they were forced in 823 to retreat ignominiously. The consequent search for a scapegoat led to the deposition of their then king, Ceolwulf, who was replaced by a rather insignificant figure, possibly an ealdorman named Beornwulf; he sought an easier prey in Wessex. At the bloody battle of Ellendun – identified as Wroughton, to the south of Swindon – Ecgbert faced down the Mercian thrust. We can imagine that he assembled his forces on the high ground around the old British hill fort at Barbury Castle nearby and overwhelmed the enemy below in a well-coordinated charge. Ecgbert won the day, but only just; his own army was already exhausted after marching from a fight with the Cornish. Nevertheless, Stenton has acclaimed Ellendun as "one of the most decisive battles of Anglo-Saxon history".[91] It brought the Mercian ascendancy to an end and marked the beginning of the inexorable rise of the West Saxons.

These were heady years. With the Mercians preoccupied in North Wales, Ecgbert had renewed Wessex expansion westwards and his bishop, Wigthegn, a former monk from Glastonbury and clearly familiar with the terrain, went with him. During the two years 823–825, Ecgbert conquered Cornwall and gave thanks for his victories by granting lands around Crediton to the See of Winchester. Given that this was Boniface's birthplace, it might well have seemed an appropriate endowment. In fact, however, adjacent land was already in the hands of Sherborne diocese, dating from well before Bishop Daniel's death.[92] The king's new grant, therefore, must have been an acknowledgement of royal appreciation for some special but unknown service that Bishop Wigthegn provided. The bishop was at Crediton when this latest enhancement of the episcopal estate was attested.

Wigthegn was not the only senior cleric with Ecgbert during his Cornish campaigns: Herefrith, who seems to have been an assistant or a suffragan bishop appointed to minister to the king's fresh conquests, was also in the field. What appears to have been developing was a diocesan structure, under Ecgbert's benefaction, whereby each shire would have its own bishop and ealdorman. These appointments, however, remained firmly under Winchester's jurisdiction: Herefrith did not sign documents without Wigthegn's imprimatur. The situation is confused by Herefrith being always listed as Winchester's bishop from 825 onwards. Did Ecgbert harbour thoughts of Wigthegn's elevation to an archbishopric, with suffragans at shire level, not unlike Offa of Mercia before him who had sought to aggrandise Lichfield?

Ecgbert's great achievement was to unite the whole of the south of England – from Canterbury to Land's End – under Wessex hegemony; and he did so just as the great threat from Scandinavia, the Vikings, was materialising. First raids in the south began in the last years of the eighth century: a local reeve (or bailiff) was murdered at Portland in Dorset when he made enquiries about Danish ships that had moored there. More serious incursions followed against the British sub-kingdom of Cornwall. It is to Ecgbert's discredit that, for a short period, he allied with the raiders to defeat the Cornish Britons during his 823–5 campaign. His bishops would have been aware of this stratagem and may have counselled it as a means for clearing out the last vestiges of Celtic opposition to Roman canonical rule. Divine retribution, perhaps, came in 836 at the Battle of Charmouth when, as the *Anglo-Saxon Chronicle* records, both Wigthegn and Herefrith were slain by the Danes.

The increase of influence that the Winchester See enjoyed during Ecgbert's reign was not at the expense of Canterbury. The King of Wessex and his eldest son, Aethelwulf, who chased the Mercians out of Kent in 825, maintained a close political relationship with Archbishop Wulfred (805–832). The latter, in welcoming the replacement of the last Mercian vassal sub-king, urged the population to accept Wessex overlordship. Ecgbert and Wulfred, as well as the next archbishop, Ceolnoth (from 833), were now able to work towards two major goals: the melding of a single Saxon kingdom and the promotion of a united ecclesiastical province south of the Humber. Their success was such that only four years later, in 829, Wulfred anointed Ecgbert as Bretwalda, or overlord, of England, including the old sub-kingdom of Northumbria. The archbishop travelled all the way from Canterbury to conduct the solemn ceremony at Winchester's Old Minster, with Bishop Herefrith in attendance. Ten years later, Ecgbert's son Aethelwulf and Archbishop Ceolnoth, surrounded by senior magnates, both temporal and spiritual, met at Kingston, the important royal centre on the Thames. There, they ratified a treaty of long-term constitutional importance: for the first time it established, in law, the right of primogeniture in royal succession. It also reconciled outstanding troublesome land disputes in Kent and enshrined the "unshakeable friendship" between king and archbishop. Also present at the ratification was Bishop Helmstan of Winchester who had just succeeded to the bishopric after Eadmund (836–7) and Eadhun (838–9), each of whose episcopates having lasted little more than two years. Sadly, we know nothing of these two men, except that ancient sources[93] claim

Eadmund was buried under the entrance to the choir in the Old Minster. There is also an intriguing reference to Eadhun in a charter issued from Kingston in 839[94]: a grant of forty hides at Shalfleet on the Isle of Wight was made conditional on the bishop's loyalty. What lay behind this is not known and, by that date, Helmstan had succeeded him. As the Viking threat grew, however, the importance of securing the offshore island would have been considered crucial.

While we lack any detailed knowledge of the Winchester bishops of the late 830s, there is strong circumstantial evidence that they played an important role in the crafting of the Kingston treaty. The wide scope of the agreement suggests that it was not conjured up overnight. Months, probably years, beforehand, the king's counsellors would have worked on its content. Consulting as necessary with Canterbury, the Winchester bishop would have been to the fore, from offering his services to break an impasse in a complicated issue of land tenure to directing the scribes who drew up drafts for the final treaty text.[95] If there were ruffled feathers at court over legalising the principle of primogeniture, the bishop would have helped smooth them down with research-based argumentation. It is evident that both king and archbishop were deeply grateful for the Winchester bishop's contribution. Ecgbert granted valuable land to his bishop adjacent to his palace just outside the old defences of Winchester. Here, the bishop was given permission to build a residence where he might receive distinguished visitors and accommodate his supporting clerical staff and archives. Long since lost during subsequent development, this building may have occupied a site close to the foundations of the medieval bishop's palace of Wolvesey.[96] From now on, the bishop would have his own household, quite separate from the communal environment of the Old Minster. Within a short time, the building would have been brought within the integral defences of Winchester as the increasing threat from the Vikings emerged.

Winchester prospers under Ecgbert

The diocese also expanded geographically, though hardly to the same extent as previously. With the blessing of the archbishop, Ecgbert confirmed that the See of Winchester had jurisdiction over the Isle of Wight and added to the bishop's endowment there. From now on down to the Reformation, the Bishop of Winchester would periodically assume the role of a lord-lieutenant leading the defence of the vulnerable south coast of England. At the same time, the bishop recognised that he and his successors owed, and should profess obedience, to the head of Canterbury province. This regularised a procedure that, in the past, had been honoured in the breach.

It was during Ecgbert's reign that the religious community of St Peter and St Paul at Winchester received a major boost to its estate and, consequently, its revenues. For the first time, we hear of the long-standing diocesan interest in Farnham; a charter issued shortly after Ecgbert's accession recorded a grant of sixty hides by the otherwise almost unknown Bishop Eahlmund in exchange for parcels of land in Wiltshire. The bishop, however, insisted that the recipient, Brithelm, should provide hospitality for him for two nights – and ten jars of honey – annually. In what looks like a shrewd move, Eahlmund added the provision that, if Brithelm wished to sell, he should give his church at Winchester first option and, in effect, re-purchase at only half the price.[97] Under Bishop Wigthegn, forty hides at Alresford, previously lost to the Old Minster's estate, were restored.[98] Following Ecgbert's victories in Cornwall and at Ellendun, royal appreciation of the Church's contribution materialised in major land grants in Wiltshire, the upper Itchen Valley, the Meon Valley and, again, on the Isle of Wight.[99]

The agreement at Kingston was the climax to Ecgbert's impressive reign, but at – for those days – the ripe old age of sixty-three, he died the year before its ratification. In the preceding months, he had withdrawn from his capital and had entrusted the responsibility for receiving and entertaining important visitors to his bishop. In this, the ecclesiastical office was taking on a new – and secular – dimension, in some respects a forerunner to that of the medieval chancellor. Proximity to the king and his royal palace incurred duties outside those that fell to other bishops. By the time of Ecgbert's passing, the See of Winchester had gained substantially in authority and prestige, in parallel with the increasing influence of Wessex. It is largely forgotten today that King Ecgbert is regarded as the founder of the English monarchy. The royal family trees acknowledge this, but it is rare that this fact makes it into history lessons at school. By the same token, during his reign, virtually unremembered bishops would establish their place in government that would increase in importance almost inexorably down to the Conquest.

Even though Winchester was, indeed, becoming an administrative hub and a stronghold Ecgbert's son, Aethelwulf, would inherit, it lacked some of the functions of a major power base. Navigable though the Itchen was, the town was still twelve miles inland and its position could not rival a latter-day Southampton, or London. It is indicative that Ecgbert had established mints at London, Southampton and Rochester, all trading ports, but not at Winchester. Moreover, many of his charters were signed at Southampton and elsewhere during his still peripatetic rule. Winchester was not, in the first instance, a commercial centre; rather, it provided the spiritual and cultural focus for an embryonic nation served by a core of scholars based at the Old Minster. The environment suited the pious King Aethelwulf and more charters started to issue from Winchester as a result. Unlike his father and in contrast to his earlier military campaigns in Kent, he became increasingly reluctant to join battle. In fact, at this point, there was less necessity for forceful tactics because the southern shires – with archiepiscopal blessing – were now ready to accept his overlordship. Even Mercia was content to draw in its horns; previously disputed Berkshire was now recognised as West Saxon.

One might consider Aethelwulf to have sat on his laurels, but this would be to ignore the early influences on his approach to statecraft. These came from tonsured men of peace: two of them, Helmstan and Ealstan, had been personally chosen by Ecgbert as his son's tutors. Their guidance helped to introduce the first known procedures for the appointment of a Winchester bishop which hitherto had remained obscure. There were now to be three vital elements: the king's desire, the pope's approval and the cathedral's assent. Thus, within a short time of his accession, Aethelwulf commanded that Helmstan should be appointed his bishop at Winchester. Florence of Worcester, quoting from sources now lost, claimed that Helmstan was then sent on an embassy to Rome and whilst there, received the pope's ratification of his appointment. Meanwhile, for the first time that we know of, a bishop of Winchester was elected by the community at the Old Minster.[100] The West Saxon constitutional approach went further and illustrates one of the unique characteristics of the pre-Conquest English Church in the wider Christian context. Even with both royal and papal approval, Helmstan's appointment had still to be accepted by the West Saxon Witenagemot as the people's choice. Only then, in 839, was Helmstan consecrated bishop by Archbishop Ceolnoth. Subscribing fully to the spirit engendered at Kingston, Helmstan declared his profession of obedience to Canterbury. He went on to say that he had been elected by the pope and "the congregation of the city of Winchester", and by King Aethelwulf, the bishops, the nobles and the peoples of the kingdom. For the first time on record, a senior prelate of the Saxon Church was declaring the full legitimacy of his appointment. In doing so, he was also proclaiming the strong ties between – and interdependence of – Church and State, and stressing the important status of his cathedral centre to boot. In a century of scant detail on the lives of the bishops of Winchester, we suddenly have evidence of their powerful precedence over all other prelates owing allegiance to Canterbury.

Stenton, however, adds that Helmstan himself wrote of being consecrated "in the illustrious place, built by the skill of the Romans, called throughout the world the great city of London".[101] This suggests that Aethelwulf's bishop was also promoting West Saxon control over a city that had long been under the influence of the Mercians. In the years to come, Wessex would benefit from this new commercial asset on the Thames, but London, being more vulnerable to Viking incursions and their occupation, could never become the Saxon capital. For all the damage it would also suffer, Winchester remained the more defensible.

Helmstan with Ealstan, who became Bishop of Sherborne, remained Aethelwulf's closest counsellors after he came to the throne. From early in the new reign, they were busy spreading balm in the still troubled areas bordering Devon and Cornwall. They persuaded their king to be generous in providing reparations to those who had suffered from the ravages of the previous decades. Evidence of their success in mellowing a young man, previously acclaimed for his derring-do against the Mercians in Kent, may be found in Aethelwulf's charter of All Saints' Day on 1 November 844, signed at the Old Minster and attested by both bishops.[102] The charter granted relief from taxes to communities around Malmesbury – at Ellendun, Elhamstede, Charlton, Minety and Rodbourne – in consideration of the damage from plundering and warfare that they had incurred. As a corollary, plans were laid by the bishops for local religious houses and churches to observe in perpetuity the daily singing of fifty psalms and to hold masses for the king and his most senior counsellors to mitigate their sins during past conflicts. The sword had been sheathed to be replaced by economic relief and generous subventions – laced with impressive religious displays.

Despite one hundred years or more of relative obscurity, the Bishop of Winchester had now emerged as first amongst equals as courtier and counsellor. He was also the trusted guardian and teacher of future kings and could induce less violent methods of government. In turn, a more benevolent regime increased the loyalty and cohesion of a once tribal population. When the great external blast hit Wessex, this was to prove a crucial advantage in turning the Viking tide.

ST SWITHUN

THE PEOPLE'S SAINT

The bridge was almost complete; only the parapets needed final touches. A small group with sacks of produce for the market was already jostling across the new structure which would put the ferryman out of business and increase profit margins as a result. And when the river was in full spate, crossing it in the skiff was not without danger. Today, all that was in the past and there was excitement in the town to try out the new facility. There had been some trepidation at first. Would the stones stay in place – hold the weight? Now they were crossing in increasing numbers and the workmen were irritated; their final embellishments were being impeded. There was an oath, then a cry: the crowd retreated. On the ground lay a basket of eggs, the old woman's week's collection. Hearing the commotion, a man who had been standing on the city shore giving instructions to the foreman came over to the woman and raised his right arm over her bowed head. Then he picked up the basket and handed it back to her; she felt the contents, first one, and then another. She gazed up at the man in wonderment – not a single egg was damaged…

The miracle of the unbroken eggshells has always been attributed to Swithun, the nineteenth Bishop to the West Saxons. He was enthroned in about 852[103] at the Old Minster a year after King Aethelwulf's crucial victory over a Danish army, somewhere between the Thames and Winchester. The site has never been positively identified. The *Anglo-Saxon Chronicle* states that it was "fought to the south of the Thames at a place called aet Aclea". Historians discount Ockley in Surrey on etymological grounds[104] and no evidence has ever been found in the vicinity. One credible alternative is Oakley, pre-Domesday *Aclei*, to the south-west of Basingstoke. Low-lying, it would have been in the path of any mid-ninth century army advancing on Winchester from the north-east. It would also have been at least two days' march from the Danish reinforcement and supply route up the Thames. In contrast, the West Saxons would have had the advantage of shorter lines of communication and locally available trained forces and militias. The result of the victory was that the Wessex heartland, which had until then only been harried by coastal incursions (including the sacking of Southampton in 842), was relieved of immediate threat. It was only delayed since the Danes would soon take to wintering on the northern coast of Kent, so that they might build up more substantial forces to strike inland in the following spring. For a little while longer, however, the prosperity enjoyed in Winchester and in the surrounding countryside during the reigns of Ecgbert and Aethelwulf could continue. The bridge over the Itchen, an important piece of economic infrastructure, was a visible sign of this. Eggshells apart, its construction is certainly dated to the period.

As Barbara Yorke has assessed him, Swithun is a shadowy historical figure, but, conversely, his career seems to have been "of the greatest importance in the development of Winchester". As far as the See is concerned, one can go further; with the exception, perhaps, of Bishop Aethelwold in the late tenth century, Swithun's prestige as Bishop of Winchester was pre-eminent. A life of Bishop Swithun, written some two hundred and fifty years after his death, places his birth in the Winchester area.[105] The name Swithun or Swithin means 'moor cleared by fire' and could describe the place of his birth; there is a Twyford Moor to the south of Winchester. Domesday, however, refers to some eighty acres of Church land at Abbot's Worthy,[106] just to the north of the city, as The Moor. Given the intensity of Saxon manorial settlement in the upper Itchen Valley, it is tempting to favour this location over that of Twyford, which has never claimed a connection with the saint. And there is a pre-Conquest foundation dedicated to St Swithun at Headbourne Worthy on the same road leading north out of Winchester.

Swithun is said to have been born of a noble family in about 806 and any education he received would have been at the hands of the body of monks, priests and deacons who formed the religious community at the Old Minster. Here in 827, while still in his early twenties, he was ordained by Bishop Helmstan. It is not clear what level of holy orders he had attained by this point; neither do we know whether he actually took the tonsure or swore vows of celibacy. Part of the understanding of being taught in a religious community, however, was a commitment by the pupil to study for junior roles in the Church. This might be as an acolyte, or candle-bearer, assisting the celebrant at Mass or, subsequently, as a sub-deacon able to undertake more administrative tasks. Neither of these 'lower' orders of ordination required vows of celibacy or cut a young man off from more secular pursuits. On balance, therefore, and given his reported early association with King Ecgbert's court, it seems more likely that he was a secular clerk, having been ordained a sub-deacon, at most a deacon, but not yet a priest. And, at the time, even priests were still able to marry.

The next we hear of Swithun is that the king valued his counsel and chose him as his chaplain.[107] This suggests that Ecgbert had noticed a talented clerk at Helmstan's side and had taken him into the royal retinue. In successive, though not entirely trustworthy, charters, Swithun is described as "priest" and "deacon", but not in chronological order. A combination of a noble upbringing and involvement at court would have engendered in him a robustly practical approach to the mounting Viking threat to Winchester. A particularly gruesome legend ascribed to him paints Swithun as the instigator of a rather less saintly exercise: it is said that he caused the heads of dead Vikings to be displayed on the city walls above the river to deter further incursions. A Danish longboat, discovered nosing up-river on reconnaissance, would have presented an easy target to patrolling defenders. The crew would have been given no quarter.

Whether or not there is any substance in this story, Ecgbert's inclusion of him among those he entrusted with Aethelwulf's education confirms that Swithun was erudite. In such times, too, military considerations were never far from the thoughts of even religious advisers who often accompanied the ruler on campaign. As already mentioned, Swithun was close to Helmstan, who encouraged his king to spend more time in Winchester and to use it as his strategic base. Swithun's close association with the city suggests that he shared this view and had registered its importance in the kingdom. He was clearly proud of his birthplace, a point which would have enhanced his reputation amongst its inhabitants.

After a decade or more at court, Swithun is thought to have chosen a more spiritual life and it is now – in his late forties – that he would more likely have submitted for ordination as a priest. It would have been an essential prerequisite for his next recorded preferment. Elected by consent of the Old Minster clergy, Swithun was consecrated as Bishop of Winchester on 30 October 852 by Archbishop Ceolnoth and, in accordance with recent predecessors, declared his profession of obedience to Canterbury. With Bishop Ealstan of Sherborne, he remained one of two principal counsellors to King Aethelwulf, apparently offering advice on ecclesiastical affairs, while his colleague majored in financial and military matters. After his early years of struggle and conquest, Aethelwulf is known to have developed a diffident streak and tired of facing both administrative difficulties and further military confrontation. William of Malmesbury maintains that the two bishops urged Aethelwulf to exert himself.[108] As even this seems to have had little effect, they were left to shoulder many of the duties of kingship themselves.

Notwithstanding Swithun's pleas, but more likely because of his stepping into the breach, Aethelwulf recorded his thanks in the form of a clutch of land grants, one or two of which would have lasting significance. Small but potentially lucrative parcels at Headbourne Worthy and Chilcomb – both close to Winchester and originally believed to have been granted by King Cenwealh in the mid seventh century – were reconfirmed as property already given to the Old Minster. Swithun also received sixty hides at Farnham, the by now traditional way of thanking Winchester's bishops! The grant was subsequently confirmed to his successors by Aethelwulf's son, Aethelbald. Farnham Castle would become an important episcopal base from the Middle Ages through to the 1920s when it was absorbed into the new Guildford diocese. By far the largest grant to Swithun, however, was the one hundred and thirty-three hides (as much as almost 16,000 acres) at Taunton, the major politico-economic bastion way beyond the boundaries of the diocese.[109] This is evidence of Swithun being regarded as a military lieutenant as well as religious counsellor.

Episcopal contribution to stability during the latter part of the reign

Something seems to have been eating away at Aethelwulf; perhaps he was distraught by the loss of his wife, Osburg, with whom he had had at least five sons and a daughter. His eldest son, Aethelstan, had also recently died. Whatever the catalyst, it was at this point that, like his distant ancestor, King Ine, before him, he felt the need to go on pilgrimage and, in 855, made the long journey to Rome. It is thought that his innate piety had caused him to consider the venture from early on in his reign, but his former tutor, Swithun, was also in a position to have encouraged him. More valuable at home, perhaps, Swithun was not invited to go with his king. During the year Aethelwulf was away, he left his two eldest surviving sons, Aethelbald and Aethelberht, in charge of the kingdom.[110] On his return journey he stayed at the Parisian court of the West Frankish king, Charles the Bald. The two kings had much in common to talk about: both faced dynastic squabbles[111] and difficulties in keeping their respective realms in one piece. Evidently they hit it off, since the much younger Charles gave his daughter Judith's hand in marriage to the elderly Aethelwulf. Doubtless, he saw the union with the twelve-year-old princess – whom he insisted should be crowned queen – as a guarantee of Wessex support in the future. For Wessex, the fortuitous legacy was Judith's subsequent role as governess to her youngest stepson, the seven-year-old Alfred. Teaching him to read Latin was to have a far-reaching and invaluable outcome. This would far outstrip any political dividend Aethelwulf had hoped to gain from the match, even allowing for the fact that she was the great granddaughter of Charlemagne. And it seems axiomatic that Bishop Swithun's hand was behind the education of the future Alfred 'the Great'.

On his return to Wessex, Aethelwulf chose to withdraw from the centre of his kingdom to Canterbury and left his eldest son, Aethelbald, to rule in the West. This move has been interpreted as a symptom of an old man's increasing piety as he drew near to meeting his Maker, together with weariness of the issues piling up before him. They were considerable: feuding had broken out between several ealdormen during his absence, there was rivalry between his sons, and, of major concern, the mounting threat from an external enemy – the Vikings. In addition, his marriage to Judith had introduced fresh domestic strain in the realm. Events moved swiftly: in 858, Aethelwulf died and, seeking to strengthen his claim on Wessex, Aethelbald soon married his widowed stepmother. A son marrying his dead father's wife would certainly have caused a sucking in of breath, especially in the Church. It also widened the rift between those who subscribed to primogeniture in line with the agreement in principle reached at Kingston – where Aethelbald now chose to be crowned in 839 – and others who were all too ready to advance the claims of Aethelwulf's remaining sons and their own influence.

Where was Swithun in all this? History is all but silent. We can state with some confidence, however, that he was a strong supporter of primogeniture and the maintenance of the nation's cohesion. After all, he would have been at Kingston with Helmstan. And, as bishop of Winchester, there can be little doubt where he wanted the centre of government to be. We cannot, however, be entirely confident that his hitherto close colleague, Ealstan of Sherborne, shared his views; he must have had qualms about Aethelbald's marriage. And his diocese was soon to rise in status as, rather than Winchester or Kingston, its Minster began to receive the royal dead for burial. It should not be forgotten that Asser, the future waspish bishop of Sherborne and King Alfred's biographer, has handed down a particular slant on the period, not least because there are few other near-contemporary sources. His commentary apart, two events underlined the realities facing the kingdom: in 860, Aethelbald died and was succeeded by the next brother in line, Aethelberht; the following year, the Danes sacked Winchester in a daring raid up the Itchen. It is no surprise, therefore, that the new king took steps to reunite Wessex; he would have had the key moral authority of Bishop Swithun in bringing this about. The bishop's later stature is the more fully understood when viewed through this political lens. Moreover, it seems likely that he was in the vicinity when a force led by two ealdormen – apparently in their king's absence – drove the Danes away from Winchester. If not actually putting heads on spikes, he would at least have ministered to the unhoused, wounded and dying.

Swithun's reputation as more than a local saint

Despite scanty references to Swithun in historical records, more than any other bishop he has come to be identified with the city of Winchester and its folklore. He promoted the erection of fortifications round the Old Minster, so that they became part of the city's defence system. Just beyond the now lost Eastgate lies the site of the first stone bridge over the Itchen which he is credited with building; his bridge survived for over nine hundred years until its replacement in 1768.[112] Miracles apart, at the time he would have been much admired for the project per se, which facilitated traffic into the town from the sheep and other farming communities among the hills and valleys to the east, including the Church estate at Chilcomb. The egg story, therefore, is symptomatic of the reverence and thankfulness with which Swithun was held by the people of Winchester and surrounding villages.

Less dramatically, Swithun inspired scholarship at the Winchester school centred on the Old Minster, where he directed the compilation and augmentation of the Latin annals. In doing so he contributed to the *Anglo-Saxon Chronicle*, but strangely, the contemporary Winchester manuscript portion of the *Chronicle* makes no mention of him. Indeed, there is only one mention of Swithun in the entire *Chronicle*, which is to be found in the Canterbury entry for 861 and merely records his death.[113] The absence of so prominent and colourful a personality from the *Chronicle* points, perhaps, to Swithun's self-effacement as its principal informant or annalist, rather than to obscurity.

Swithun's reputation has come down through the ages as a man of humility and piety – always ready to visit and pray with the sick. However, there was also clear-sighted practicality: during his episcopate, he encouraged the building of new churches funded out of the growing prosperity enjoyed by greater Wessex and the comparative peace of its interior. Impressively, he is also thought to have persuaded King Aethelwulf to part with one tenth of his lands as a gift to the Church – tithing on a grand scale. For his part, when a new church was to be dedicated, Swithun would walk – not ride – through the night to ensure that he arrived in good time. Sadly, few if any, of these often wooden foundations have survived.

Popular in his time, it was long after his death, dated to 2 July 862 by Florence of Worcester[114] rather than 861 as in the *Anglo-Saxon Chronicle*, that his miraculous potential was fully recognised. On his deathbed he is said to have bidden three colleagues who were keeping watch to inter his earthly remains outside the Old Minster.[115] Here they would be trodden on and rain from the eaves would pour upon them. One assumes this was some token of humility. According to William of Malmesbury, the chosen spot was outside the north wall of the Old Minster towards the belfry tower. Unsurprisingly, over the next hundred years the tomb's exact whereabouts were forgotten by most people.

It was during Bishop Aethelwold's episcopate in the second half of the tenth century that the legends began to burgeon; the weather folklore about St Swithun's Day, 15 July, for example, is well-known down to the present day:

> "St Swithun's day if thou dost rain
> For forty days it will remain
> St Swithun's day if thou be fair
> For forty days 'twill rain na mair."

Weathermen will say that there is some meteorological sense behind the saying and will talk of 'blocking highs', and there are other parts of Europe where similar forecasts apply.[116]

The traditional explanation for the rain story is that the saint was angered by the decision in the latter half of the tenth century to move his body inside and erect a shrine to his memory. But the issue is rather more complicated. It was while Bishop Aethelwold was rebuilding the

Old Minster that the opportunity arose for the translation of Swithun's remains to a more salubrious site. One of Aethelwold's clerks, Eadsige of Winchcombe, who may have borne a grievance about being turned out of his quarters during the Minster's renovation, pointed out where Swithun lay – in the path of an extension planned by the bishop. At about the same time, a ceorl – a freeman of the lowest Saxon class – claimed that his prayers to Swithun had caused the hump on his back to disappear. More and more miracles were reported and King Edgar (944–975) ordered Aethelwold to move Swithun to lie beneath an elaborate feretory at the east end of the New Minster.[4] Without the grave in the way, of course, work on the western extension to the church was able to proceed.

It may have poured with rain on the day of his removal (15 July), but in the ten days that followed, two hundred people claimed to have been healed; in twelve months the number was countless. Impressed by this, Bishop Aethelwold obliged the monks at the Minster to assemble and to give thanks at each reported miracle. Unsurprisingly, this caused dissension and tradition has it that Swithun sent a posthumous rebuke to the protesting clergy – but not necessarily in the form of persistent rain. It did not cause him to refrain from working miracles and William of Malmesbury actually attested to having witnessed one of them.[117] Perhaps the most famous story of all was the legend of Queen Emma's survival of ordeal by fire. In the first half of the eleventh century she was accused of adultery with the then Bishop of Winchester,[118] and also of fraudulent land deals. Two centuries later, she is recorded as having agreed to undergo compurgation by walking over nine red-hot ploughshares. That she passed the ordeal unscathed was attributed to her pleas to St Swithun, who had appeared to her the previous night and had assured her all would be well. For good measure, the crowd watching also prayed to the saint for her deliverance. There is probably no substance to the story whatsoever: Emma was descended from Vikings and was the great aunt of William the Conqueror; she had married first a Saxon and then a Danish king. Given these antecedents, why would she acknowledge the

---

4   A bier surrounded by iron railings.

power of a Saxon holy man? It is possible some latter-day nationalist thought was at work.

In fact, contemporary accounts suggest that Swithun's translation was in accordance with his wishes. It was certainly what the people wanted, and their object of reverence and pilgrimage was declared a saint by popular acclaim – with no reference to Rome. There is a further dimension to Swithun's initial burial. As already noted, Winchester was sacked the year before his death and the Old Minster was severely damaged, almost certainly unroofed by arson. The grave, therefore, would have been exposed to the elements wherever it lay. When the time came, a suitable shrine was erected to provide a fitting memorial. Just as Swithun was moved at the time of the building of the New Minster, so Bishop Walkelin (1070–1107) had him transferred into his new Norman cathedral on 15 July 1093. Sadly, the feretory was damaged by accident in 1241 and the saintly bones were exhibited on 17 May to draw in funds for the repairs. Finally, the shrine was destroyed in 1538 during the Dissolution of the Monasteries. According to the contemporary audit, the value of the silver – not gold – retrieved for King Henry VIII's treasury was 2,000 marks (about £762,000 at today's prices). In recent years, Swithun's skull has been rediscovered at Evreux Cathedral in Normandy, having previously been taken to Canterbury by Bishop Aelfheah (984–1005) on his appointment as archbishop. How it came to rest in Evreux is not known.

Considering the lack of contemporary detail of Swithun's life and the historian's necessary resort to speculative accounts written in the late tenth century,[119] the saint has accrued a substantial following. There are some fifty-eight Anglican parish churches dedicated to him; this is on a level with worthies such as St Augustine of Canterbury and St Thomas Beckett. A number of Roman Catholic churches are also dedicated to him. The spread of these in England stretches as far north as Lincolnshire. He is remembered overseas – from Stavanger Cathedral in northern Norway, which claims to hold one of his arms, to a remote parish in Barbados. In Winchester, he has been the subject of many a pageant and has given his name to one of the most prominent girls' public schools in the country.

Ironically, the church dedicated to him in Winchester sits over Kingsgate, until recently the last surviving ancient thoroughfare into the old city.[120] Nowadays, people pass below – not over – this memorial.

ALFRED'S BISHOPS

The survivors threaded their way through the breaches in their town's defences and gasped at the widespread destruction. Here and there they came across the bodies of those who had not been so fortunate. There had been some elation when the rescue force had sent the Danes packing to their longboats, but now spirits were depressed. Houses were burnt to the ground, royal and episcopal palaces loomed out of the smoke as blackened skeletons and, horror of horrors, the Old Minster, still standing amongst the carnage, had lost its roof and furnishings.

The story of the destruction of Winchester in 860, after being put to the Viking torch, has slipped almost unnoticed through the pages of the history books. The effect of such devastation on the surviving population and local economy, however, is not hard to imagine.

Contemporary accounts[121] imply that a firestorm raged through the town reducing the highly flammable wood and thatch buildings to ash. Even if the shell of Cenwealh's Old Minster, built two hundred years earlier, was constructed substantially of stone, it would have suffered terribly, since at least its roof would have been supported by wooden beams. A similar fate must have overwhelmed the wooden framework of the royal quarters. Worse, and with longer-lasting consequences, was the burning of the Old Minster's library and the destruction of countless historical documents that had supported Winchester's reputation for scholarship. The only major stone works had been the remains of the Roman walls which had once surrounded the old *civitas*. There were substantial gaps in this defensive perimeter after stone had been removed over the centuries for Saxon projects, not least the construction of the Old Minster itself. Never seriously threatened since the fifth century, the town's defences – where augmented – would have been simple earthworks surmounted by wooden palings. Indeed, the heads of any slaughtered Vikings would probably have been stuck on stakes rather than perched on surviving walls.

Where was the king? The *Anglo-Saxon Chronicle* sets the date for the sack of Winchester at 861, but late 860 is now generally accepted since scribes then started each year in September at Michaelmas. King Aethelberht was probably still away in Sherborne burying his predecessor and elder brother, Aethelbald. Hence the Danish attack could not have happened at a worse time, during a period of mourning. With the new king away and no large defending force left in the town, Winchester was attacked by the crews of a Viking squadron. They had advanced up the Itchen in search of provisions for the winter in an area which had so far escaped their ravages. Although too late to save the town and many of its inhabitants, two local unknown nobles, described in the *Chronicle* as ealdormen, and their hastily gathered militias, chased off the marauders. This suggests that the Danes were not a major force, but rather that Winchester had been left vulnerable and offered easy pickings.

Where was the bishop? There is no mention of him, either at the time of the attack or during the rescue operation. He might, of course, have been with the young king, but contemporary timings are confused. Writing centuries later, Goscelin considered that Swithun did not die until 862, so it is possible that he returned in time to wreak vengeance on Viking corpses, hence the legend of impaled heads. In the chaos, however, no one had opportunity to provide chapter and verse, although the local population's reverence for their 'saint' is unquestioned. Regrettably, all the Anglo-Saxon chronicler in distant Canterbury says is that Swithun simply "passed away" sometime in 861. And in the aftermath of the destruction, his successors Ealfrith (c862–c871) and Tunbeorht (872–878) fare even less well in the *Chronicle* – they are not even mentioned. For the next fifteen years or more Winchester is no longer the centre of political or military activities, at least as far as the official record is concerned. Many of those trained to write the annals may have been killed and their papers destroyed. Scholarship and government suffered equally, and, during the ensuing years, administration was conducted peripatetically elsewhere. With the king's palace burnt down, the court had to seek refuge outside Winchester in one or other of the royal centres, deeper into Wessex. Sherborne, with its abbey founded by St Aldhelm in 705, would have been an obvious substitute for the Old Minster. Away from Viking access by river and the burial place of King Aethelred in 871, Wimborne might have substituted, as well Wantage, his younger brother Alfred's birthplace. Both could have offered the court temporary sanctuary until a time when Winchester might be rebuilt. This dispersal, however, was hardly conducive for scholastic continuity and the annalist's work.

In the immediate aftermath of the Danish attack, Swithun's successors would have had their hands full in conserving what was left of the books and records of the monastic school. Hardly the stuff of history and yet the very absence of an historical account speaks volumes about the misfortunes of Winchester during this period. It is difficult to do justice to Bishops Ealfrith and Tunbeorht. If, as one must suppose, they were following their increasingly beset king, military events were moving too fast for their reputations to become established. By the time Wessex fortunes recovered, they had died and were forgotten. Moreover, the 'great' champion of the Saxons – Alfred – was to overshadow his ministers and advisers in all areas of government, secular and ecclesiastical.

The Viking threat assumes a new dimension

The warfare that dominated the next decade or more also directed attention away from Winchester. From the mid-860s, the Danes increased the dimension of their attacks on the British Isles: instead of coastal raids, short-term incursions and wintering over, they landed a large army on the mainland which began methodically to eliminate the independent Saxon kingdoms. They started with East Anglia and moved on to York, which they occupied and held despite counter-attacks by the Northumbrians. Within two years, the Danish host had also descended on Mercia, whose king, Burgred, the brother-in-law of King Aethelred of Wessex, called for help from his kinsman. A temporary peace was bought in 867 and the Danes moved away to finish off the East Anglians. Joining up with fresh reinforcements arriving from Scandinavia, they fought a series of engagements with King Edmund and eventually captured him. Whereupon they humiliated him, tying him to a tree before puncturing him with arrows St Sebastian-style, and finally beheading him. Such a fate awaited any Christian leader who put up a fight against the Vikings and was cornered by them. For his religious fortitude, he was canonised as St Edmund the Martyr and, during the tenth century, his body was translated to Bury St Edmunds.

In the autumn of 870, it was the turn of Wessex. With the enemy establishing their headquarters near Reading, Aethelred and his remaining brother, Alfred, found themselves fighting to defend present-day Berkshire and northern Hampshire. Repulsed at Ashdown, the Danes retired towards Winchester but encountered further strong Saxon resistance at the drawn Battle of Basing. The size and military professionalism of the Danish host against the increasingly uncoordinated Saxon shire levies meant, however, that Aethelred and Alfred were compelled to firefight, never quite knowing where the next blaze might break out. The following April, Aethelred died and Alfred started his reign inauspiciously by losing to the Danes at Wilton in May.

The coming of Alfred

It could hardly have been a worse time for Alfred. Not only did he face a major threat, but throughout his kingdom there was famine following a "pestilence" which carried off humans and animals alike. It may well have killed Bishop Ealfrith[122] who would have ministered to the sick and dying. Many clerics over the centuries have died from disease caught from the bodies of the souls in their pastoral care. The widespread sickness in the south and some timely financial inducement from Alfred encouraged the invaders to move away to seek fresh pickings, firstly in London, before returning north to put down a revival of resistance in Northumbria. By the autumn of 873, however, the Danes were established on the Trent and had forced the Mercian King, Burgred, to flee to Rome. Thus, the pope of the day was informed of the dire heathen threat to Christianity in the Saxon kingdoms but was totally powerless to do anything about it. And neither of the Canterbury archbishops of the period – Ceolnoth and Aethelred – has left much of a mark on history.

From the ealdorman to the ordinary villager in the path of the Danish rampage, the situation was dire. The Danes, too, clearly considered that the plight of their intended victims meant they could afford to fight on two fronts. Leaving one half of the host to subdue the north, in the autumn of 875, they sent the other, under Guthrum, from the Midlands to Wareham in Dorset. There has been little explanation why Guthrum should have so extended his lines of communication, but one possibility is that he was compelled to track down the wily Alfred, who was reluctant to commit his disorganised forces to a set piece battle. The king was also seeking to deflect the Danes away from the Wessex heartland. During the following year, the two sides fought a series of minor engagements in the West, neither gaining the advantage. After a reverse in Devon and running short of supplies during the summer of 877, Guthrum retreated from Exeter to Gloucester. Alfred's tactics appeared to be paying off. The following January, however, the Danes moved on Chippenham where they routed the Saxons, forcing Alfred to take refuge amongst the Somerset Levels, on the Isle of Athelney. Nearly seventeen years since the sack of Winchester, the kingdom was all but obliterated.

Against all the odds, the fight back now began. It would lead to the neutralising of the Viking peril for nearly a century and the birth of Wessex as the basis for English unity. Within half a day's ride from Athelney, Alfred's bishop, Tunbeorht, is thought to have owned a farm at Montacute, once known as Bishopston or, more descriptively, Bishopscomb.[123] The very term, *comb*, meaning a wooded hollow in a hillside, suggests a refuge or safe haven where the king might have been able to summon his advisers, temporal and spiritual, for a secret council of war. The still extant Bishopston tithing is situated on and around a once revered promontory – St Michael's Hill – affording a wide view of the surrounding countryside. Alfred's biographer, Asser, states that the king also sought shelter in "the woodlands" of Somerset.[124] If impenetrable Athelney was the last-ditch defence in winter, was 'Bishopscomb' the place where a counter-offensive was planned for the spring? We cannot know, but it would have provided a discreet meeting place where the king's senior counsellors could have gathered without attracting the attention of Danish scouts to Alfred's hideaway in the marshes. And the bishop would have naturally been a key member of the assembly.

While some of his followers might have harried Danish lines of communication in the early spring, for a more ambitious thrust, Alfred needed to collect his forces and supplies from the shires and concentrate them at a place where he could fight at best advantage. This was not something conjured up: it would have required careful planning and the deployment of a network of messengers. Who better to give advice on this than Bishop Tunbeorht? He would have been able to use his clergy to host and refresh mounted couriers deployed to population centres throughout the kingdom? At this point, too, his own diocesan estate still stretched from eastern Somerset to western Kent, taking in parts of present-day Dorset, Gloucestershire, Wiltshire, Hampshire, Berkshire, Surrey and across the Thames into Oxfordshire. That so many levies mustered at Ecgbert's Stone at such a critical time speaks volumes for the underlying cohesion of Saxon society, but the Church was the glue that held it together. What followed was the comprehensive victory over Guthrum at Ethendun (Edington), near Trowbridge, in May 878 and, within a few weeks, Guthrum's baptism at Wedmore in Somerset, with Alfred as his godfather. No one has identified the cleric who officiated at this major conversion to Christianity, but the unsung Tunbeorht would have been the man on the spot. Of all the bystanders, he would have been conscious of the symbolism and the parallels with the baptism by his venerated predecessor centuries before of another pagan leader. That, too, had brought peace and stability.

Tunbeorht died within a year of Ethendun, perhaps for the same reason that other leaders, like King Aethelred or Swithun, had "passed away" soon after a military campaign or skirmish. What contemporary chronicles do not describe are the privations endured during long months of fighting, let alone any wounds suffered. If Tunbeorht was with his king, as seems likely, the conditions he would have faced would have been exhausting, especially for an older man.

Bishop Denewulf

Interestingly, his successor was a much younger man and, it is said, illiterate, at least at the time of his consecration.[125] The Winchester tradition has it that Alfred met his future bishop, Denewulf, while in Somerset: the latter had been driving a herd of swine into the forest to feed on acorns. The two men had fallen into conversation and the king had been impressed by the straightforwardness and simple common sense of the herdsman. He took Denewulf into his immediate retinue. The story has been embellished and combined with Asser's description of Alfred letting a woman's cakes burn.[126] It was Denewulf, so the story goes, who entered the hut just after she had boxed the king's ears and revealed Alfred's identity. Another version claims that Denewulf was actually the woman's husband. Stripping his elevation of its colourful legend, the new bishop's lack of education points to a dearth of better qualified candidates and to the socio-military priorities of the time. Alfred had to choose a man whom he could trust to administer a diocese forming the backbone of his kingdom.

Whatever the truth, Bishop Denewulf was ordained, consecrated and installed at Winchester within a year of Ethendun and held the diocese until his death in 908, as recorded in the *Anglo-Saxon Chronicle*. His humble origins may not have endeared him to surviving clergy in Winchester, used to his well-educated and tonsured predecessors. Be that as it may, Alfred encouraged his bishop into literacy; indeed, it is likely that they both received instruction in Latin from Asser, a Welsh monk from St David's. Again, it should be noted that the king was drawing in a scholar from the west, not from Canterbury or Winchester. In 885, Asser was invited to join the depleted circle of scholars at Winchester, and it was he[127] who assisted Alfred in his translation of St Gregory the Great's treatise *Pastoral Care* from Latin into the vernacular. On its completion, Alfred sent jewelled pointers or aestles to each of the bishops in Wessex, *"pour encourager les autres"*, along with a copy of this work. To date, seven of these have come to light, the most famous being 'Alfred's jewel' discovered in 1693 at North Petherton, only eight miles from Athelney Abbey. The aestle is described as a "masterpiece of goldsmith's work formed round a tear-shaped slice of rock crystal" that bears an enamel plaque illustrating a figure said to depict the sense of sight. An open-mouthed mythical animal is at one end into which a pointer made of bone or ivory was once inserted. The language construction of the inscription "Aelfred mec heht gewyrcan" ("Alfred ordered me to be made") is Mercian and would have been a gift crafted by someone in the retinue of Ealhswith of Mercia, Alfred's queen.[128] Denewulf, as a probable recipient of an aestle, was, however, literate enough to be sent to Rome shortly before his death, by Archbishop Plegmund, to deliver the money collected by the Church, subsequently known as 'Peter's Pence'.[129] For the first time since early in the century, the Bishop of Winchester was being sent on provincial business to the Vatican. Denewulf's Latin must have been good enough by then for such a mission.

Asser makes no mention of Denewulf in his biography of Alfred, but the latter was still in office when Alfred's son and successor, Edward the Elder, founded the New Minster – immediately adjacent to Cenwealh's church – as a mausoleum for his father and kinsfolk. The three 901 charters show that the new community was expected to serve the spiritual interests of the royal family; the incumbents were to say prayers daily for the souls of both Alfred and Edward. The Old Minster, however, remained the bishop's seat and was served by irregular canons, many untonsured.[130] Scholarship, administration and pastoral care, rather than monasticism, remained as Alfred's priorities in contrast to his son's new edifice where the emphasis was on the dead rather than the living. Having survived his early years by the skin of his teeth, Alfred's principal concern was to reconstitute the very fibre of his kingdom. One cannot escape the conclusion that whoever was Bishop of Winchester in the reign of Alfred the Great, he would have been overshadowed. Apart from his strategic and tactical genius and his wisdom in governance, Alfred elected to be a religious leader in his own right. In turn, Denewulf was chosen for administrative competence rather than piety: there was no time or opportunity to consult with the comparatively insubstantial Archbishop at Canterbury or distant Rome – at least, there is no mention of these processes in the record. In the face of a continuing threat from the Danes, however, the Church would have been only too glad to have had such a royal champion.

Alfred was not unappreciative. Within a year of Denewulf's appointment, the king granted him in person eight hides at Ruishton ('the settlement where the rushes grow') just to the east of Taunton.[131] It is possible that Alfred was rewarding Denewulf's family, who may have come from the area. In an age of rebuilding, the bishop would have profited from the thatch material that this small estate could offer. There was, however, no repetition of the largess enjoyed by the fighting Bishops Herefrith and Wigthegn during King Ecgbert's reign. The only other land settlement affecting the diocese under Alfred is an unclearly dated reversion of over one hundred hides in total at Chisledon (near Swindon) and Hurstbourne Priors (south of Andover) in exchange for a slightly smaller total centred on Cholsey in Oxfordshire, Hagbourne near Didcot, and Basildon overlooking the north bank of the Thames in Berkshire.[132] This redistribution does not make much sense, unless one takes into account the known destruction of Basildon during the Danish rampages. Was the bishop being asked to take a personal interest in rebuilding projects close to the king's heart? There can be no other explanation for such a random selection.

Only seventeen land charters have been identified for Alfred's twenty-eight-year reign. There are small grants early on to Chertsey and Malmesbury Abbeys and to the new foundation at Shaftesbury. Shortly after his victory at Edington, another new foundation at Athelney benefited from the gift of ten hides at Long Sutton.[133] Barbara Yorke has noted[134] how during the later years of the reign, a number of episcopal properties were leased out to laymen or simply lost. This may, in part, be explained by a weakened clerical cadre and administration stemming from the sack of Winchester, with secular authorities having to step in to manage estates. When Denewulf sought to reclaim land at Alresford –

presumably that granted by King Ecgbert – held from the Church and forfeited to the Crown after the lessee had been convicted for adultery, the bishop had to buy back the property for one hundred and twenty mancuses of gold, a substantial sum probably paid in the form of bullion rather than coin.[135] Later, the Old Minster was compelled by Alfred and his son, Edward the Elder, to lease an estate at Beddington in Surrey. This provoked an anguished cry from Denewulf that the king should not make further unwelcome demands on the episcopal estate in case it diminished essential income for the upkeep of the house it supported.[136] Denewulf's protest could not have been entirely ineffectual since Beddington was certainly back in episcopal hands at the time of Bishop Aethelwold's death in 984. Perhaps surprisingly, the bishop was not remembered in Alfred's will, dated to 885.[137] That said, the king distributed his not inconsiderable wealth principally to his family; the important places in his life – his birthplace at Wantage and, of course, Edington – were handed to his wife, Ealhswith. A substantial sum was also given to the Old Minster, probably as the expected funding for the New Minster to be built during his son's reign. Overall, this wise and truly 'great' man probably judged that the Church was already well enough endowed.

Alfred died in 899 aged only fifty and was buried in Winchester. He has been compared favourably with Charlemagne, a possible role model, because of the visionary aspects of his reign. His greatness was rooted in the Christianity which in previous centuries had civilised what otherwise would have been an unenlightened society where the strong arm ruled. By the second half of the ninth century, the king, though assailed on all sides, could draw on the legacy of the early Winchester bishops who had contributed so much to the mores and legal framework of the state and had also built the foundations of a parish structure to assist with local government. During his youth, before the Danish maelstrom hit Wessex, he was also imbued with the lessons in statecraft handed down by Helmstan and Swithun. Illustrious as he was, Alfred benefited substantially from the often, unsung cohesion constructed by spiritual as much as secular forces. Fully occupied by military, legal, cultural and social responsibilities, he appears to have been more than content to leave the Church to govern itself in the hands of trusted prelates of whom we know little. But then, it is also impossible to identify any of Alfred's secular counsellors.

THE BISHOPS OF EXPANSIONARY WESSEX

Inch by inch the stone lid of the coffin ground aside. Those gathered round watched in silent reverence as the mummified remains of the saint were revealed. Leathery skin and strands of hair still covered his skull and, through the frayed cloth that covered the cadaver's body, tissue could be seen still clinging to the skeleton. The lid was then laid to one side: a small delegation advanced led by a crucifer. They carried an exquisitely embroidered maniple[138] and stole which they placed carefully on the saint. Prayers said, the lid was replaced.

The year was 934 and the place was probably close to the site of Durham Cathedral where Cuthbert, arguably England's premier saint, still lies. The episcopal adornments had been made at Alfred the Great's foundation in Winchester, the Nunnaminster, where his widow, Queen Ealhswith, had retired after his death.[139] They had been ordered by Aelfflaed, the first of King Edward the Elder's three wives, and presented to Bishop Frithstan, who had worn them over his white robes until his death two years before, in 932. For these vestments to have been placed on a man so venerated as Cuthbert, Frithstan must have been held in high regard.

Bishop Frithstan

His very name, with its combination of 'frith' (peace) and 'stan' (stone or place), suggests that Frithstan was born of a devout family, but nothing is known of his origins. He received his education at the Winchester School where he came under the direct influence of the Benedictine monk, Grimbald. In 885, this famous scholar had been attracted to Alfred's court from St Bertin's monastery, near St Omer in France. It is a mark of the extent to which Winchester's scholastic reputation had been re-established that Grimbald subsequently declined the offer of the See of Canterbury; instead, he remained to inspire the next generation, accepting Edward the Elder's appointment as the first abbot of his just completed New Minster standing adjacent to Cenwealh's church. It seems likely that Frithstan was a monk at the Old Minster and was engaged in the arrangements for, if not the construction of, this celebrated Saxon edifice, so hard-heartedly destroyed by the Normans shortly after the Conquest. He could also have been at Southampton in 903 when Edward issued the founding charter, complete with grants of approaching three hundred hides up and down central Hampshire to guarantee New Minster's financial security.[140]

Frithstan was one of seven bishops consecrated on the same day in 909 by Archbishop Plegmund, an event which reflected a major reorganisation of the dioceses of Wessex. During the ninth century, assistant bishops, sometimes known as shire bishops, had been appointed to help care for remoter parts of Wessex. During the height of the Danish threat, too, Sherborne's influence had perforce eclipsed that of damaged Winchester, at least temporarily. But with the deaths in the same year of Alfred's long-serving Bishop of Winchester, Denewulf, and biographer, Bishop Asser of Sherborne, the ideal opportunity presented itself for reordering the two rambling dioceses. Sees were now established for each of the Wessex shires: Cornwall (Truro), Devon (Exeter), Somerset (Wells), Wiltshire/Berkshire (Ramsbury), Sussex (Selsey) and Dorset (Sherborne). Although Winchester lost its western extremities – but not its estates – it retained all Hampshire and Surrey and still stretched east along the south bank of the Thames to Rochester's boundary inside Kent. One or two of the new dioceses, however, were to prove financially unviable and, before the end of Saxon rule, Cornwall had been placed under Exeter and Ramsbury united with Sherborne. Winchester's geographical position and close access to London ensured that the diocese remained first among equals. Despite its reduction in size, Winchester also retained its scholastic eminence and, importantly for several centuries to come, its wealth.

The arrival of Edward the Elder brought some noteworthy additions to the diocesan estate. In 904, the king signed off a charter at Southampton to Denewulf and his retinue ('familia') which exchanged forty hides at Portchester for a similar tract of land at Bishop's Waltham; this would eventually become the attractive fortified palace and retreat – a favourite with many medieval bishops and their successors down to the English Civil War – in south-east Hampshire.[141] In the same year, Denewulf and his household received a grant of privileges for the monastery at Taunton in exchange for several parcels of land in Somerset and Wiltshire.[142] Touchingly, in the last few months of his life five years later, the king "and the community" granted the elderly bishop a lease of three hides at Tichborne from the local diocesan estate.[143] Was this a retirement package? There were, moreover, conditions attached: the lessee was expected to supply vitals to the Old Minster and with his death the land was to revert to his cathedral.

The opening years of Frithstan's episcopate witnessed a consolidation of the bishop's hold on a number of well-known Hampshire settlements, now small towns and beauty spots.[144] Next to the king, Bishop Frithstan and his successors were recognised as the greatest landlords in the Wessex heartland with financial buoyancy more than assured. Above all, in what was to be an age of conquest and expansion, Winchester's bishop represented the central control of a widespread web at home while the king was away on his campaigns. He was no longer expected to provide blessings on the battlefield, but rather to be a mainstay in the army's absence and the principal adviser at a court increasingly based at Winchester. With Edward the Elder and his successors now embarked on achieving hegemony over all England and requiring stability on the home front, the prestige and influence of their bishop back in the recreated capital was bound to grow.

Alfred's son and grandson take the offensive

Edward the Elder's reign started inauspiciously with a rebellion staged by his cousin, Aethelwold, son of Alfred's elder brother, Aethelred I.

Centred in the potentially rival town of Sherborne, the opposition to Edward's succession lasted for three years and there is reason to believe that Bishop Asser played an active role. Although his near-contemporary account of Alfred's life added colourful detail on the reign, it also included some waspish comment from which it would appear that he nursed divided loyalties. As Sherborne's bishop, he would hardly have been an idle bystander while a young pretender conspired against Alfred's son and heir. This interpretation might help explain why Sherborne was so reduced during Archbishop Plegmund's diocesan reorganisation, a move which re-established Winchester's seniority. In the previous century, the successors to St Aldhelm had inherited a scholastic tradition which had rivalled Winchester. But however many bishops Archbishop Plegmund had consecrated, it was Edward the Elder in Winchester who ordered their placement. By 909, too, he had encouraged the purchase by Saxons of large tracts of land held by Danes north and north-east of the Thames, behind which came a Christian missionary impetus, launched from Winchester – not from Sherborne. Hand in hand, the same year also saw a renewal of hostilities with a combined Wessex and Mercian army harrying the Danes as far north as Northumbria and forcing them to sue for peace.

The following year, a decisive Saxon victory against the Danes at Tettenhall in Staffordshire opened the way for the great expansion of Wessex. This major push was consolidated by the strong alliance between Edward and his sister, Aethelflaed, the 'Lady of the Mercians', who ruled in Mercia from 911 until 918 after her husband's death. During this period, Edward consolidated his hold on London, Oxford, Bedford, Hertford and Cambridge, advancing into Essex. Before the end of the pre-harvest campaign in 917, he had killed the Danish East Anglian king and several of his senior commanders at the Battle of Tempsford to the north of Huntingdon[145] and now dominated the Midlands. Aethelflaed's death did not delay his progress through Nottingham, Tamworth and Lincoln: in the following year, all the earls of Mercia had accepted his overlordship. When Aelfwynn, Aethelflaed's daughter and only contender for the Mercian throne, was carried off to Winchester, Wessex and Mercia became one. By the autumn of 919, Edward had fortified his northern borders and had received tributes from Raegnald of York, Ealdred of Bamburgh on the Northumbrian coast, and from the kings of Scotland and Strathclyde. No other Saxon king, including Penda and Offa, had gained such sway.

The only account of Edward's military and political achievement appears in the West Saxon Annals, so it is little wonder that he is portrayed as heroic. He could not, however, have made such great advances without the firm support of the Church and, as with Swithun before him, Frithstan was the man who controlled the record. As a reputedly humble man, he was content to edit the deeds of others without detailing the part he played himself. But it must have been substantial. The ceremony at Cuthbert's tomb two years after Frithstan's death is surely testament to the reverence with which he was held, as well as a propaganda stunt.

Bishop Beornstan

His successor, Beornstan, became bishop in 931, the year before Frithstan died. We know from the *Anglo-Saxon Chronicle* that Frithstan, not the archbishop, consecrated Beornstan in Winchester on 29 May. We might infer from this that the elderly bishop was feeling too frail to continue his pastoral duties. But Frithstan's contribution to Wessex expansion and influence would not be complete until after his death, when his beautiful vestments were laid out in St Cuthbert's tomb at Durham.

Edward the Elder died in 924. His eldest son, Athelstan, was crowned on 4 September 925 at Kingston in Surrey and very much within Frithstan's diocese. Kingston had become the traditional venue for the coronation of Wessex kings, although Edward and his son Aelfweard were buried at Winchester. Their bodies were carried from Cheshire and Oxford respectively, a clear indication that Winchester, rather than Sherborne or Wimborne, was now considered the royal mausoleum. The *Chronicle* does not say who crowned Athelstan, but Frithstan would surely have buried his father. Within a few years, Athelstan had emulated Edward by taking over York and subduing Northumbria. He then pressed on into Scotland and it was during his progress north in

934 that he stopped at Durham. Here, he delivered Frithstan's beautifully embroidered vestments for the adornment of Northumbria's cherished saint. Not only was he resealing an old alliance, but he was matching Winchester's re-emerging excellence in art and culture to the traditions of the old northern realm. Evidently aware of his own kingdom's history, Athelstan reprised Cynegils' axis with Oswald in the time of Berin, blessing it with a symbolic religious demonstration of spiritual authority. The vestments remain on display at the shrine of St Cuthbert in Durham Cathedral, complete with the text stitched into them: "For the revered Bishop Frithstan". It is pleasing to note that several of Frithstan's books survived until William of Malmesbury was writing in the twelfth century. Moreover, there is evidence of a cult surrounding his memory from two martyrologies written a hundred years later.

Frithstan's feast day was celebrated on 10 September, and he was canonised by popular acclaim. The exact spot for his tomb has never been discovered,[146] but one person would certainly have prayed over it: his successor, Beornstan. He was another disciple of the scholar-monk Grimbald and was said to have spent long nights kneeling in prayer at tombs in the cemetery. His saintly and ascetic behaviour also attracted a cult later in the century. The story was told that during one night's mass for the souls of the departed, he had just rounded off his psalm singing with a 'requiescent in pace' when the sound of a mighty multitude beneath the earth responded 'Amen', doubtless frightening and inspiring those present in equal measure. During the two and a half years he served as bishop, Beornstan would wash the feet of the poor and serve them daily with food from his table. This close identity with the teachings of Christ contrasts sharply with the meaning of his given name: 'bear' or 'warrior-like'. Born in about 870, he might well, of course, have been the son of one of Alfred's brave captains in the field.

For much of Beornstan's episcopacy, however, the warriors were in the north bringing the Scots to heel. King Athelstan would have been more than content to leave behind a bishop who would do his best for the common people and pray day and night for the souls of his distinguished ancestors in the Winchester mausoleum. Sadly, Beornstan died on 1

November 934, All Saints' Day, while on his knees. It is said that he had retired to his private chamber after a day's work attending to the sick and poor. When he did not appear the next morning, his servants assumed that he had been praying at great length for all souls and so did not venture into his chamber until the evening of the next day. There they found his lifeless body.

Of all the Winchester bishops, Beornstan is credited with a unique legacy. What claims to be the oldest charitable foundation in the country was probably the result of a bequest from him for the continuing care of the poor of his city. Across the road from King Alfred's statue in the Broadway stand St John's House and Chapel, parts of which date from 935, the year after Beornstan's death. In his time the thoroughfare was known as Bucchestret (Buck Street), now Busket Lane. Beneath St John's House there is an Anglo-Saxon vaulted kitchen which may have formed part of the original alms-house. The charity was refounded in 1289 and has since continued, uninterrupted, to provide relief for the poor and needy. Since 1984 it has been known as St John's Winchester Charity and houses nearly a hundred residents. Fittingly, Bishop Aethelwold declared some thirty years after Beornstan's death that he had received a vision in which he was told that his predecessor enjoyed equal glory in Heaven with Berin and Swithun; he should receive similar honour on earth. Another version has it that Beornstan announced his own beatification. Although his feast day is recorded as 4 November, he was in fact never canonised and his memory was quickly eclipsed in the tenth century by the more colourful cult of St Swithun. Such is the way of the world.

Beornstan's piety fits into a sadder side to Edward the Elder's and Athelstan's glorious deeds on the battlefield. The victims of nearly thirty years of continuous warfare on the boundaries of Wessex – the dead and wounded and widows and orphans – added to other privations and swelled the problems of poverty in the city. While in the surrounding countryside, farmers and landholders both large and small may have enjoyed prosperity in a peaceful kingdom at home, the poorer parts of the capital would have resembled a soup-kitchen economy. And the bishop's quarters were only five minutes' walk away. The St John's

Charity was a brave attempt to address the endemic problem in the royal city.

What kind of a place was Winchester in the mid tenth century? Its defences were surer, even if stone walls were not yet complete. The vulnerable approach up the Itchen seems to have been plugged by Alfred's creation of a naval force in the Solent which grew in strength during Edward and Athelstan's reigns. The destruction of 860 would have long since been made good and there were now royal quarters just outside the city limits where Hyde Abbey would later stand and, also, just two or three miles to the north at King's Worthy. Despite their campaigning, both Edward and Athelstan much preferred to be in the south and held councils regularly within the Winchester diocese. Interestingly, only one council was held in the Canterbury area from the mid ninth to the mid eleventh centuries, which again suggests that the Bishop of Winchester was always more closely in contact with the English overlord than the archbishop.

Apart from its military and diplomatic achievements, Athelstan's reign impresses for the literacy of the clerks who served him. It has even been said that the British civil service can trace its origins back to Athelstan. But clerks first needed to be educated. It was Winchester's several religious centres and assiduous bishops that produced a corps of scholars to draft the charters and laws of the day. Such laws contain traces of humane thinking which might well have come from men of gentler persuasion who were in a position to use their influence with the king. In the face of a wave of thievery during a time of recovery from continuous warfare, Athelstan's legislative deterrence recognised that young persons under the age of fifteen could not be held fully responsible for their criminal acts, an approach which compares favourably with today. As the kingdom continued to expand during the tenth century, so the inevitable demand for prestigious Winchester-trained clerks increased. Complete with its already noted school of religious art and illumination, St Swithun's priory, based on the Old Minster like St Augustine's at Canterbury, was becoming a forerunner of the great European universities. As an abbot in his own right, the Winchester bishop was a prototype scholastic chancellor.

Bishop Aelfheah I

The installation of Aelfheah (the first of two bishops of this name) in 934 coincided with a growing awareness of a need to regulate monastic life more closely. Aelfheah was a Benedictine monk before his consecration, but where he came from is not known. We do know something of his appearance, for his name includes the suffix 'heah' meaning 'tall', and he bore the nickname 'the bald'. There is a suggestion that he had spent some years on the Continent and had also lived as a hermit. Perhaps during this early period of his life, he learnt of new ideas beginning to percolate out from the great European monastic houses. At any rate, he became convinced that the role and status of cloistered monks should be more clearly distinguished from the role of secular canons or clerks who had enjoyed far more contact with society at large, including those in government. Aelfheah's arrival at Winchester coincided with the dominance of the West Saxons over former Mercian territory north of the Thames and the parallel surge of Christianity into the Danelaw.

His appointment preceded by some years the enthronement of Archbishop Oda at Canterbury in 942. It is Oda who is usually credited with having spurred the revitalisation of the Benedictine Rule in England. Indeed, not previously a monk, he is known to have asked the reformist abbey of Fleury on the Loire for supply of the monastic habit which he subsequently wore. Fleury had so emulated the Cluniac reforms introduced by Abbot Odo[147] that it earned the reputation of being "a bright example of the purist monastic life". However, it is known that Aelfheah was already thinking along similar lines a decade before and was influencing young men who would, in turn, carry out the great monastic reforms of the second half of the tenth century. Before his elevation, Archbishop Oda, said to have been the son of a Dane, was bishop of the newly created See of Ramsbury and would have received encouragement from his senior neighbour. It was Aelfheah, too, who ordained two future saints, Dunstan and Aethelwold,[148] on the same day and went on to prepare them for their subsequent work and pastoral authority. Under Aelfheah's instruction, both men became monks and were introduced to King Athelstan, who appears to have taken a direct interest in their progress.

Just as Cynegils and Berin had collaborated in the mid seventh century, so now the latter-day Wessex kings and their bishops were working closely on the deepening of Christian influence in areas north and south of the Thames basin. During his episcopate, Aelfheah and the Old Minster continued to receive land from the king in Berkshire, Hampshire, Somerset and Wiltshire. Such grants were designed to bolster the finances of the bishopric for pastoral purposes, not to increase the personal wealth of holy men. In turn, the bishop could hand on revenues accrued for the repair and improvement of monastic houses – particularly in those areas of Mercia which had been ravaged during the long struggle against the Danes. Alfred had rebuilt Winchester and endowed several religious houses in the city's vicinity; as the kingdom expanded under his successors, so the rebuilding of many a ransacked monastery or nunnery elsewhere ensued. The king's instrument was his bishop of the day who also encouraged the exchange of intellectual ideas between Christian centres. And in this movement the Old and New Minsters were the hub of an expanding complex of religious houses with an increasing interchange of obedientiaries and other monastic inmates – as we shall shortly see in the study of Aelfheah's successors.

Like Frithstan and Beornstan, Aelfheah was revered for his holiness; but he was also a persuasive preacher and accredited with the gift of prophecy. He followed in Swithun's steps by walking to parish churches during his visitations. According to legend, on one such occasion he was returning to Winchester with his protégé, Dunstan, and as they passed the ruined church of St Gregory,[5] Aelfheah proposed that they should say compline together. As they did so, a large stone fell off the roof and landed between them but left them unscathed. An incident which might have happened to any passer-by, but it grew in significance when the individuals that escaped harm were so obviously God-fearing men.

---

5   Not identified, but probably within ten or so miles from Winchester.

Sadly, while legend has survived, contemporary sources provide scant detail of Aelfheah's work during the seventeen years of his episcopate. The Anglo-Saxon chronicler, Bishop Aethelwold perhaps, clearly understood him to be an important figure, since he drew attention to the coincidence of the bishop's death in 951 on the same day as that of St Gregory – 12 March.[149] Hailed subsequently as a saint by the Anglo-Saxon Church, Aelfheah's feast day was celebrated on that day at Winchester. Tellingly, it has also been celebrated at St Albans, a strong Mercian religious centre which clearly appreciated his pastoral attention. His cult would certainly have been encouraged by St Oswald who became bishop of St Albans in 960. The nephew of Oda of Canterbury, Oswald, was another great proponent of reform in the era of English monastic renewal that was about to begin. As Hunt states in his survey of the English Church before the Conquest, "this movement seems to have had its origin in the teaching and influence of Aelfheah, bishop of Winchester".[150] The spark was lit by the royal patronage that could attract and encourage innovative talent, an element Canterbury did not possess on the spot at the time.

ST AETHELWOLD

MONASTIC REFORMER AND LITURGIST

High up in the Alpine pass, a small group of travellers staggered into the windblown snow, their teeth chattering from the cold. One of their number lay on a rigged-up sledge which attendants struggled to pull along. They had lost count of how many hours the storm had raged and could barely see in front of their faces. As night fell, they could only halt and huddle round the prone figure covered in furs to protect him from the icy blast. When dawn eventually broke and the sun reappeared at last, it was already too late; the new Archbishop of Canterbury had perished of the cold on his way to Rome to receive the pallium of office. It was late in the year of 958 and Aelfsige (the first of three of the name) had been preferred to the highest office in the English Church, the first bishop of Winchester to be so honoured. When his surviving companions returned to England with news of his death from exposure, there were many who considered that God had punished Aelfsige for his sins. The would-be archbishop's death and that of his king the following year were to facilitate a change in religious life in large parts of England for centuries to come.

The bad reputation Aelfsige was to receive from posterity had more to do with politics than with his personal morality. As we have seen, his immediate predecessor, Aelfheah, was revered in Mercia, but Aelfsige was identified with the Wessex heartland. Moreover, the backdrop to his episcopacy portrayed increasing tension between groups of nobles within the vastly expanded kingdom. They had more time to jockey for influence now that external enemies were largely subdued. The untimely death of the king since 939, Eadmund, on the feast of St Augustine, 26 May 946,[151] at the hands of a criminal who was assaulting his steward, had also disrupted the continuity of post-Alfredian achievement. The succession of Eadmund's younger brother, Eadred, the 'weak-footed', to the throne was an opportunity for malcontents in the newly conquered north to renew their resistance, despite initially swearing fealty. No sooner had the northern magnates – including Wulfstan, the highly political Archbishop of York – done so than a prominent scion of the royal house of Norway, Eric Bloodaxe, arrived in Northumbria in 947. Driven from the Norwegian throne after a short but violent reign, Bloodaxe now sought his fortune across the sea as had many an exile – political and economic – before him. His arrival provoked rebellion amongst those, many of Norse origin, who resented Wessex dominance. Eadred was forced to lead the Wessex army north once more to secure an uneasy settlement, but for the next few years his hold on Northumbria remained uncertain.

When it came to appointing Aelfheah's successor at Winchester, therefore, Eadred's concern was to have a bishop at his council who would have more interest in matters of state than his saintly predecessors – and was a man of Wessex. Thus, Aelfsige was almost certainly the personal choice of King Eadred; the monkish – and Mercian – Archbishop of Canterbury, Oda, was given little say in the decision. At the time of Aelfsige's installation at Winchester in 951, plots were still being hatched in the north. The following year, Eadred was even compelled to order the arrest of Archbishop Wulfstan for his continuing involvement in them. Although a fellow prelate, Aelfsige would have been party to this move, whatever Archbishop Oda's thoughts on the matter.

Bishop Aelfsige – a contrast to his predecessors

A secular deacon or clerk in the royal household with no record of a monastic background, Aelfsige appears not to have taken the tonsure, let alone vows of chastity. In contrast to his saintly predecessors, Frithstan, Beornstan and Aelfheah, his early career more resembles that of Swithun. There are two charters from Edmund's reign (939–946) granting Aelfsige

– as "minister" – large areas of land in North Hampshire and Wiltshire.[152] King Eadred added two rather smaller parcels to his "most faithful" minister's estate.[153] Two years after his appointment to Winchester there is a further charter from Eadred to Aelfsige as "minister" and "his wife, Eadgifu". There is no confirmation that this is the bishop, but in the increasingly political atmosphere of the Wessex court, it is a credible assumption.[154] The grants of lands to Aelfsige and other courtiers continued the policy of building up the king's influence in areas which had once been under Mercian sway. There is one possible clue to the bishop's origins. His name survives at Alice Holt, 'the wood belonging to Alfsi', that is the shortened version of Aelfsige. It remains today near Farnham under the management of the Forestry Commission.[155] Again, this fits with someone whose forbears were already landed gentry: there is a reference in Aelfsige's surviving will to his father's estates.[156]

Although Eadred was able to stabilise Northumbria in 954 and to expel a resurgent Eric Bloodaxe, he was already a sick man and died childless the following year. His successor was Eadwig, a wilful youth and the elder son of the late King Eadmund. On the night before his coronation, Eadwig left the state banquet prematurely and was subsequently found dallying with two women, Aethelgifu and her daughter Aelgifu. The man who discovered the young king's behaviour was the devout Dunstan, whom we have already met as the late King Eadmund and Bishop Aelfheah's protégé promoted to the abbacy of Glastonbury. Eadwig ignored Dunstan's remonstrations and expelled him from court – and into exile at Blandinium Abbey in Flanders. Aelfsige, on the other hand, appears to have indulged the young man and remained at his side. Again, this suggests that the bishop was a complete contrast to his predecessors.

Whether the incident was a factor or not, one thing is evident: Eadwig was unsympathetic towards monastic life and saintly writings, so he would have been indifferent at best to a man like Dunstan whose reputation as a reformer had grown during his fifteen years at Glastonbury. Dunstan shared the views of Oda of Canterbury and was tipped as his successor. Aelfsige, on the other hand, was no admirer of Oda and continued to serve Eadwig. He probably conducted Eadwig's eventual marriage to Aelgifu, which was then annulled by Oda in 958 because, according to the *Anglo-Saxon Chronicle*, husband and wife were "related".[157] Loyalty, however, was at a premium, for in the latter half of 957, first the Northumbrians then the Mercians had withdrawn their fealty to Eadwig in favour of his younger brother, Eadgar. Aelfsige remained Eadwig's man and when Archbishop Oda died the following summer, the young king promoted his bishop to Canterbury, without apparently relieving him of Winchester, not the last time this would happen. The *Anglo-Saxon Chronicle* skates lightly over these events and makes no mention of Aelfsige as archbishop; nor does it name him and his immediate successor, Beorhthelm, as Bishops of Winchester. Indeed, the Winchester manuscript claims that Oda died in 961 and was succeeded immediately by Dunstan,[158] an early example of censorship, glossing over an awkward period in Church and royal Wessex history.

While the promotion of Aelfsige to Canterbury demonstrates how dominant the Wessex kings had become in matters of Church leadership, Eadwig's high-handedness provoked a storm of criticism from those who had expected Dunstan to succeed as archbishop. Identified with his king, Aelfsige was also reviled: he was accused not only of simony, the purchase of additional office, but of actually insulting Oda's tomb before departing for Rome. Little wonder then that the news of his demise in the Alpine snows was attributed to God's punishment for his wickedness. How immoral Aelfsige really was, those who skated over the history of his episcopacy do not say. There is one, probably misleading, glimpse of his humanity, or last attack of conscience: in his will, which survives in the Winchester Cartulary, he declared that all those penally enslaved working on his personal demesne should receive their freedom. But this appears to have been a routine response to a resolution agreed at the Synod of Chelsea in 816 which called on bishops, on their death, to free all individuals who had served them in manumission. Aelfsige's will was careful not to mention the slaves working on his family estates.[159]

Before he died on 1 October 959, Eadwig had appointed a further archbishop and another bishop at Winchester. To Canterbury he promoted one of his favourites, Byrhthelm, Bishop of Wells, and to Winchester, Beorhthelm, whom he had described in three 956 charters respectively as his faithful priest, kinsman and bishop-elect, clearly another loyal courtier cleric.[160] Beorhthelm had been elevated to Selsey in 656 and the suggestion is that he was translated to Winchester in 960. But Eadwig's death brought his younger brother, Eadgar, to the throne, a man of completely contrasting views where the Church was concerned. From early in his life, Eadgar had taken note of the dereliction of religious houses, in large part brought about by continuous warfare and neglect. He was a ready convert to the need for monastic reform, a great admirer of Oda and Dunstan and had secured the latter's return to Wessex from the Continent before Eadwig's death. One of his first acts was to give Dunstan the Sees of Worcester and London – ironically, with no cries of simony or pluralism on record – and in 960 he returned Byrhthelm to Wells as too weak a personality to hold the primacy. He then appointed Dunstan as archbishop in his stead. Although we do not know what happened to him, Beorhthelm at Winchester did not last long either. In 963, Eadgar raised Aethelwold, the Abbot of Abingdon and close confederate of Dunstan, to be the bishop in his capital. A new alliance of secular and ecclesiastical powers had been forged which would modernise the legal system and revitalise the Anglo-Saxon Church.

Aethelwold's early career

Much is known and has been written about Aethelwold, who was consecrated at Winchester by Archbishop Dunstan on St Andrew's Eve, Sunday 29 November. We are fortunate in having two contemporary chroniclers of his life and times: Aelfric, who came under his direction at Abingdon, and Wulfstan, writing a little later, who was precentor at the New Minster. Like Dunstan, Aethelwold came to maturity in the royal household and was born, probably about 908, to a prominent and devout family in Winchester. At sixteen, the traditional Saxon age of manhood, he entered King Athelstan's service as a comitatus (follower). The king noted his religious zeal and commended him to the instruction of the balding, and learned, Bishop Aelfheah, who officiated when Aethelwold was tonsured and then ordained as priest. From an early age, therefore, Aethelwold was imbued with the scholarly and disciplined environment he would have found at the Winchester School, at the time under the direction of a devout bishop. Marking him out as well-grounded in religious knowledge and sharp-witted, Bishop Aelfheah likely saw him as a future holder of the Winchester See.

It is noteworthy that Aethelwold and Dunstan were ordained on the same day, probably in about 938 when they would have reached the canonically acceptable age of thirty. Bishop Aelfheah, incidentally, was probably Dunstan's uncle.[161] Aethelwold joined his friend, by now the Abbot of Glastonbury, in 944 as dean or prior of the house; he was, therefore, set in charge of monastic discipline from an early stage in his career. Their friendship, however, went back many years. It is said that Aethelwold knew Dunstan was being bullied by his less well-motivated peers and consoled him in the face of their taunts. Born into a devout family at Glastonbury, Dunstan was seen as a prig by the worldlier sons of courtiers in Winchester basking in Wessex ascendancy. The story is told that rough-housing young nobles bound him hand and foot before rolling him into the mud. While Dunstan was still recovering from this humiliating episode, Bishop Aelfheah sought to relieve his depression by suggesting that he would be better suited for the religious life. Dunstan, however, still had hopes of marriage and ignored the advice. He then fell dangerously ill, and the bishop supervised his recovery with Aethelwold in close support, after which Dunstan accepted Aelfheah's counsel to take monastic vows. Dunstan then withdrew to Glastonbury with King Athelstan's sanction and lived an ascetic life in the ruins of the once famous and ancient monastery destroyed by the Danes. By the time Aethelwold arrived, the house was beginning to thrive again under Dunstan's revived spirits. Both men had studied not only theological works, grammar and poetry, but could also turn their hands to illuminated writing and work in precious metals. Aethelwold also seems to have had a special interest in horticulture and produced food for the table. Using their practical skills, they were able to lead by example and direct their growing community in vigil, prayer, fasting and general austerity during the continuing work on rebuilding a previously moribund abbey. In an age of warfare and internecine strife, one catches a glimpse of young men disenchanted by secular materialism and aggression, two early pioneers of the 'good life'.

After a few years at Glastonbury and conscious that English monasticism was far behind developments on the Continent, Aethelwold petitioned to pursue his studies abroad. His wish was refused by Eadgifu, King Eadred's mother and dowager queen as Edward the Elder's third and last wife – and by Dunstan himself. Instead, the king respected his mother's wishes and gave Aethelwold his own religious house, a then small but old congregational institution at Abingdon, served by secular clerks. Here he was provided with the opportunity to develop his ideas among the local people. On his arrival there he found the buildings and those who served them to be in a wretched state, with income decimated by the loss of two-thirds of the estate to successive kings. Within a year or so he had sent to Glastonbury for reinforcements of both monks and clerks who were ready to submit to monastic discipline; he also persuaded Eadred to return lands sufficient to endow the creation of a monastic house.[162] A substantial contribution came from Eadgifu. Eadred visited Abingdon to see the progress and was entertained along with the large body of Northumbrian thegns who had accompanied him. According to Aelfric, Eadred ordered the doors to the feast to be shut so that no one "might shirk his drink". The carousal lasted all day, but at the end of it Aethelwold's cask of mead had "failed not, nor wasted more than one hand's breadth", whilst the Northumbrians ended up "as drunk as hogs".[163]

Aethelwold's endeavours were not without accident: during the building work a heavy post fell on him, breaking some of his ribs and throwing him into a pit. Nevertheless, he recovered from his injuries and retained royal patronage, even after the less reliable Eadwig came to the throne. His own ability as a craftsman furnished the abbey with three gold and silver crosses, an organ and, founded by his own hands, two bells. Sadly, the crosses were destroyed during the civil wars of Stephen and Matilda in the twelfth century. In addition, the *Abingdon Chronicle* tells us that he devised a wheel overlaid in gold and hung with little bells, which he would flourish at festivals to excite the devotions of the worshippers.¹⁶⁴ The regimen Aethelwold introduced at Abingdon was based on the practice he had followed at Glastonbury, since he was still unversed in the reformed Benedictine Rule observed by the great tenth century houses on the Continent.

Aethelwold made up for this deficiency shortly after he arrived at Abingdon by sending one of his former Glastonbury clerks – Osgar – to the abbey at Fleury to learn how the Benedictine Rule should be applied. On Osgar's return to England at the beginning of Eadgar's reign, Aethelwold introduced the Rule at Abingdon which became the first religious house in the country to put such reform into effect. The Rule was different from that followed by the seventh- and eighth-century Wessex foundations in that it stipulated what a monk should be doing at virtually any time of his day. Indeed, Aethelwold even wrote down in minute detail what the Abingdon monks should eat and drink each day, albeit their diet would have been healthier than Spartan.¹⁶⁵

Aethelwold becomes bishop

Aethelwold was never going to be left in a relatively insular society; not with his friend Dunstan at Canterbury and a new forward-looking king. Indeed, it was Eadgar's specific order which placed Aethelwold at Winchester in 963, although Dunstan would have been more than happy with the appointment of his old friend and colleague. Their joint concern for religious reform, however, was resisted by those – chiefly nobles in Wessex – who had lost power they had enjoyed under Eadwig. Over several decades of instability and disorder during the Danish incursions, strong warlords, and the Crown itself, had encroached on former Church lands. The same families had started the centuries-old tradition of placing younger sons and unmarried daughters in religious houses where their living in wartime could be protected and, in peace time, luxurious. The ways of the flesh subsumed the demands of the spirit, not least in the great scholastic institutions at Canterbury and Winchester. Even Oswald, a strong supporter of reform, had only become headmaster of Winchester Old Minster School through his uncle Oda of Canterbury's substantial financial backing. The Minster was firmly in the hands of the rich secular clergy and Oswald dined well.[166]

The new bishop's first act was to expel the secular clerks from the Old Minster and to send to Abingdon for a body of monks led by Osgar to replace them. The rich clergy resisted, but Aethelwold's appeal to Eadgar brought about their eviction through the intervention of a king's thegn named Wulfstan. He made them an offer they could not refuse – "either be gone or assume the monastic habit". Aethelwold, as bishop, automatically became abbot of the newly reformed house and Osgar succeeded him at Abingdon. The year after his consecration, Aethelwold drove out secular clergy from Chertsey Abbey in Surrey and Milton in Dorset.

The expulsion of the secular clergy excited bitter feelings which induced plots to remove the bishop by foul means. There is the story of a possible attempt to poison him but, when afflicted by severe stomach cramps over a meal, Aethelwold lay down and the pains subsided "through an exercise of faith". With Eadgar's authority behind him, Aethelwold turned to the New Minster where he appointed another disciple, Aethelgar (later Archbishop of Canterbury c988–990), as abbot and again threw out the secular clergy. The inmates of the Nunnaminster founded by Alfred's widow, Queen Ealhswith, were not spared: they too were obliged to live as *mynchens* (like monks, from the Anglo-Saxon noun *mynecen* meaning monk) in accordance with the Benedictine Rule under a new abbess, the godly Lady Aethelthryth.

This sweeping away of old and bad habits and introduction of a conscientious regimen epitomises the change in style and substance between the reigns of Eadwig and Eadgar.

With his own backyard put in order, Aethelwold set out on tours of the north-eastern shires, again with the force of the king's authority behind him. He selected abbots and established bands of monks at Ely,[167] Peterborough (previously known as Medeshamstede and in total ruination when Aethelwold first visited the site), and Thorney in Cambridgeshire, among a number of other places in East Anglia and the Wessex heartland. Way beyond his diocesan border Aethelwold became, in effect, a 'visitor general' for the king who supplied much of the funding for new buildings and granted land to ensure the future prosperity of the religious communities – on condition that they held strictly to the Benedictine Rule. Aethelwold imposed the discipline and punished transgressions severely "with stripes", according to Aelfric, while remaining generous to the faithful and adding funds from his own estate. He was instrumental in promoting the wide spread of Benedictine houses in England, which survived until the Reformation. Visitation was formalised after the Conquest when strong emphasis was placed on the fealty owed to the king by an abbot for his temporalities. Increasingly, the bishop was expected to oversee the activities of the religious houses in his diocese, but as centuries wore on, the responsibility became a chore to be delegated to officials, not forgetting the fees and expenses charged.

Eadgar's reign witnessed a further major boost in the property income of the English Church. Of his one hundred and sixty four identified charters, just over a half concerned the transfer of land to ecclesiastical control. The principal beneficiaries were monastic houses, several of which lay within Aethelwold's diocese or were closely associated with him before and during his episcopate.[168] By far the largest recipient of Eadgar's largess was Winchester: no less than twenty-six charters added to (approaching two hundred hides), restored or confirmed the holdings of the bishop or those of the two minsters in the capital. This compares with only two for Canterbury and one for St Peter's Westminster, the site on which the great abbey would one day stand. From Eadgar's time onwards, the Winchester See had a secure hold on a raft of villages surrounding the town and swathes of land along the river valleys of Hampshire and further afield. Aethelwold's role was central in this enlargement of the diocesan estate and the monks and clerks in the cathedral scriptorium provided the necessary skills in legal writing to record this. On a number of occasions, we also see the bishop given custody of land later to be handed on to a religious house once it was sufficiently competent to manage it. This usually meant when a trusted abbot had been appointed. Such an additional episcopal responsibility was often exercised after the

Conquest when a diocese fell vacant. It was abused in the run-up to the Reformation, notably by Cardinal Wolsey.

A strict disciplinarian

Aethelwold, however, was far more than an estate manager. He appreciated that war had not only ruined the ancient monastic foundations but had also undermined their scholastic basis and discipline; many would-be monks at the start of Aethelwold's episcopacy did not read Latin and their ransacked libraries could not re-edify the minds of even those eager to learn. Hence, Eadgar and his queen, Aethelthryth (not to be confused with the abbess of the same name), commissioned Aethelwold at a synodic council in Winchester – attended also by Dunstan – to supervise the production of a Benedictine *Concordia Regularis* in English. The resulting work was concerned chiefly with liturgical observance and drew its substance from the eighty statutes drawn up in 817 by an assembly of Benedictine abbots at Aix-la-Chapelle. These were then blended with the customs Osgar had learnt from his experiences in Ghent and Fleury. Nonetheless, there was some adaptation for English usage: the preface is decidedly national in tone: the king was accorded supremacy in monastic governance; and elections of bishops, abbots, abbesses and priors required the royal assent. The monarch became the preferred arbitrator in cases of dissent and his bishops, many already abbots of their cathedral clergy, were required to be monks. The impetus behind the reforms was also very English and reflected a less rigid society than that pertaining after the Conquest.

There is no evidence of papal intervention; Rome had long since left the English Church to do things its own way. King and prelates worked together: Eadgar is credited with the foundation of forty monasteries, with scant reference to his Witan. Once more the Church was being used as a unifying instrument in political and economic terms, not just for Wessex, but for the whole extent of the territories now under the sway of *Rex Anglorum*. For its part, the Church benefited greatly from the partnership and was richly endowed: Aethelwold himself received Sudbourne Manor in Suffolk for his work on the *Concordia* and immediately handed the property over to Ely Abbey.[169] Monarch and bishop working together in Winchester dealt harshly with secular clergy, even with those who had previously held good title to their lands and revenues. In contrast, Dunstan allowed secular clergy to remain in service at Christ Church, Canterbury, as did St Oswald, Bishop of Worcester, and later Archbishop of York.

Aethelwold was less concerned with the regulation of parish clergy, which was the subject of sixty-seven canons approved during Eadgar's reign. Here it was the softer influence of Dunstan, rather than Aethelwold's sternness, that was at work. There was, for example, no proscription of marriage; rather, the concern was to discourage misconduct such as the Anglo-Saxon vices of drunkenness and concubinage, while at the same time improving security of tenure for parish priests. Aethelwold saw a clear divide between those who entered the monastic life and the rest of society. He was not afraid to speak out if he considered individuals were seeking to blur the edges, even if they were connected to royalty. In 962, Wulftrud, a nun at Wilton Abbey, bore King Eadgar's child, a daughter called Eadgyth. Wulftrud promptly returned to her nunnery as a penitent taking the child with her and, in due course, became abbess. Eadgyth also took her vows and was known for her devout conduct, except in Aethelwold's eyes for one thing: she dressed as befitted a king's daughter. The bishop considered her apparel not to be that of a bride of Christ, to which Eadgyth retorted that her thoughts were as much with God as though she wore a goatskin and that her Lord regarded the heart rather than the raiment.

The story indicates that Aethelwold's view of monastic life attracted derision from some quarters and, with the death of Eadgar in July 975, an anti-reform movement revived, particularly in Mercia. Here monks were driven out at Winchcombe[170] and former secular residents and their wives were reinstated. In East Anglia, however, Aethelwold's reforms were stoutly defended by the nobility, one of whom appeared before the bishop in bare feet to confess his assassination of an opponent. Rather than receive his penance, Aethelwold declared him a champion of the Church. In parallel with Dunstan, he also supported the legitimacy and succession of Eadgar's son by his first wife, Edward.[171] In spite of the latter's violent outbursts, which offended many of the prominent Wessex nobility, the prelates stood up against the claims of those who favoured Aethelred, the less than ten year's old son by Eadgar's third wife. Aethelwold assisted Dunstan at Edward's coronation at Kingston in 975.

Perhaps the greatest legacy Aethelwold left to Winchester – but sadly only to last just a further hundred years – was the reconstruction of Edward the Elder's New Minster, including a tall tower with ornate and colourful carvings. What was started at the beginning of the tenth century as a planned major structure seems to have come to a halt, perhaps because of other secular preoccupations, not least the secular occupancy of the building. Aethelwold emulated his earlier work at Glastonbury and Abingdon, and the New Minster was ready for its rededication on 20 October 980. The ceremony was attended by the then King Aethelred who came over to Winchester from his palace at Andover. The procession was led by Archbishop Dunstan "with his snowy hair and angelic face", the tall, gaunt figure of Aethelwold immediately behind him. Great builder and source of generous endowments for church furnishing though he was, chroniclers testify to Aethelwold as a "benevolent bishop" ready always to sell off rich ornaments to provide for the poor in time of famine.

It was during the reconstruction of the New Minster that St Swithun's remains were rediscovered and translated within its walls. In his promotion of Swithun's reputation, as with other holy men of the past, we see a shrewd mind at work. This was, after all, the man who was quick to present his king with a freshly discovered piece of parchment attesting to ancient ecclesiastical rights and to require their restoration. This he did in the case of the charter found at Medeshamstede which declared the abbey free from all royal and secular jurisdiction. Aethelwold was a wily propagandist, a spin doctor of his age, whose political aims were always in pursuit of the Church's best interests.

Much less is known of his later years, in part because he appears to have withdrawn from public life and to have concentrated on his love of teaching the young. But by the time of the New Minster's dedication he must have been in his seventies. His many years of addiction to the ascetic life aggravated his failing health, brought on by a probably cancerous bowel condition and tumours on his legs. He was reputed to have eaten neither meat nor fowl, except for three months when Dunstan prevailed on him to vary his diet during a severe bout of illness. Aethelwold died on 1 August 984 at Beddington in Surrey, once the site of an ancient wooden church under the patronage of local Saxon nobility and long associated with Winchester diocese. This suggests that he was lodging there briefly or had retired to a personal demesne that lay within reach of Kingston and with access to the well-trodden route between Winchester and Canterbury. That his body was then taken to Winchester burial in his New Minster might indicate that he was en route and was therefore accompanied by a retinue. His earthly remains were translated to an imposing shrine raised by his successor, Aelfheah II. A twelfth-century entry in the *Abingdon Chronicle* claimed that some of the bishop's relics were by then in the hands of the abbey. As with Berin and Dorchester, the propaganda value of Aethelwold's earthly remains – and income derived – was immense.

The breadth of Aethelwold's achievement and interests is belied by his reputation as a monastic reformer. Throughout his life he was devoted to the arts and sciences. He wrote a treatise on the circle which he addressed to the mathematician Gerbert of Aurillac in the Auvergne,[172] who was credited with introducing Arab concepts of arithmetic and astronomy into European thought. It is typical of Aethelwold that he should have had a scholastic relationship with the man who reintroduced the abacus into Western usage. Back in his Old Minster he directed the creation of a pair of organs, which according to legend made a sound that could be heard all over the town. Fourteen bellows served the lower register and a further twelve the higher – pumped by seventy men and supplying wind to four hundred pipes. The two players thumped their respective set of keys in unison and could produce seven notes and the 'lyric semitone'.[173]

As John Crook has pointed out in his history of the Winchester choir schools,[174] some sort of educational institution at the Old Minster was in being from the late seventh century. According to Asser, King Alfred's youngest son attended lessons there. The 'alta schola' was still based at the cathedral down to the Reformation. With the arrival of Aethelwold – like his friend Dunstan, an enthusiast for music – it is more than likely that his resourcefulness led to the recruitment of a first 'dedicated' choir from the schola. Aethelwold's *Regularis Concordia*, moreover, prescribes the duties that the young boys ('pueri') and novices should perform during daily services. There is reference to a 'right-hand' and 'left-hand' choir, later to be known as 'cantori' and 'decani', singing antiphonally. This, of course, explains why even today cathedral and many church choirs still sing from pews opposite each other. Crook, however, emphasises that there is no evidence that the eleventh-century *Winchester Troper*,[175] a set of over one hundred and fifty plainchant melodies, was sung by boys rather than monks. But we can safely assume that Bishop Aethelwold encouraged Precentor Wulfstan to produce excellence in the chanting that made the Cathedral Mass so compelling. For the reader interested in enjoying a reproduction of the sound that rang round the Old Minster in the later years of Aethelwold's episcopate, Mary Berry's direction of *Christmas in Royal Anglo-Saxon Winchester*, sung by Schola Gregoriana of Cambridge, is a must.[176]

Aethelwold travelled widely, was a popular preacher and said Mass up and down the kingdom. Sometime in the 970s he commissioned a benedictional – a collection of prayers spoken by the bishop for the one hundred and sixteen festivals of the liturgical year at the breaking of the bread during the Mass. The work is considered the most important surviving example of the illustrated manuscripts produced at the Winchester School during the tenth century and, in some ways, documents Aethelwold's life and priorities. Amongst its one hundred and nineteen pages and thirty miniature illustrations may be found prayers for the intercession of St Swithun, St Etheldreda of Ely and St Vedrast, a sixth-century follower of the Benedictine Rule. The craftsmanship in producing the Benedictional is usually attributed to a monk, probably from Abingdon, who served as Aethelwold's chaplain until 973 when he was preferred to Thorney as Abbot.

Given the longevity of his episcopate – twenty-one years – and the extent of his influence during the great ecclesiastical reforms of the later tenth century, Aethelwold's contribution to the Saxon Church was probably greater than any other pre-Conquest Winchester bishop. Indeed, the pre-eminence of the Winchester School and its riot of colourfully illustrated manuscripts, together with his promotion of reverence for a long line of holy predecessors, entrenched Saxon culture so that its influence lasted well beyond the Norman predations post-1066. Buildings might be pulled down, but ideas are rarely scotched. It is a fortuitous accident of history that Eadgar, Dunstan and Aethelwold were so neatly contemporaneous. Church and State worked in harmony to create the benevolent, largely prosperous and resilient society that characterised Anglo-Saxon England, for all the suffering it had to bear under Eadgar's incompetent successor, Aethelred II.

ST AELFHEAH

MARTYR

Anaesthetised to their cruelty by copious consumption of wine, the Vikings lurched over to the mess of blood and gore lying in the corner. They kicked the body beneath the pile of ox bones; its groans were barely audible. One of the Vikings, who had hung back to watch his comrades, picked up an axe and smashed it down on the man's bruised head almost splitting it in two; so died the first Archbishop of Canterbury to suffer martyrdom. The story of the bone-throwing savages has grown with the telling, but one thing seems certain: Archbishop Aelfheah refused resolutely in the face of a lingering and excruciating death to abjure his Christian faith or submit to the financial demands being made of him and those in his pastoral care. He was also the second Bishop of Winchester to be elevated to Canterbury and a far worthier one at that.

Aelfheah, often rendered as Alphege, was also known as Godwine, but he was not related to the prominent Sussex family of that name who later resisted the Norman invasion and provided the last Anglo-Saxon king. He was born in 954 at Weston in Somerset of noble parentage and, against the wishes of his tearful widowed mother, left home for the monastic settlement at Deerhurst in Gloucester. The only sign of its existence today is the largely Saxon church of St Mary dating back to AD800 and possibly earlier. An important Mercian outpost, its principal claim to historical fame was as the venue in 1016 for the treaty between Edmund Ironside (King Aethelred's robust son) and Cnut, which partitioned England. We may not know why Aelfheah abandoned a secular life, but his decision coincides with a general wave of fervour for the spiritual life without which Dunstan's and Aethelwold's monastic reforms could not have succeeded. He must have been in his teens when he moved to Glastonbury where he was thought to have later acted as prior. Still not satisfied that he was serving God with sufficient devotion, he was attracted to Bath, possibly for the much-delayed coronation there of Eadgar as "King of the English" in 973. The highly symbolic ceremony, which drew on Eadgar's appreciation of the spectacle and substance of Emperor Otto the Great's enthronement, would have drawn large crowds. Tradition has it that Aelfheah built a hut nearby and, rather like Diogenes and his tub, lived as a hermit. His example attracted a following, including some prominent individuals who sought his advice; others provided him with subsistence.

If he was in the vicinity at the time of Eadgar's coronation, reports of his piety would certainly have come to the attention of Archbishop Dunstan and Bishop Aethelwold, and this may have led naturally to his later preferment. Florence of Worcester recorded Aelfheah as Abbot of Bath Abbey.[177] This late-seventh century foundation was promoted as an imposing monastery by Offa of Mercia but fell into decay during the Viking period; it was refounded in 970 with further endowment.[178] Aelfheah is thought to have been appointed by Dunstan to Bath in about 980 and was credited with the introduction of strict observation of the Benedictine Rule in the teeth of strong opposition. But his support from King Aethelred II, who had succeeded to the throne two years before, was constant, as shown by his grant in 984 of three and a half hides at Radstock in Somerset. His zeal for monastic reform and his firm action at Bath, together with experience of the royal court, would have been marked out by Archbishop Dunstan and Bishop Aethelwold as ideal qualifications for Aelfheah's succession in due course to the Winchester See and supervision of several important religious houses.

The Winchester manuscript of the *Anglo-Saxon Chronicle* tells us that Aelfheah "occupied the bishop's seat in the Wessex capital on the feast day of the two apostles – Simon and Jude – 28 October 984", two months after Aethelwold's death. Archbishop Dunstan had consecrated him several days earlier in Winchester. With the two main enforcers of the Benedictine Rule – Eadgar and Aethelwold – out of the way, some secular clergy and a number of monks resisted Aelfheah's appointment, but Dunstan held firm to him. The new bishop did not disappoint, for he promoted devout and well-educated men to take charge of roles in the diocese and religious houses. Notably, these were the prominent ecclesiastical historian and homilist, Aelfric, to Cerne Abbey in Dorset in 987 and Wulfsige, whom Aelfheah may have met at Glastonbury, to the See of Sherborne in 992. Aelfric repaid the compliment by including Aelfheah in his *Lives of the Saints*, from which we can derive glimpses of the bishop's priorities.[179] The appointments demonstrate the continuing influence of a Winchester bishop beyond the borders of his diocese.

By the start of Aelfheah's episcopate, Aethelred 'the Unready' had been on the throne for six years and the stability and expansionism of the several preceding reigns were being eroded by increasing disorder. It has been said[180] that Aethelred behaved like a man who was never sure of himself, a condition possibly stemming from the unfortunate circumstances surrounding his brother's death at Corfe and his succession to the throne.[181] It should have helped to have the reassuring presence in the early years of his reign of the ageing Bishop Aethelwold, who appears to have preferred him to his 'martyred' elder brother, Edward. The bishop and the Old Minster received their reward for the support they had given: five charters within four years of Aethelred's succession granted land at Crondall in north-east Hampshire, on the Isle of Wight, and at Portsea and Titchfield in the south-east of the county. Thereafter, however, apart from the site of the future minor house of St Denys, near Southampton[182] and some minor confirmatory charters, the bishop and the diocesan estate received no further endowment. Meanwhile, just over half again of the reign's identified charters concerned gifts to the Church. Among them were important endowments of the two great London religious centres, Westminster and St Paul's. The 894 charter in Westminster's favour actually took land away from Winchester, a harbinger perhaps of the eventual transfer of government from the old Anglo-Saxon capital.[183]

With men like Aelfheah to call on for advice, the king was hardly "Redeless" – without council. But the bishop's close identity with Dunstan, the king's dead brother's former supporter, seems to have distanced him from Aethelred. Furthermore, Aelfheah's priorities were pastoral, not secular. Four years before his arrival in Winchester, however, word that England was once more a divided camp had reached the old enemy and Viking raids recommenced. At first these were pinpricks, raids mostly on the south coast and completed before English forces could arrive in time to protect the locality. It was a reversion to tactics of the early ninth century and a complete change from a situation whereby a Saxon king could bring a usually smaller Viking force to bear in a set battle. With the advantages of shorter lines of communication and a network of fortified places, the Saxons would have stood a good chance of decisive victory in any straight fight. During the years of peace under Eadgar, however, the Saxon military system had deteriorated, increasing the kingdom's vulnerability to Viking attacks from different directions. Ironically, while the Vikings became bolder at the prospect of easy pickings, the Saxon heartland remained largely unaffected – at least for the moment.

Unlike Alfred, Aethelred was not the man to visualise a military strategy which could deter the enemy. In the face of misgivings from his advisers, including Aelfheah, his recourse was to build on an idea devised years before by one of his more distinguished predecessors. In his will of 956, King Eadred had left £16,000 to his people "that they may be able to buy relief for themselves from famine and from the heathen army if they need". It was never meant to be used as a sum with which to buy off the Vikings. Nevertheless, Aethelred chose to use the growing wealth of the Wessex hinterland to fund subsidies to the Vikings, later to be known infamously as Danegeld – or the giving in to politico-military blackmail of an aggressor. Under Aethelred, the laudable tolerance during Eadgar's reign of the Nordic customs and culture of those immigrants – often converts to Christianity – who had been allowed to settle in the Danelaw since Alfred's time mutated into a surrender to the brutish behaviour of their pagan cousins coming afresh from Scandinavia. Neither Aethelwold nor Aelfheah would have seen any wisdom in such a policy.

The first major use of Danegeld was made in 991, after a Viking force under a scion of the Norwegian royal house and a lapsed Christian, Olaf Tryggvason, trounced the ealdormen of Essex at the saga-recorded Battle of Maldon and threatened the Wessex heartland.[184] Aethelred bought peace at a cost of £10,000, a vast sum at today's prices, but only half that the king felt obliged to pay out two years later. This second tranche, however, was at least in parallel with a treaty which brought with it a promise from Olaf that he would never return as an invader. What in fact was a major diplomatic coup was achieved through the intercession of Bishop Aelfheah. He had travelled with a senior Wessex ealdorman, Aethelweard, to Southampton to meet Olaf and his kinsman, Swein Forkbeard, who had moored their nearly one hundred longships in the Solent. Through Aelfheah's entreaties, Olaf agreed to accompany him to Aethelred's hunting lodge at Andover on the upper reaches of the River Test, having first taken hostages aboard his ships. Aelfheah continued to reason with Olaf during the thirty-mile journey, probably in part by boat, and secured his reconversion to Christianity. Following feasting on the excellent local trout and mutton, no doubt, the once baptised Olaf was confirmed by Bishop Aelfheah and, in the treaty signed with Aethelred, agreed to return to Norway never to raid England again. What argumentation turned his mind, we cannot know, but the agreement with Olaf – on which he did not renege – must have recalled the traditions of the first evangelist to the West Saxons and led to the Norwegian prince's active engagement in the Christianisation of large areas of Scandinavia and Northern Germany.

The years that followed witnessed a further build-up of Viking raids with Aethelred responding by launching mindless and savage forays as far north as Strathclyde. He was clearly not listening to Aelfheah or his equally skilled and tough archbishop, Aelfric (995–1005), who had been one of Aethelwold's pupils at Abingdon. Aelfheah himself never identified with policies of appeasement. In 992, he had encouraged two of his fellow bishops, Aescwig of Dorchester and Aelfstan of London, to lead a fleet against the marauders in the absence of firmer leadership from the then timid Archbishop Sigeric. As Dunstan's successor in 989, Sigeric had tried to use the diplomatic influence of the papacy to blunt the Viking threat. He persuaded Pope John XV to intercede between Aethelred and Duke Richard of Normandy, who had been providing the protection of his harbours for his Nordic cousins. The resulting treaty lasted but a few months before it was broken irreparably by both sides. The archbishop's good intentions were a misperception.

Had Aethelred respected the judgement of his senior bishop at court, as Alfred, Athelstan or Eadgar would have done, the kingdom might have rallied. But each year the Vikings returned for more. In 1005, the redoubtable Archbishop Aelfric[185] died and Aelfheah was elected unanimously as his successor at Canterbury, testimony to the respect with which the country, if not Aethelred, held him. Taking St Swithun's skull with him, he would have followed the old pilgrims' way along the North Downs to Canterbury. Here he found his cathedral served only by monks, his predecessor having cleared out the secular clergy. As before in Winchester, Aelfheah would have met with resentment from those who had lost their protected livelihood, but still lived locally.

Aelfheah journeyed to Rome in 1006 to receive his pallium of office from Pope John XVIII, a man not known for his awareness of events in northern Europe. He could have expected little material support from the pontiff for his vulnerable position so close to the Kentish coastline. On his return to Canterbury, however, Aelfheah followed Aethelwold's example and promoted cults of saintly men of the recent past, notably Dunstan, as models for devotion to God. He commissioned his former junior at Bath, the monk Adelard of Ghent,[186] to write a biography of his much-loved predecessor, to be delivered in the form of lectures at Christ Church. He was instrumental in the Witan's recognition of St Wulfsige of Sherborne whom he had promoted while at Winchester. He is also known to have encouraged new liturgical practices at Christ Church, possibly prompted by his long years at Winchester listening to the organs of the Old and New Minsters competing with one another for sound as much for melody.

The chroniclers of the age were naturally more preoccupied by the constant warfare provoked by a succession of ever larger Viking hosts which ravaged fifteen counties – some repeatedly – during his archiepiscopate. The English Church, however, continued to stand its ground during a period of uncertainty and disorder: in 1008 Aelfheah presided at the national synod at which the saintly but robust Archbishop Wulfstan of York castigated "the English" for their loose morals, which he implied were the fundamental cause of the ills that now afflicted the country.

Three years later, Aelfheah's physical vulnerability was sharpened by the arrival of a Viking army which overran Kent and laid siege to Canterbury. The story goes that the city was betrayed after a short struggle by Archdeacon Aelfmaer, whom Aelfheah had previously rescued through ransom. Resentment of some kind must have lain behind this act, but its result was a Viking demand of £48,000 in return for their withdrawal. Aelfheah was seized and a separate ransom was demanded for his release; he was taken as a prisoner and transferred "as a roped thing" by sea to Greenwich. Others with him were soon ransomed, but Aelfheah refused this option and was held for seven months at Greenwich, where he continued to reason with his captors and preach to them. After winter months without plunder and facing an obduracy which denied them gold, several Viking leaders lost patience with their prisoner. During a drunken orgy on 19 April 1012, they put Aelfheah's faith to the supreme test. The archbishop continued to refuse to allow the people to pay for his delivery.

His acceptance of martyrdom had an amazing effect. One of the Viking leaders, recorded as Thurkill and possibly identical with a man called Thrum, who is the man supposed to have used his axe to put Aelfheah out of his misery, had earlier remonstrated against the archbishop's maltreatment. He was so impressed by Aelfheah's conduct that he had been baptised the night before the orgy. He is said to have intervened to ensure that the corpse was taken to St Paul's in London, rather than be thrown into a pit or overboard. News of the manner of Aelfheah's death spread to other Viking bands and shocked many, to the extent that forty-five Norse long ships submitted to Aethelred and promised to help defend his realm. The shock waves spread into

Scandinavia and Germany, where evangelists were able to demonstrate how Aelfheah's bearing and dignity were very much an emulation of Christ crucified – in whom he had placed all his trust. In pagan peoples this was a surprisingly effective message, bravery beyond standard expectations. In the Danelaw, moreover, Aelfheah's example strengthened Christianity which had already taken root amongst the farming immigrants. They were impressed, too, by the work of religious houses set up or reformed by Aelfheah's predecessors which had increased the homogeneity of a still culturally diverse population. The point was not lost later on King Cnut in his efforts to reunite the English and build a wider empire than that of any of his Saxon predecessors. In 1016, he caused Aelfheah's body to be translated from Southwark to Canterbury in much pomp and display. It was reburied close to the high altar in Christ Church where it is still marked today.

Aelfheah was canonised by Pope Gregory VII after some dispute over his sanctity between Archbishop Lanfranc (1070–1093) and his future successor Saint Anselm (1093–1114), who rebuilt Aelfheah's neglected shrine. Out of contrition late in life, Lanfranc commissioned a biography of the martyr by Osbern, a monk of Canterbury. Despite the hagiographic content, Osbern based his account in part on a contemporary record written by the German Thietmar of Merseburg.[187] This provided the detail we have of Aelfheah's death and chronicled the wide effect it had. Aelfheah's cult received a further boost when an opening of his sarcophagus showed his earthly remains to be incorrupt. Apart from Augustine of Canterbury, Aelfheah is the only pre-Conquest divine whose reputation was large enough for him to be included in the Norman calendar of saints; his feast day is celebrated on the anniversary of his death – 19 April. His twelfth century successor, Thomas à Becket (1162–74), is believed to have prayed to Aelfheah just before he became the second martyred archbishop.

In suffering without complaint a horrible death for his beliefs, Aelfheah demonstrated a kind of courage that the Viking culture of heroism had rarely encountered before. As such, it provided a turning point in English history. In the following years down to the Norman Conquest, the Saxon state, including its Norse immigrant population, became increasingly unitary, not least out of respect for a Church leadership which had been willing to sacrifice itself on behalf of the ordinary person. As Christ preached: greater love hath no man than this, that a man lay down his life for his friends.[188] Aelfheah's friends were the ordinary people in the street and in the countryside.

THE BISHOPS ON THE EVE OF THE CONQUEST

A key figure in the fifty or so years before the Norman Conquest was Queen Emma, successively wife of Aethelred the Unready and Cnut.[189] She is, perhaps, best remembered for the legend of her ordeal by fire which she underwent voluntarily as compurgation. This was for accusations said to have been made by the Norman Archbishop of Canterbury, Robert of Jumièges,[190] that she had been intimate with Aelfwine, Winchester's bishop from 1032 to his death in 1047. According to the legend, two bishops held the ageing queen by the hand as she walked barefoot across nine red-hot ploughshares – four for her personal compurgation and five for the long-dead bishop – and emerged without injury. The story was further embellished by the claim that Emma had prayed the night before to St Swithun, who had then appeared to her and promised she would be unharmed. The result was that Archbishop Robert was banished in 1052 and the king, Edward the Confessor, Queen Emma's eldest son by Aethelred, accepted a whipping as penance for not supporting his mother. The drama has more to do with political infighting between Saxons and the growing number of influential Normans introduced into Edward's court than fact. It is, however, in striking contrast to the drab and poorly recorded background of the Winchester diocese during this period – however tendentious the story's origins. It also obscures parallel constitutional development which laid the foundations for English government institutions that would survive the Norman Conquest.

After the whirlwind years of Aethelwold's reforms and Aelfheah's departure from the diocese, it was not unnatural that the affairs of the Winchester See should become more low-key and less record-worthy. Aelfheah's immediate successor, Cenwulf, also reduced continuity considerably by dying within months of his consecration in 1006. He was, however, a man of some stature in the Church hierarchy who, had he lived, would have attracted more prestige to his diocese. He had replaced Ealdwulf as Abbot of Peterborough Abbey (formerly Medeshamstede) in 992 on the latter's preferment as Archbishop of York.[191] Peterborough's contemporaneous historian Hugh Candidus[192] described Cenwulf as remarkably learned and eloquent but, sadly, no books have survived ascribed to him as author. The suggestion is that Cenwulf used his pen to correct the works of others. However, Abbot Aelfric of Eynsham,[193] known as 'Grammaticus' for his volume of pastoral and biographical writing, thought sufficiently highly of Cenwulf to dedicate his life of St Aethelwold to him. Sadly, there is no similar work on Bishop Cenwulf from which to learn of his family background and early life.

During his abbacy he directed the building of a protective wall around St Peter's and converted his monastic settlement into a local defence point; it became a haven for the population in the surrounding countryside who would otherwise have been at the mercy of marauding bands of Norsemen. In fact, Peterborough derives its status as a 'burh' from this time. Cenwulf's election to Winchester, however, is clouded in some mystery since it was said that he obtained the See by simoniacal means.[194] Quite why the accusation was made remains obscure, but there would still have been resentful secular clergy in Winchester to make trouble over a relative stranger's election just as there had been at Aelfheah's consecration. Conversely, several bishops had been allowed to retain their previous office as abbot, at least until a suitable successor might be found, and there is no indication that Cenwulf had previously held another See. Archbishop Aelfheah announced the death of his successor at Winchester during his visit to Rome in 1006 to collect his pallium, confirming that Cenwulf's episcopate was the shortest for the See on record.

Of Cenwulf's successor, Aethelwold II, we know hardly anything other than that he is thought to have held the See until about 1014. These were troublesome years and the main contemporary source – the *Anglo-Saxon Chronicle* – devotes most of its account to constant warfare. This was waged between increasingly demoralised Saxon forces under the feckless King Aethelred and the rampant Danes and Norwegians, egged on periodically by the dukes of Normandy, their distant cousins. Aethelwold, however, would have witnessed the laying waste of large swathes of his diocese and must have ministered to the countless refugees falling back on the Winchester defences. When the Danes sacked Winchester again in 1013, Aethelwold may have been one of their victims, but as with Swithun one hundred and fifty years before, there is nothing on record to say that this was so.

Florence of Worcester claims that he died in 1015 but there is no royal charter evidence from 1012, when Aethelwold's signature last appears, until 1016; such was the chaos in government. Between these dates Prince Aethelstan, King Aethelred's eldest son by his first wife Aelfgifu, died on 25 June 1014, having included in his will the gift of "a black stallion" to Bishop Aelfsige, Aethelwold's successor.[195] It is likely, therefore, that Athelstan knew and respected Aelfsige as his tutor at court. The entry might suggest, too, that Aelfsige II's succession was a year earlier than the not always reliable Florence of Worcester records. One might also ask what use a bishop would make of a finely bred horse. Is it indicative of a courtier priest more used to the secular life than the cloister? Swithun, Aethelwold I and Aelfheah – on their ponies or going by foot – would not have had use for it, except to sell on for money to give to the poor.

Aelfsige II appeared amidst the sad situation that had produced the martyrdom of Archbishop Aelfheah, the widespread poverty induced by stringent taxation raised to pay Danegeld and the comprehensive collapse of English defences. Moreover, the English throne itself was under dire threat from King Swein 'Forkbeard' of Denmark who had already won the allegiance of the north and support from the Danelaw. With the surrender of Winchester and London and other centres of Wessex power, King Aethelred fled to Normandy at the end of 1013 and Swein would have usurped him but for the latter's untimely death on the following 3 February. Aelfsige II would have been a first-hand witness to these events, but the Winchester text of the *Anglo-Saxon Chronicle* sheds no light on what he saw – or did.

During the ensuing breathing space, those leading Englishmen who remained in the field opened a dialogue with their exiled king. Thanks largely to Emma, his queen, Aethelred remained under the protection of her brother, Duke Richard II of Normandy. Indeed, Emma, supported by Abbot Aelfsige of Peterborough (from 1006 to 1055), had preceded her husband in seeking refuge and would have opened up diplomatic entreaties for Norman support. Correspondence crossed the Channel in which Aethelred promised to govern more justly. In reply, the English nobles summoned him back, so that an agreement on the way ahead might be forged. Cautiously, Aethelred first sent his eldest son by Emma, Edward – later to be known as 'Confessor' – to negotiate, but then returned to England in the spring of 1014 to accept the allegiance of "all the councillors, both ordained and lay". In words of what sounds like bravado, he declared that every Danish king should be outlawed from England forever.

It seems unlikely that the Bishop of Winchester at the time, whether Aethelwold II or Aelfsige II, was absent when the councillors accepted the king's return to England. Tempting as it might be to think otherwise, Aelfsige II was not identical with the queen's companion, the Abbot of Peterborough, who was busy anyway on the Continent collecting the arm of St Oswald. While both bishops might have been expected to identify with the Saxon opposition to Danish-Norman infiltration, as holders of the Winchester See, they would always have been the king's bishop, whoever he might be.

Aethelred's return changed nothing. A further £21,000 was handed over to the Danes, now led by Swein's second son, Cnut. While the latter harried Dorset, Wiltshire and Somerset, Aethelred went east to savage Lindsey in present-day Suffolk. Some months later, during 1015, Aethelred held a great council at Oxford during which he was accessory to the killing of two leading thegns of the northern Danelaw, Siferth and

Morcar, and confiscated their estates. His third son by Queen Aelfgifu, Edmund 'Ironside', angered his father by promptly carrying off Siferth's widow. He sought refuge in the Danelaw, securing the allegiance there of several leading nobles. What Aelfsige thought of this family rift is not recorded, but we can imagine that his loyalties, as the royal bishop, would have been strained into disillusion and despair.

Aethelred died on 23 April 1016 in London, some thirty-eight years after ascending the throne – one of the longest of all reigns and perhaps the most tragic. The scene was now set for the final showdown between the English and the Danes. The English had been expecting a seaborne attack on London launched by Cnut from his base at Poole harbour. Gaining the allegiance of parts of the Danelaw and support from disgruntled Mercians, Edmund Ironside was acclaimed king by the men in London and by elements in the south-east. But, only a few days later, a larger assembly at Southampton reflected the mood of the Wessex heartland and swore fealty to Cnut. Amongst the gathering were several bishops and abbots, and it seems likely that Aelfsige was with them, all disenchanted with Aethelred and anticipating more of the same from his progeny.

Edmund, however, was a complete contrast to his father and acted swiftly and decisively to bring Wessex to heel before raising an army strong enough to face Cnut. He abandoned London to Cnut's ships; yet, after a couple of drawn battles at Penselwood (near Gillingham) in Dorset and Sherston in Wiltshire, he was still strong enough to march back north of the Thames and to surprise the Danish defences downstream. The Danes abandoned the north bank but entrenched themselves down on the south side of the river from where they beat off Edmund, who was obliged to fall back on Wessex to raise more troops. After further engagements in which the Saxons seemed to be gaining the upper hand, Cnut and Edmund faced each other finally at Ashingdon in south-east Essex – on St Luke's Day, 18 October 1016. During the battle, the unreliable Mercian levies led by the treacherous ealdorman Eadric fled and, cutting down the flower of the English army including bishops, abbots and ealdormen, Cnut won an outright victory. Edmund escaped and his continuing popularity in the country persuaded

Cnut to parley: the two men met on Ola's island in the Severn, adjacent to Deerhurst where St Aelfheah had first studied. Here it is likely that Bishop Aelfsige stood anxiously on the bank while the two leaders, according to several accounts, first engaged in single combat and then, close to exhaustion, agreed to share the spoils of England; Edmund took Wessex and Cnut the rest. Within two or three weeks – on 30 November 1016 – Edmund died, possibly of the effects of wounds received or, more dramatically as legend would have it, by a fatal stabbing to his posterior as he squatted over the cesspit. Cnut was acclaimed king of all England and began a reign in which law and order was reestablished, thus creating a stability during which the Church could come into its own once more.

Until the armed struggle had been brought to a conclusion, the role of the Church leadership was eclipsed. Cnut, however, was no heathen; on the contrary, he accepted that the Church was the glue which could be used to bind society back together. The records do not say what personalities influenced him in this belief, but he would have relied on the counsel of his royal bishop, who is likely to have had early diplomatic contact while Cnut was based at Poole. It was the Bishop of Dorset who was listed among the dead at Ashingdon, not Aelfsige, who seems to have remained at Winchester. There is nothing specific, but circumstantial evidence suggests that Aelfsige's sympathies had rested with Cnut. The new king certainly appears to have appreciated them since, while Winchester did not benefit greatly from Cnut's grants, Aelfsige's name as attestor appears on more of the forty-four royal charters of the reign than any other prelate, save Canterbury. Unsurprisingly, therefore, Aelfsige is one of three divines – along with Archbishop Aethelnoth and Bishop Bryhtwhine of London – mentioned as leading Cnut's staged procession bearing St Aelfheah's relics from Southwark to Canterbury on 15 July 1023. This was royal propaganda at its best, aimed at assuaging the bloodlust[196] of Danes and Saxons generated over hundreds of years and recognising the three still most prominent prelates in the kingdom.

Some eighteen months after he succeeded Edmund, Cnut called together all the Wessex, Mercian and Danelaw ealdormen, along with the two archbishops and the shire bishops. The gathering took place at Oxford in 1018 and, although Aelfsige is not mentioned, the Winchester hand is evident from the outcome. It was agreed that the constitution of the realm should be based on the laws of Eadgar, so heavily influenced by St Aethelwold, and not some Nordic design. This decision was enshrined in Cnut's charter of 1020 which pointed up the role of the shire bishops in the settling of legal disputes and was a general exhortation to people of all ranks to keep God's law. It was still very much in line with Ine's late-seventh century laws, so closely influenced by Bishop Haeddi. The new constitution received a seal of approval from Pope Benedict VIII who is remembered for his decree that priests should not marry – another of St Aethelwold's prominent canons. The charter enshrined the liberties of Wessex dating from Ine and became a model for post-Conquest legal frameworks culminating in Magna Carta.

Aelfsige II died at Winchester in 1032 and was succeeded by the "king's priest", Aelfwine, so wrote the Anglo-Saxon chronicler. Eighteen years before, Prince Aethelstan's will had mentioned Aelfwine as another of his beneficiaries – the recipient of "a horse with harness".[197] The fact that he was also described as Aethelstan's chaplain indicates that he was, like his predecessor, a long-serving member of the royal household, an important qualification for elevation to the See of Winchester. He would certainly have held office in one or other of the Minsters and, as a tonsured monk, is believed to have been sacristan,[198] the keeper of vestments, valuables and holy relics. This was a position of great trust given that the Old and New Minsters had become mausoleums for the House of Wessex as well as for several revered bishops.

Although we know little of Aelfwine's origins, there is more than a hint that he was of mixed Norse or Norman parentage. Otherwise, he would not have been so close to Cnut; nor would he have had the king's Norman wife Emma's approval. He became a figure of influence and power during the latter years of Cnut's reign and, like his predecessor, attested the lion's share of the king's charters, usually appearing after the two archbishops – and above London. This evidence is in line with Winchester's position as the centre of legal drafting and writing in the later Anglo-Saxon period. Given that the day-to-day business of government was often dominated by land transactions, the clerks from the cathedral servicing the court had to develop an understanding of property law, one of the key elements in any society seeking stability. The king and his bishop must have appreciated this factor, particularly where war and disease had brought sudden death and property law had to be extended to wardships and legacies, as well as the ownership or occupation of lands and buildings. It is from this administrative retrenchment during a period of comparative peace and stability that the formation of a king's chancery, or office – and the appointment of his head of staff, or chancellor – originates in the early eleventh century. All the signs are that with the Wessex, or rather English, capital now settled at Winchester, a literate bishop appointed to the See was always going to fill the role of the king's senior-most counsellor – even if the term 'chancellor' had not yet been recognised. This continuity was demonstrated by Aelfwine's surviving influence during the tyrannical but short reign of Cnut's son, Harthacnut (1040–42).[199]

Aelfwine's career really took off after the accession of Emma's son, Edward, in 1042. There are still surprisingly few sources for the period and mention of the bishop in the chronicles is a rarity.[200] Thanks to some helpful detection by Dr J L Maddicott,[201] we have a persuasive account of Aelfwine's role in the replacement of the deranged Harthacnut by the moderate Edward, later revered as the saintly 'Confessor'. From a Latin translation of Anglo-Saxon legal material made in the early twelfth century, he identifies how Aelfwine and Earl Godwine instigated the return of Edward to England in 1041. The same passage records that Edward and his supporters met "the thegns" at *Hursthevet* where he promised – as his father had done in 1014 – to defend the rights of his people and to forbear from oppression. Without assurances from men of Aelfwine and Godwine's stature, Edward's landing in England would have been foolhardy: his brother, Alfred, had been murdered there early in Harthacnut's reign. Dr Maddicott also clarifies the picture further by locating *Hursthevet* (a sandy spit of land) at Hurst Head on the south-west Hampshire coast and well inside the Winchester diocese. This identification fits neatly: Edward – like Berin four centuries before – sailed from the Seine basin; the all but inundated peninsula afforded means for a quick getaway had the reception party been hostile, and it was just such an isolated location favoured in the past – and would be in the future – as the venue for a tentative armistice or peace settlement.

As we have seen repeatedly in this account, the new king was not slow to register his gratitude for the crucial support of his bishop. While Harthacnut was probably dying, it was the king-making trio – Emma, Godwine and Aelfwine – who witnessed his last charter. Edward's first known charter dated to 8 June 1042 was attested by Emma, Archbishop Eadsige and Aelfwine. The new king was then crowned on 3 April the following year at Winchester, the first use of the cathedral for such an illustrious occasion for a hundred years or more and at least eight episcopates. Indeed, in previous centuries Kingston had been the preferred site for coronations. There are, of course, several reasons why Winchester should have been chosen, but the prestige accruing from the event cannot be disputed. From then until his death in 1047, Aelfwine's name appears on twenty-one of twenty-two charters of the period, far more than any other prelate.[202] At the same time, he received further significant endowments, including Witney manor (thirty hides) in Oxfordshire in 1044,[203] one of the richest in England. Its connection with the diocese of Winchester lasted until the eighteenth century and its facilities provided a convenient stopover for medieval bishops – usually occupying high office – when travelling to some meeting or trouble spot in the North. The warmth of Edward's relationship with his bishop is revealed in the wording of the Wintney charter: "to his familiar bishop" as "a reward for the faithful service by which he has faithfully shown obedience to me". Aelfwine's diocese benefited from three further grants in 1045–6 adding twenty-one more hides to the diocesan estate. As Dr Maddicott considered: "judging by the charter evidence, no other bishop approached Aelfwine's standing or benefited so greatly from Edward's generosity".

What of Aelfwine's relationship with Emma, Edward's mother? While he must certainly have been on more than nodding terms with

Cnut's wife, it is unlikely that he was her lover. The story first appears in the *Winchester Annals* attributed to Richard of Devizes, a cathedral monk writing in the late twelfth century.[204] He used it to glorify the Winchester Church and St Swithun at a time when 'Englishness' was coming back into vogue. The tales of Robin Hood tweaking the Norman tail also originate from this time. According to Richard, too, Edward had to appear in Winchester in disguise before his coronation, presumably in case supporters of Harthacnut were still lingering in the capital. If so, Bishop Aelfwine would have been party to the ruse and his palace a refuge for the aspirant king. Over a century later, Emma's compurgation ordeal became the subject of a ballad said to have been sung at the enthronement in 1333 at Winchester of Bishop Adam Orleton. The king at the time was a young Edward III and it was during his reign that the Round Table, still hanging in Winchester castle hall, was manufactured and tales of Camelot, Guinevere and Lancelot circulated. Orleton's heart was quite literally left in the city: he decreed that his vital organ should be placed in the cathedral after his death. This was all pageantry, hardly truth.

There is usually, however, an element of truth behind any legend. In the case of Emma and her alleged misconduct with Aelfwine, some ground for the story could date back to 1043. This was when Cnut's widow appears to have supported the claim of King Magnus of Norway to the English throne, as a strong man to keep Cnut's Anglo-Scandinavian imperial legacy intact, instead of the unreliable blood of her first husband, Aethelred. Tough lady as she was, she would have had reservations about Edward's gentler qualities. Edward, however, was already married to Earl Godwine's daughter, Edith, and Emma's opposition to his succession only incensed the Wessex nobility. There was certainly a confrontation during which Edward and leading Saxon earls rode into Emma's Winchester home — the site of the surviving medieval Godbegot restaurant in the High Street — and confiscated all her lands and property. She must have been in her late fifties by then and was put away, according to the legend, in Wherwell Priory, a Benedictine nunnery halfway between Winchester and Andover which had been endowed by King Aethelred II in 1002.[205] The trout-rich waters of the upper Test, on which the long-lost house stood, would have attracted Saxon nuns long before then. Again, the legend is wide of the mark, since it was Emma's daughter-in-law and wife of Edward the Confessor, Edith, who was sent to Wherwell. There is no record of Emma's whereabouts after her disgrace, and it is more likely that she lived quietly in old age at Winchester until her death in 1051. There, as a long-serving member of the court, Bishop Aelfwine would have ministered to the dowager queen, albeit he died four or five years before her.

There is one glimpse of Aelfwine's true regard for women. The prolific hagiographer Osbert of Clare wrote a life of St Edburga of Winchester in the mid-twelfth century.[206] Almost as an afterthought, he makes a special reference to Aelfwine's assistance to the nuns of Nunnaminster during his episcopate. St Edburga, daughter of King Edward the Elder, spent virtually all her life during the first half of the tenth century at the then newly founded nunnery. Her example of Godly chastity was later exalted by Aethelwold I. As with Swithun, it was he who arranged for Edburga's relics to be translated within the Nunnaminster from her previously humble resting place out in the open. But while the cult of St Swithun attracted growing popular support with the regular miracles attributed to him – including protection of Queen Emma – it was St Edburga's emulation of the Virgin Mary which seems to have impressed the more devout sections of society. St Aethelwold had a stern view of how nuns should behave. Perhaps Aelfwine was of a similar opinion, in which case he might have suffered the gibes of those still in support of clerical marriage, particularly if he was known to keep close company with the politically risqué Emma.

Aelfwine died in 1047: the *Anglo-Saxon Chronicle* couples the event with the "severe winter of that year". His death brought Stigand to Winchester, a man whose misfortune it was to be still in office when the Norman Conquest swept away Saxon vestiges of power. Not surprisingly, his reputation did not stand a chance in the eyes of posterity. Unlike his immediate predecessors, Stigand's prominent position at court, and in the country as a whole on the eve of the Conquest, meant that much more was said about him – and negative comment recorded – by those who sought to justify the Norman usurpation. He has come down to the present-day as a figure of doubtful character, ironically with the result that we have more detail of his life.

Stigand is thought to have been born sometime after 990 in East Anglia, at or close to Norwich which was already a shire town with strong trading links across the North Sea. In some respects, the geographical position on the River Yare resembles that of medieval Winchester at the head of the then navigable Itchen. Stigand's name is strongly suggestive of Norse origins, but his younger brother was called Aethelmaer with its more Anglo-Saxon ring; subsequent chroniclers claim they were born to noble parents. The likelihood is that they were the progeny of a mixed marriage – a Danish father and an Anglian mother. Domesday shows Stigand, Aethelmaer and their sister having held extensive property in the Norwich hundred before sequestration by the Normans.

The family would certainly have been affected by Swein Forkbeard's sack of Norwich and the surrounding countryside in 1004, and they would have had to find refuge from the privations suffered during the great famine the following year. If they had survived these terrible visitations, the parents of the two brothers would have been obliged to contribute substantially towards the £30,000 Danegeld levied in 1007. Their sons would certainly have been old enough in 1010 to witness the return of the ravaging Danes, wherever they were living. Exposure at an impressionable age to any one or all of these events would have left their mark on Stigand's character, inducing wiliness, shrewdness – in short, an instinct for survival.

There is no record of where Stigand received his education and training for ordination. Ely, with which he had a long association, would have been an obvious choice given its great reputation under several abbots, including Leofsige (1029–44). In his time, no one was admitted to the monastery unless they were good scholars and men of high birth with families expected to add wealth to the foundation. Stigand certainly took the tonsure, as depicted in the Bayeux Tapestry's scene of Harold II's Coronation and, for all the several accusations of greed and ambition, he never married or was openly licentious.

Stigand is first reported reliably as an ordained clerk working at Cnut's court in the early years of his reign. How was he recruited? It is known that Cnut was especially attracted to the monasteries of East Anglia and that it was his custom to spend Candlemas (2 February and the end of Christmas celebrations) every year at Ely where he enjoyed the choral presentations. While endowing monastic churches, however, Cnut would have been looking for clever scholars who could serve him in the running of a realm stretching by the end of his reign across large parts of Norway and Denmark. As we have already noted, under Athelstan, Eadgar and Cnut, their chaplains, or clerks, appear increasingly as an organised body – an embryonic civil service – employed in the affairs of state and particularly in the drawing up of royal writs issued under the king's seal. The expansion of his empire brought Cnut into contact with many of the leading continental rulers of his day and he needed men who understood foreign affairs to counsel him in this field. Stigand has attracted the accolade of diplomat.

One possibility is that Stigand served Edmund Ironside in some way during the months after the latter's marriage to Siferth's widow, when he sought refuge in East Anglia from his irate father, Aethelred. Was Stigand, as an East Anglian, present at Deerhurst in 1016 in some junior role and a ready hand in the drawing-up of the divisions of power during the short-lived joint rule of Edmund and Cnut? If Cnut was shrewd enough to marry Aethelred's widow, Emma, he was surely able to spot those amongst Edmund's entourage who could also be used in his grand design.

During the early 1960s it was fashionable to extol the achievements of the Anglo-Saxons, itself a correction of earlier admiration for the ruthless efficiency displayed by the Normans. A long line of distinguished historians paid tribute to the social structure and unified kingdom that William the Conqueror took over. England, however, was still only superficially a nation with the north barely accepting the authority of a king based in the south and Mercia bridling against Wessex overlordship, a rivalry which went right back to the opening pages of this account. Added to these regional fissures, there were competitive families, typified by the Godwines of Sussex who strove for greater influence in the kingdom. In the throes of Aethelred's weakness against external enemies and his mercurial behaviour at home, the Godwines would also have entertained designs on the throne itself, through marriage or, if the opportunity arose, by force.

It was Cnut's administrative genius, however, that restored for the length of his reign a veneer of order in what had become a divided and lawless society. During this time, he nurtured and strengthened the bonds of his kingdom: as already noted, the law was based on that laid down by King Eadgar with the full blessing of the Church; and, in return, he endowed the Church and determined its leadership. His household was filled with men of literacy and proven capability, the bulk of whom were priests who had foresworn the ties of marriage and were wedded instead to his service. In return, many of his clerks in holy orders could anticipate promotion to the episcopate. Within these ranks we find Stigand as a royal chaplain who was appointed in 1020 to build and minister to a commemorative stone church at "Assandun". This is clearly identified with Ashingdon, the site of the climactic battle between Edmund Ironside and Cnut only four years before. As "his own priest", Cnut was promoting a man who had already served him well in the ordering of the realm and in the adoption of English legal codes; Stigand was also a man of the Danelaw.

Stigand did not stay in Ashingdon long: having farmed out his duties to a local priest, he returned to be with his king. In 1023 he must have appreciated the royal purpose behind the pomp that accompanied the translation of St Aelfheah's bones to Canterbury and may have been involved in the preparations. He is not mentioned accompanying the king on his campaigns in Scandinavia in 1025 and probably remained at court, where he was to become a close confidant of Queen Emma – like Bishop Aelfwine. In addition, he had been appointed as chaplain to Prince Harold 'Harefoot', Cnut's son by Aelfgifu of Northampton and, in the eyes of the world, illegitimate – although older than his half-brother, Harthacnut. This office placed Stigand in the centre of a potential political storm over which of the royal offspring should succeed their father.

Given Stigand's reputation as a diplomat, it is possible that he accompanied the king on his visit to Rome in 1027 to attend Pope John XIX's[207] coronation of Conrad II of Germany as Holy Roman Emperor. We simply do not know. At the very least, however, he is likely to have been involved in drawing up argumentation used to persuade the pope that incoming Archbishops of Canterbury should not have to pay steep fees for collecting their pallium of authority, considering the expense they incurred in travelling to Rome. On his return from the Holy City, however, Cnut rode north into Scotland where, after a show of force, he received King Malcolm's submission. There is some later suggestion that Stigand had diplomatic ties with Scotland and may have accompanied Cnut there. It might not have been his only visit – as we shall eventually see.

Cnut's death in 1035 caused a division in Stigand's loyalties. He appears to have chosen to leave Harold Harefoot, who had been acclaimed king by a large section of the nobility, particularly in the Danelaw, and joined the twice-widowed queen in Winchester. Emma, together with the Godwines and many of the other Wessex nobility, favoured her legitimate son, Harthacnut, but he was still in Denmark where he had been sent as his father's viceroy. A compromise was reached between the rival parties in early 1036 at Oxford, whereby Harold would remain regent in England but would leave Emma at Winchester – now the seat of the nation's treasury – to maintain her son's interest in Wessex. The following year, matters came to a head when Aethelred's son, Alfred, also by Emma, came back to England from Normandy, but was refused permission to visit his mother in Winchester. By now, however, the scheming Earl Godwine had transferred his allegiance to Harold, who had seized the treasury, and was instrumental in the detention, blinding and death of Alfred at Ely.

In the wake of a massacre at Guildford of six hundred of Alfred's supporters and Emma's flight to Bruges, Stigand chose to join up with the Godwines at Harold's side. The king was, after all, the man on the spot and had Stigand's homeland behind him. Wily tactician that he was, Stigand could not have foreseen that the winter of 1037–8 would carry off Aethelnoth, the Archbishop of Canterbury, and three other prelates in as many months. Harold looked to his court clerics for replacements and appointed to Canterbury "the king's priest", Bishop Eadsige, who had been consecrated as suffragan in Kent three years earlier. Stigand also expected promotion to fill the vacancy left by Bishop Aelfric's death in East Anglia. Whether Harold's support was only lukewarm or there is truth in the story that the Dane Grimkettel outbid him for the impoverished See of Elmham (later Norwich), Stigand was disappointed. Rather than returning to his birthplace, he was obliged to remain in service at court and await another opportunity for preferment.

Stigand fared no better after Harold's death in 1040 and during Harthacnut's two-year reign. With the succession in 1043 of Aethelred and Emma's son Edward the Confessor, his luck changed. According to the *Anglo-Saxon Chronicle*, "Stigand the priest was blessed as bishop for East Anglia", Grimkettel having meanwhile secured the ancient See of Selsey on the Sussex coast. Stigand, however, seems to have lost Elmham again briefly during the spat between Emma and Edward over the competing claim of the Norwegian strongman, King Magnus, to the throne, a quarrel that the mother was always bound to lose. Her former counsellor kept his distance and was not only rewarded with reinstatement at Elmham in 1044, but became head of Edward's royal chapel and, as such, the king's chancellor and custodian of the royal seal. Many a Winchester bishop would be appointed to these offices in the centuries to come.

For the year 1047, the *Anglo-Saxon Chronicle* describes Stigand as Edward's "bishop in the north" when he was appointed as Aelfwine's successor at Winchester. The promotion may well have been a show of gratitude for some successful feat of diplomacy in the king's troublesome relations with his northern vassals. However, in his choice of Stigand as his royal bishop in the ancient capital, Edward was recognising a proven administrator, not least of treasury expenditures. He confirmed him as his chancellor, a position that many of his post-Conquest successors would occupy. As a man who earned the reputation of being thoroughly decent and clean-living, Edward was hardly likely to have chosen a blackguard as his senior counsellor and bishop.

Stigand remained in this key position at Winchester during the subsequent struggles between the king and the Godwines over the increasing Norman influence in the realm. The influx of Norman appointments and settlers may be traced back to the end of the tenth century when Aethelred the 'Redeless', beset by Norse invaders, sought an accommodation with the dukes of Normandy. He married his second wife, Emma, the sister of Duke Richard II, in 1002, and this connection had provided her husband with a bolt-hole during the worst moments of his reign. There was a price to pay, however, in the form of favours, gifts of land and appointments at court. Cnut had also brought in men from the Continent, but this was to improve the mettle of his English clerks whose abilities had declined in the years of chaos under Aethelred. It was by no means to ingratiate petty rulers across the Channel. When Edward the Confessor came to the throne, however, he brought with him from Normandy a fresh influx of advisers and clerks from the land where he had spent much of his life. To the annoyance of the English nobility, his favourites were rewarded with gifts of land and accepted at court.

The last straw for the Saxon nobility was the succession in 1051 of Robert Champart as Archbishop of Canterbury. He had served as Bishop of London from 1044 after being brought over from his abbacy at Jumièges, richly endowed by the dukes of Normandy. Edward had also appointed another Norman as Bishop of Dorchester in 1049 and had lined up a third to take Robert's place in London.[208] It was all too much for the English camp led by the Godwines who had served Edmund Ironside against his mercurial father, Aethelred, and had earned the respect and gratitude of Cnut. As we have seen, they were key players in Edward's ascent to the throne. By the death of Archbishop Eadsige on 29 October 1050, however, Edward had come to resent Godwine's influence and was estranged from the latter's daughter, Queen Edith. A key element in the quarrel between king and magnate was Edward's decision to appoint Bishop Robert, since it overruled the Canterbury monks' election of one of Godwine's kinsmen. To make matters worse, Archbishop Robert, a zealous reformer and staunch defender of Church privileges, accused Godwine of encroaching on lands of the archbishopric and sought to recover them. He also encouraged a whispering campaign with the king to remind him of Godwine's role in the murder of his brother Alfred. And the legend of Queen Emma's dalliance with a former Bishop of Winchester may also have originated as salacious gossip at this time, although as we have already noted, it was largely spurious.

Matters came to a head when Edward summoned Godwine to attend him in Council at Gloucester on 8 September 1051 to answer charges that he had refused to punish the citizens of Dover for an alleged outrage against Count Eustace of Boulogne.[209] To Edward's surprise, Godwine arrived in Gloucester a few days early with an armed retinue and demanded that the king should dismiss charges against him, including complicity in the death of Alfred. Edward reacted robustly and summoned his own allies, declaring Godwine to be a rebel. Civil war loomed but, fortunately, wiser heads on both sides urged restraint. A truce was agreed underpinned by an exchange of hostages.

It seems that one of these wiser heads was Stigand,[210] whose links both in the Danelaw, where several of Edward's allies came from, and to the Godwines made him an important intermediary. Edward, however, was in the stronger position and obtained support for Godwine's exile: it is thought that Stigand was asked to convey the message to the earl informing him of his banishment, while also allowing him time to withdraw his family and personal fortune gracefully. During the months that followed, Godwine and his sons recruited mercenaries from their bases in Bruges and Dublin, funded by treasure they had been able to take with them from England. In September 1052, the Godwines returned with a powerful fleet and faced Edward across the Thames. Again, Bishop Stigand, whose episcopal sway still extended to the South Bank, entered as intermediary, securing a truce and a meeting of the Council in London on 15 September 1052. This time there was a sapping of support for Edward and, realising the odds were stacked against him, Archbishop Robert withdrew to Normandy, taking his pallium of office with him. The Council, led by Stigand, and the northern earls Leofric and Siward persuaded Edward to restore Godwine and to expel several leading Normans from England. In recognition of his diplomatic and administrative services, Stigand was appointed Archbishop of Canterbury by Edward without any recourse to the pope and was retained at the king's side as his royal Bishop of Winchester. The Witan's decisive support for Stigand's promotion is in sharp contrast to its ambivalence over his earlier appointment to Elmham and again suggests that he was, by now, well-regarded.

History has judged Stigand ill on two counts: his replacement of a living incumbent was uncanonical; and by remaining Bishop of Winchester he had become a pluralist, an offence against the laws introduced by Pope Benedict VIII (1012–24). These sought to prevent the multiple holding of high office in the Church. The record does not show Stigand to have been simoniacal, although tradition has also accused him as such. On the first issue, however, it should be remembered that Stigand was Edward's personal choice as a politically acceptable appointment of a long-standing royal servant; in contrast, Robert of Jumièges was clearly unacceptable to the Saxon nobility and, if there is any truth in the Emma legend, had spread scurrilous rumours about a respected lady. In England, too, the king had long been accustomed to making his own clerical appointments or influencing the election of men he wanted set in place – in the face of a weak and often preoccupied papacy. As to the charge of pluralism, Stigand was by no means the first to be accused of holding two senior offices and he would hold both until 1070 when William the Conqueror had no further use for him. Stigand's elevation, therefore, should be seen much more as a reflection of royal respect for his ability than personal greed. That said, the royal bishop was not above the accumulation of wealth and position for himself and his family: he retained several abbeys, including Ely, for several years, and he had already secured the See of Elmham for his brother, Aethelmaer, in 1047.

There can be little doubt that there was some sucking of teeth in the Church at Stigand's preferment: the Abingdon text of the *Anglo-Saxon Chronicle* recorded literally, and inaccurately, that "there was no archbishop in the land" in 1053.[211] Based at Christ Church Canterbury, two or three decades after the Conquest, the chronicler Eadmer suggested that "a man might not wish to receive his (Stigand's) ministrations lest he seem to put a curse in place of blessing". Another, albeit twelfth century, writer described the Canterbury See as vacant as late as 1060, while William of Poitiers, a Norman scribe, considered it was the replacement of Robert of Jumièges that had roused Duke William's wrath and acted as the catalyst for his decision to invade England. Stigand was also excommunicated by five successive popes: this, however, is a less impressive statistic than it sounds, for the papacy in the mid eleventh century suffered from short-lived incumbencies and intense disputes over succession. And it is not clear how seriously the excommunication was meant to be taken, other than to remove his authorisation to consecrate bishops. This did not prevent Stigand consecrating mitred abbots at Christ Church (1061), Bury St Edmunds (1065) and Ely (1066). When, after pressure from Earl Harold Godwinson,[212] Stigand's appointment was accepted in Rome in 1058, he was able to consecrate two English bishops. Unfortunately, within a year, his patron Pope Benedict X was deposed and does not now even appear in the approved Vatican list of papal succession. Indeed, he was declared an antipope. Benedict was replaced by Nicholas II who, tellingly, called a synod in Rome at which the investiture of bishops was forbidden without papal authorisation – the start of a thorny issue between successive kings and popes. Stigand's case must have been in the minds of those who attended and in 1062 a new pope, Alexander II, sent legates to England to investigate the matter. They returned to Rome after consulting King Edward and other notables but refrained from spurning Stigand; they certainly did not recommend his removal at the time.

Nevertheless, it was Archbishop Ealdred of York who consecrated the saintly Wulfstan at Worcester in 1062 and was chosen by Earl Harold to dedicate his new minster at Waltham in Essex in 1060.[213] Sadly, there is no mention of Stigand's presence at the eight days of celebrations and feasting marking the event. Having tested the political waters in England and with greater problems in its relations with the Holy Roman Emperor, the papal curia seems to have tolerated a situation it was in no position to change. Had not the English Church always had a tendency to go its own way?

For his part Edward seems to have been more than able to live with his 'royal archbishop' and proven diplomat: he had already set Stigand the task of identifying a suitable heir to the throne, the Confessor being without issue and the last of the line. King and archbishop had fixed their attention on a surviving son of Edmund Ironside, one of two sent into exile by Cnut in 1017. It would have been under Stigand's direction that the 'Atheling' (prince of the royal blood) Edward was located in Hungary in late 1054. The preferred choice indicates further the appreciation Stigand had of political factors: Edward the Atheling, a popular king's son, served nationalistic purposes and could lock out other potential overseas contenders. Like Stigand, the Atheling was also the progeny of a mixed marriage, since his mother, Siferth, was the widow of the Danelaw thegn Edmund Ironside had married. Ealdred, the then Bishop of Worcester, was sent to the German Emperor, Henry III, to seek his help in contacting the Hungarian king, but a dispute between respective rulers prevented progress for the time being. In October 1056, however, the emperor died and the effort to find the Atheling was renewed, this time with Earl Harold leading a delegation to Cologne where he lobbied the new emperor, Henry IV, and the Bavarian pope, Victor II.[214] Sadly, all the diplomatic investment in bringing the Atheling to England was thwarted by his death after arriving in London in 1057. But all was not lost, since his son, Eadgar, had come too and it would have fallen to Stigand to supervise his tutelage for future kingship.

The search for a successor to the Confessor gives the lie to the story propagated by William of Poitiers that King Edward had nominated Duke William of Normandy. It also sheds another light on the Norman propaganda sewn into the Bayeux Tapestry depicting Harold's apparently accidental landing adjacent to the Norman coast in 1064 from whence he fell into William's hands and was obliged to swear fealty. Time, however, was not on the side of the English, for within less than eighteen months King Edward had died. Stigand was with the Confessor during his illness in late 1065 and, as the *Vita Edwardi* records, was at his deathbed on 5 January 1066 when he would have witnessed the king's fevered ravings concerning the future of his realm and designation of Earl Harold as his successor. As chancellor, Stigand was quick to appreciate that England, with rebellions in the North and covetous eyes in both Normandy and Scandinavia, needed a strong man. However legitimate his claim to royal blood, Eadgar, the Atheling's son, was still an inexperienced boy. Like Cnut before him, Harold's competence as a military leader and administrator outweighed arguments concerning blood line.

Norman chroniclers, keen to denigrate the defeated Saxon king, claim that Stigand crowned Harold II at Westminster on 6 January 1066 within hours of Edward the Confessor's burial. The Bayeux Tapestry also shows Stigand standing on Harold's left and names him as "archieps". But the more reliable – and Saxon – John of Worcester records that Harold chose Archbishop Ealdred of York,[215] translated from Worcester in 1062 for his consecration. Earl Harold would have been as concerned as anyone to legitimise his claim to the throne, more so than for any wish to ingratiate troublemakers in the North. Both Ealdred and his successor at Worcester, the saintly Wulfstan, were Harold's spiritual advisers at a time when his kingly soul sought reassurance; Stigand, in contrast, remained his political adviser and de facto chief minister.

This is not the place to discuss the rights and wrongs of Duke William's invasion of England on 28 September 1066. Suffice it to say that William of Poitiers' claim that his master had the full backing of Pope Alexander II to rid England of an illegitimate king and an uncanonical archbishop has been assessed as largely propaganda. Alexander was embroiled with his own problems in the face of a Holy Roman Emperor who did not recognise him and an antipope, Honorius II, who is also not included in the Vatican's list of succession. What is clear, however, is that without substantial popularity Harold could not have raised such support for his lightning campaign against the Norwegian invader of Northumbria, Harold Hardrada, and Earl Tostig, the king's rebellious brother. Where Stigand was during Harold's great victory against Hardrada and Tostig at the battle of Stamford Bridge on 25 September is not recorded. However, as Harold's senior adviser, he would have been party to the flow of intelligence which allowed his king to steal a march on the invaders. As the Confessor's former "bishop in the North", Stigand must have had a network of contacts which serviced this flow.

Neither do we know whether he was with his king at Hastings on 14 October, like the Abbot of New Minster and a number of his monks, most of whom died in the battle. It is more likely that he remained at Westminster directing the king's secretariat in the coordination of logistics. When news of Harold's death reached London a day later, Stigand was already there and in a position to marshal counter-measures along with Archbishop Ealdred and the surviving English leaders. Resistance to the Normans did not collapse immediately after Hastings and the Atheling Eadgar, supported by his archbishops, fended off William's first attempt to enter London. But with the surrender of the royal treasury at Winchester by the Confessor's estranged widow, Edith, all hope of funding a major military counter-attack was lost. Stigand would have been the first to know of this development and quickly appreciated the implications: he sought out William, who was encamped at Wallingford, and submitted to him.

When William returned to Normandy in March 1067, he took with him the Atheling Eadgar, the still influential earls Edwin and Morcar, and "Archbishop Stigand", as the *Anglo-Saxon Chronicle* attests. William did not, however, depose the archbishop: on the contrary, he saw to it that Stigand was received honourably at churches and abbeys in his duchy. The Conqueror even permitted Stigand to consecrate Remigius, a Norman monk serving at Canterbury, as Bishop of Dorchester in 1067 or 1068, although this may have been due to the Archbishop of York's indisposition or preoccupation. In the conduct of state business, Stigand is known to have attested two charters at Pentecost in 1068 with his signature appearing above that of the Archbishop of York. He was still witnessing charters in the following year. William was shrewd enough to appreciate the power Stigand represented as a potential rallying point for the Atheling and as a potential financier of revolt from his personal fortune. Archbishop Ealdred certainly crowned William on Christmas Day 1066 at Westminster, but the Conqueror permitted Stigand to appear at his left-hand side – as he had done at the coronation of Harold II. So far, little had changed in Stigand's status.

There is no evidence that Stigand schemed against William, although Dean Kitchin[216] thought that he might have escaped with the Atheling to Scotland and then found his way to Ely. If so, he would surely have joined forces with Hereward the Wake in his fenland uprising in 1070–71. It is more likely, however, that William used Stigand on some diplomatic mission to Scotland to secure his northern borders. However uncanonical, his half-Saxon archbishop was, after all, a man well-versed in Anglo-Scottish relations throughout the previous five reigns. This would have bought time until William was ready to use more forceful methods against the Scots, as he did in 1071–2.

Down to 1069, William left the English Church more or less to its own devices, judging that it could deliver public acquiescence. Apart from Remigius of Dorchester, in fact, the episcopate remained unaltered. Abbeys were left under English control and, in his scriptorium, Stigand continued to direct the clerks who had served the Confessor; charters issued used the Old English language. Stigand's possession of vast tracts of land stretching over ten shires was also left intact, including fourteen manors in Norfolk. Here, even one of William's leading supporters, Roger Bigod, was obliged to pay rent to the archbishop for his manor at Forncett. And as far as uncanonical matters were concerned, William left it to Rome to make the first step in any process for Stigand's removal from Canterbury.

Whatever his original ambition, the outbreak of rebellion in 1069 determined the Conqueror to accelerate the pace of 'Normanisation'. The uprising of the English earls Edwin and Morcar was crushed and the lands of the fallen distributed to Norman knights, a process which had begun after Hastings. This, however, was not the only factor sealing Stigand's fate. The death on 11 September 1069 of Archbishop Ealdred – during the course of the savage Norman suppression of the North – left England without a properly constituted metropolitan. The arrival of a papal delegation in England the following April fits with the timing required for news of the vacancy to reach Rome, and for subsequent deliberations in the Curia. There followed the despatch of couriers to William seeking his good offices in the welcome of a legation to adjudicate on what should be done to correct the anomalous nature of Stigand's succession to Canterbury. The papal commission's proceedings at Winchester under Ermenfrid, Bishop of Sion (in Switzerland) and a man who enjoyed princely status, have not survived, but the result was the deposition of Stigand and his brother, Aethelmaer of Elmham, along with most of the other Saxon church leaders. It was a clear-out of most of the ethnic episcopal bench, not just the sacking of Stigand.

Despite his fall, Stigand was allowed to keep some of his temporal holdings, including the large manor of East Meon in Hampshire – some 8,600 acres. Opinion, however, is divided on what really became of him: during the compilation of Domesday, he did not receive a single mention in his home county of Norfolk, in contrast to Hampshire where his former ownerships are at least acknowledged. The Winchester tradition records that he died on 22 February 1072 after being imprisoned in the old capital. According to Dean Kitchin, he was buried somewhere in the grounds of the Old Minster: it is probable that one or more of the mortuary chests in Winchester Cathedral contains many of Stigand's bones, ironically jumbled up with those of Queen Emma, Bishop Aelfwine and several other near contemporaries. After his death, rumours emerged that Stigand had been found with keys round his neck bound to a writing desk containing details of a hoard of treasure. This provoked speculation that he was protecting Saxon funds against the day of a successful insurrection to oust the Norman invaders. William of Malmesbury, however, believed that Stigand was granted a small sum from the Treasury, but spent nothing of it and became a recluse, resisting all pleas from his friends, including the late Confessor's wife, Edith, who urged him to dress and live more comfortably. There is even the suggestion that he starved himself to death in protest against William's treatment of him, albeit he must by then have been about eighty years old.

It is generally agreed that Stigand was a man who acquired wealth with which he could purchase high clerical office but, as we have seen, he was not always successful in this. To complete the picture of his advancement, one has to appreciate his worth to successive rulers from Cnut to William I. Moreover, there is a munificent side to Stigand. Richard of Devizes[217] recorded in the *Winchester Annals* that Stigand was well-regarded at St Swithun's: he had conferred rich gifts on Ely and on St Augustine's, Canterbury, while the Old Minster received a large cross with the figures of St John and the Virgin Mary, richly adorned with gold and silver bought out of money he had received from Queen Emma. It was hung over the nave of the new Norman cathedral built in the last quarter of the eleventh century. Needless to say, such treasure would have been purloined during the despoliations of Henry VIII, if not before.

It is pointless to speculate what might have happened to Stigand had Harold II won at Hastings, but it is more than likely that a Saxon king would have left him in situ until his retirement or death. Stigand was no saint, but the saintly Wulfstan of Worcester, whom the Normans left to die in office in 1095, described him to the newly consecrated Archbishop Lanfranc as "*Stigundus vestrae excellentiae praedessor*" ("Stigand, predecessor of your excellence"). In this, Wulfstan was not only confirming that Stigand had been the recognised Archbishop of Canterbury but was using the formal (*vestrae*) rather than familiar (*tuae*) when addressing a Norman. Stigand, however, simply did not fit in with William's designs for the subsumption of the Norman and English Churches within his feudal and centralising system of military government. That Stigand survived at all after Hastings is testimony to the strong influence of the English Church and his personal abilities. In the end, however, this long-serving servant of the state, along with all but two of his fellow prelates from the Confessor's time, had to be swept away if William were to achieve his ambitions. Nevertheless, the belief remained, as expressed by William of Malmesbury, that Stigand was "a prelate of notorious ambition, who sought after honours too keenly". Did Stigand not pass though things temporal and thus lose the things eternal?[218] The question might have been asked of many a political prelate who came after him.

The fate and subsequent reputation of Winchester's last substantive Saxon bishop fell into the hands of the victors at Hastings. There were many in Rome, too, who rejoiced at Duke William's military success because it afforded the opportunity to bring into line a national Church which had for many years sought to plough an independent furrow. From failure or refusal to pay Peter's Pence, through a distinctive liturgy to an unwillingness to discourage clerical marriage and promote celibacy, the Anglo-Saxon Church of England, helped by geographical remoteness from Rome, had to be brought to heel. The strong arm of William the Conqueror provided the means for achieving this. Stigand's anomalous position as Archbishop of Canterbury was a symptom of a much wider issue between the Papacy and the English crown that would not be settled until the Reformation.

A LOOK FORWARD

According to a mid-twentieth century local legend, Adolph Hitler ordered the Luftwaffe not to bomb Winchester; it was said that he wished to be crowned king in the Cathedral. However apocryphal the story, it holds a ring of truth. Certainly, no bombs were deliberately dropped on the city – albeit German aircraft running away from the RAF discarded a couple of loads on North Walls and also on neighbouring Kings Worthy – while for nights on end the southern sky could be seen burning red as, twelve miles away, the centre of Southampton and the docks received yet another pasting.

A selective reader of European history to support his loathsome claims of Aryan supremacy, the Austrian corporal was also steeped in Wagner's musical interpretation of Rhenish mythology. It is more than likely that he had picked up on Winchester's special place in England's cultural and early constitutional development and had heard of the Order of the Garter. A man who used pageantry and uniforms as tools of government would have found a way to adopt 'Camelot' and the Round Table as his own. After a successful invasion, Winchester, with its spacious parade ground a few hundred yards from the Westgate,[6] could have emulated Nuremberg. Moreover, with one of the longest naves in the world, the majestic cathedral would have served as a fitting venue

---

6   Charles II's palace still stands on the east bank of the main line railway cutting. It is now converted into well-appointed apartments, but in its time, housed the Green Jackets who used the vast central square as a parade ground fit for their 144 steps per minute marching drill.

for a dictatorial dreamer's coronation. We know enough of the Fascist-leaning appeasers who lay not far below the surface of 1939–40 society in England to appreciate that a well stage-managed festival in the old Saxon capital could have helped sugar the pill of German occupation. Just who on the Anglican and Roman Catholic episcopal benches would have been prepared to carry out the office, not forgetting Edward Windsor standing in the wings, is speculation fit only for a novel, but much fortitude would have been required to resist the compulsive pressures to oblige.

Such notional ambition is in striking contrast to William the Conqueror's decision to hold his own coronation not at Winchester, the Saxon royal capital, but in Westminster Abbey. As would soon become apparent, his concern was to suppress the Saxon identity, not to promote it. Was not the new abbey closely associated with Edward the Confessor who was, after all, half-Norman, unlike the full Saxon-blooded late 'usurper', Harold Godwinson? Both Hitler and William recognised that the choice of venue mattered where great and symbolic events are envisaged. Both men were ruthless: in the Conqueror's case he was intent on 'de-Saxonisation'. This meant not just the replacement of individuals in secular authority, but a clear-out of the entire episcopate, save the saintly Wulfstan, Bishop of Worcester, until death could replace him. This was not all: the Treasury might remain at Winchester, a rather more easily secured base than London, but impressive Saxon edifices, dating back many years before the first Norman cathedrals, had to be destroyed to make way for the new regime's visible might. Within twenty years, the Old and New Minsters had been replaced by a cathedral with footings believed to have extended even longer than the structure standing today.

People are replaced or die, materials decay; ideas and conceptions, however, linger and, if worthwhile, survive. Despite all the upheavals of the Norman occupation, the See of Winchester retained much of its prestige and wealth down to the Reformation. As Domesday confirms, the episcopal estate built up over four hundred years remained intact; the only change was a new style of management. Even after London had gone ahead in the pecking order – within two or three decades – Winchester would continue as the wealthiest ecclesiastical prize in the country. In turn, this would attract men of great influence from within and outside the kingdom; almost invariably, the appointment would be made out of royal gratitude for service to the realm.

Under the new feudal system, however, the king would underline the fact that he now owned all the land and that a bishop was only a tenant-in-chief during his period in office. When the See became vacant through death or translation, the temporalities reverted back to the Crown and, during any interregnum, revenues were to be farmed by the king's official appointees, not the diocese. Moreover, a new bishop, like his secular peers, would be required to pay a substantial fine when receiving back the temporalities – after swearing an oath of loyalty. Royal abuse of interim custody of episcopal lands and varying interpretations of how deeply a man of God's conscience might genuflect to the king would introduce major tensions between Church and State for centuries to come. Such disputes had largely been absent under the Saxon monarchs. There was a further dimension: unlike Hitler, who would have felt he had the Papacy in his pocket in one way or the other, William owed his new throne in some measure to support he had received from Rome. A succession of strong popes, too, regarded the Conqueror as a potential ally in reining in an English Church which had often gone its own way – from the appointment of prelates through to non-payment of papal dues.

At Winchester, we have seen how in the closing years of Anglo-Saxon England, the 'royal' bishop came to occupy the position of chief counsellor and minister in government. Although post-Conquest successors might be appointed to senior secular posts, one element, inevitably, remained constant and increasingly important – the geographical extent of Winchester diocese. Saxon records fail to identify the ealdormen and captains who defended the south coast in the ninth and tenth centuries; in contrast, after the Conquest, we come to know more and more about the great military defenders of the realm, both secular and spiritual. Of these, although no longer invariably chief counsellor, the Bishop of Winchester remained a crucial figure in the control and defence of the south. Moreover, with a diocese stretching up to the south bank of the Thames, he had ready access to the court, even after London had replaced the Saxon capital. For much of the Anglo-Saxon period, the bishop could be a pastor based in the heart of his diocese. From the late eleventh century onwards, he was increasingly drawn away from his cathedral city and often became little more than an absentee. After all, he would have a residence only a short boat ride from Westminster and the Tower of London – at Southwark Palace.

During the Saxon centuries, the record tells us little about the management of the episcopal and monastic estates. Yet as the many writs attest, the Bishop and the Prior of St Swithun's respectively were already in possession of vast tracts of Hampshire, Surrey, Wiltshire and Somerset, even extending as far as Oxfordshire. The Conqueror and his successors did not consider it necessary to cut the diocese down to size, at least not while the feudal relationship continued. We do not know who the reeves and bailiffs were down to the Conquest, but they surely existed. As records improved, from Domesday into the twelfth century, so names and functions became clearer. Furthermore, with secular demands on his time and whereabouts, so the bishop's household would grow and vicars-general would have to be appointed frequently. Suffragan bishops, however, were introduced much later.

Feudal service brought with it an additional side to a bishop's expected duties and responsibilities: the man of God would be required to provide horse and foot soldiers to support the king's host in time of war or civil strife. Post-Conquest bishops would also have to gather a standing force of gentlemen-at-arms to act as escorts on the increasingly insecure roads up to London and around the diocesan estate. Although Swithun and other Saxon bishops might have had their military moments, it is impossible to imagine an Aethelwold or Aelfheah surrounded by other than prayerful and scholastic clerks – let alone dressed in chain-mail.

The Winchester bishop would also take on an international role. King William was hardly likely to appoint an inward-looking Saxon to succeed Stigand; instead, the Norman and Angevin holders of the See would often retain interests or feudal duties across the Channel. The diocese was also an important commercial asset, being one of England's major wool-producing areas with key markets in the Low Countries, another vital element in external relations. These outward-looking diplomatic and mercantile aspects in the work of a Winchester bishop culminated in several of them in the lead-up to the Reformation becoming the forbears of what we now call a foreign secretary. Durham might attract the title of Prince-Bishop and can still wear a ducal coronet, thanks to his prime secular function of securing the North against the Scots from a province which lay outside the old Anglo-Saxon system of shire government. In contrast, Winchester's external interest would widen multifariously as the centuries rolled by, tempting one or two bishops to tilt at archiepiscopal ambition and at the office of papal nuncio, or legateship, not to mention a cardinal's hat or two. In return, Rome was to look to a number of Winchester prelates to provide close insights into the workings and personalities of the Westminster court. The inevitable conflict of interests would become a burden that would afflict several bishops and would leave one or two in great fear for their souls.

Cosmopolitan links and diplomatic involvement, of course, were not new. From the seventh century onwards, men like Agilbert and, later, Daniel, were central figures. Under the post-Conquest dynasties, however, this aspect mutated into a greater preoccupation with the balance of secular power in Europe. A more pastoral emphasis would eventually return during the nineteenth and early twentieth centuries and, for all its ancient history and tradition, the Winchester diocese has in more recent times attracted a reputation for promoting links and sustenance to those working to spread the Gospel overseas. While Berin and Haeddi might have been dismayed at the grossly secular and opulent activities of their medieval successors, they would surely smile with pleasure at the subsequent emphasis given at both diocesan and parochial levels to the encouragement of those in the mission field. At the same time, however, they would have to accept that their licence from the Saxon monarchy to extend the influence of Christianity in Wessex came with a price to be paid in the form of secular service by their post-Conquest successors down to and beyond the Reformation. Temporal authority and custodianship were always going to rival and sometimes undermine the purpose and behaviour of a bishop as set down in Titus 1:7–9: he should be "blameless, as the steward of God", forsaking "filthy lucre". Alas, as the head of a house with substantial delegated secular power, the Winchester bishops that came after the Conquest would find it increasingly difficult to live up to this Biblical directive.

ENDNOTES

St Berin – A Missionary Bishop from Rome

1. A/S Chronicle (text A): the entry for 634 raises the question whether Berin might have arrived a little earlier. D. P. Kirby (The English Historical Review January 1965 – Vol, 80 No. 314 pp) points out that King Oswald, who ascended his throne in 635, is unlikely to have travelled south for Cynegils' baptism until at least 636. I am aware of the fluidity in the dating of early Anglo-Saxon history, but in telling the story, have accepted the A/S Chronicle at face value. It is the sequence that is important.
2. Barbara Yorke: *Oxford Dictionary of National Biography* (2004). Having sailed in the waters, the author can attest to the strength of the tide and prevailing wind. He once tacked all day from Chichester harbour to Cowes without making any progress against a stiff south-westerly. But as soon as the tide changed the boat surged ahead and overshot its destination. It is likely, therefore, that Berin's helmsman had to beach the boat to await a favourable tide before proceeding up the Solent to Hamtun.
3. See Barbara Yorke: *Proceedings of Hampshire Field Club and Archaeological Society 38* (1982) 75–84.
4. Cynegils was a great great grandson of Cerdic the Saxon who brought his people to the Solent area in 495. He came to power in 611 (ASC texts A and E).
5. J. N. L. Myres: *The English Settlements* – Oxford University Press (1986) – based on the Winchester excavations led by Martin Biddle during the 1960–70s.
6. Margaret Deanesly: *The Pre-Conquest Church in England* – Black (1963) – pp77–8.
7. Bede contended that, before he left Rome, Bishop Birinus had promised Pope Honorius "he would sow the seeds of our holy Faith in the most inland and remote regions of the English, where no other teacher had been before

him." (Bede: *Ecclesiastical History of the English People* – book three, chapter seven, p153 in Penguin edition of Leo Sherley-Price's 1955 translation.) Taken literally, well beyond southern Albion.

8   William Hunt: *A History of the English Church from its Foundations to the Norman Conquest (597–1066)* – MacMillan (1899).

9   Pelagianism was Rome's great worry. Active in Palestine in the early years of the fifth century, Pelagius preached against the divinity of Jesus and contended that good works alone were sufficient to bring an individual into a state of grace. Earliest sources for the conversion of 'England' emphasise baptism in Berin's mission; that is, the rising from death to new life, through the washing away of sin as an admission to God's grace and implicit salvation through Christ's death and resurrection.

10 The Council of Chalcedon (451) had resolved that Christ was both human and divine. During the following two centuries, the question was increasingly asked: did Christ, therefore, have two wills? Honorius I argued that it really did not matter: he ridiculed "those bombastic and time-wasting philosophers" who, in weighing up the two natures of Christ, "croak at us like frogs". For his pains, he was dubbed a Monothelite, a believer in one will. From this distance, the charge looks risible.

11 Romano-British names are common in what is now central Hampshire; for example, Andover, the Candovers and Micheldever.

12 ASC (text A) has three mentions of the name 'Gewis' and his offspring starting in the year 552. Cerdic's descendants fell out with one another frequently and settled in different areas. By 634, however, Cynegils was looking to his northern frontier rather than pursuing his earlier westward conquests.

13 An inter-war pageant placed Cynegils' court quite wrongly in the city. See also G W Kitchin: *Winchester (Historic Towns Series)* – Longmans Green (1891) p6.

14 For details of the now virtually lost but once important road from Silchester to Dorchester, see C Cochrane: *The Lost Roads of Wessex* – Pan (1969) pp93–95.

15 The bishop's seat, derivation of the word 'See' (Webster's dictionary).

16 Professor Yorke deploys cogently in her 1982 article the argument that the Old Minster is of a date at least a decade later. She concedes that, while the major excavations at Winchester Cathedral in the 1960s and 1970s under Martin Biddle established that the construction remained unaltered until the tenth century, it is impossible to establish exactly when the original church was built.

St Agilbert – The Diplomat from Paris

17 Sir Frank Stenton: *Anglo Saxon England* – Oxford University Press (1971) p129.
18 The Lindisfarne Gospels date to the late seventh/early eighth centuries and were the work of one hand. They were written in Latin, but in the early tenth century they were translated into the vernacular, the earliest text of its kind. In later centuries, such enterprise would have been condemned as heretical.
19 ODNB: P Fouracre (2004), among others.
20 As mentioned in my introduction, one has to beware of taking Bede as 'gospel' when there is an absence of other sources. Romans and Celts both believed in the essence of Christ's death and resurrection. Dating and tonsures were side issues.
21 Erchinoald (died 658) became Mayor of the Neustrian Palace in 641.
22 ASC text F (649). The detail does not appear in the Winchester-written text A.
23 Arthur Mee: *Hampshire with the Isle of Wight* – Hodder and Stoughton (1939), p373.
24 Bede, writing only a few years after the Synod, provides a detailed account in his history but there is room for scepticism about his bias (Book 3 Chapter 25).
25 See Lapidge, Blair, Keynes and Scragg (edit): *The Blackwell Encyclopaedia of Anglo-Saxon England* – 1999, pp155–7 for an account of the respective and complicated lunar calculations of the disputing parties.
26 Bede (Book 3 Chapter 25 pp187–8).
27 Bede (Book 3 Chapter 28).
28 Bede (Book 3 Chapter 7).
29 Leon Levillain: *Etudes merovingiennes – la charte de Clotilde 10 Mars 673* (1944).

Wine and Lothair – The First Saxon and the Last Frankish Bishops to the West Saxon Kingdom

30 As noted already, the site was largely deserted for much of the sixth century; people moved back in during the middle of the seventh.
31 Bede (Book 3 Chapter 20) calls Deusdedit a South Saxon, possibly meaning a Saxon from the south (Sussex). Stenton (p122) records him as a "West Saxon". The point remains that the Church was already filling its senior posts with 'English-born' clerics.
32 Bede (Book 3 Chapter 7).
33 The consecration would likely have been doubly offensive since Chad had originally supported Celtic traditions. And it has been suggested – without a shred of evidence – that the two Celtic supporting bishops came from Cornwall, still outside Rome's control. Wherever they came from, there would have been a question mark over their laying on of hands to confirm that the new bishop should be entrusted with the pastoral care of a diocese now firmly within the Roman sphere of influence and in no need of Celtic sponsorship.
34 Ibid.
35 Purchase of Sees was well-known in Frankish Gaul. See Wood and Stephens: *The Bishops of Winchester* – Warren (1907) p5.
36 Ibid.
37 The chests have recently been refurbished, when they were temporarily out of public view. After due consideration, the cathedral authorities consented to DNA testing at Bristol University. The 'Winchester tradition' stems from the fifteenth century monk, Thomas Rudborne, whose account *Historia Major Fundatione Ecclesiae Wintoniensis* was based in part on a lost manuscript, *de Basilica Petri*. Rudborne attests to Wine's burial in Winchester.
38 As opposed to Earconwold (died 693), whose relics were preserved at St Paul's in London.
39 Bishop Fox (died 1528) stipulated in his will how quickly his body should be disposed of. If he died in the morning, he should be interred the same afternoon; if he passed away in the afternoon, he should be buried the next morning.
40 See King Athelstan's visit to the shrine of St Cuthbert (died 687) at Durham in 934 when he adorned the saint's cadaver with Bishop Frithstan's vestments.

41 *Ora et labora* (pray and work) is the motto of the Benedictines, whose conventual life stems from their founder, St Benedict (c480–547). By the mid-seventh century, his 'Rule' was being adopted by monastic houses in Frankish Gaul but had still to arrive in England. In parallel, the shorter Rule of St Columbanus placed a strong emphasis on absolute obedience. It is difficult to judge what set of rules the Winchester community followed in these early days.

42 See the Electronic Sawyer, directed since its inception by Simon Keynes at Trinity College, Cambridge. The annotated list and biography was first published by the Royal Historical Society in 1968. Additional research and updating of the resource was carried out by Susan Kelly of King's College London, with more recent work by Rebecca Rushforth and others. Cenwealh's undated and spurious charter is reproduced at S229. Whatever its origin, the Winchester connection with Downton was ancient, even if contested by prior and bishop respectively. Its early existence would explain why Winchester held so large an estate (as much as 100,000 acres or more) deep in Sherborne, later Ramsbury/Salisbury diocesan territory. The earliest genuine charter for Downton, however, is dated to 948 (S540) and appears to have been a re-confirmation of an earlier grant.

43 Ibid: S1164 granted by King Cenred and dated between 670 to 676.

44 Bright: Early English Church History – Oxford (1888) p267.

45 Malmesbury's library was extensive by the eleventh century, so William would have had access to earliest documents about the history of his house. Sadly, what he did not know, he often made up!

46 See G T Dempsey in *Speculum*, Vol. 57 No. 4 (October 1982) p846. Dempsey considers that the book would have been brought in by Archbishop Theodore.

St Haeddi – A Holy Estate Agent

47 *Crockfords Clerical Directory*.

48 *Oxford Dictionary of Saints*: D H Farmer – Oxford (1997 edition).

49 William of Malmesbury: *Gesta Pontificum* based on a letter from Aldhelm to Haeddi which William would have read in his abbey's archive.

50 Deanesly: *The Pre-Conquest Church in England* – p195.

51 Bede: Book 5 Chapter 18. It is quite likely that Bede received a first-hand

account of Haeddi from Aldhelm's monkish friend, Pecthelm, who became bishop of Whithorn in south-west Scotland and close to Jarrow.
52 J. E. A. Jolliffe: *EHR*, Vol. 50 No. 197 (January 1935) p1935. It may be found on Esawyer at S1249 and is generally considered to be authentic.
53 M. Lapidge: *EHR*, Vol. 90 No. 357 (October 1975) p817.
54 John Leland (c1503–52), the antiquarian, was commissioned by Henry VIII to make a survey of ancient records held in the monasteries about to be dissolved and at college libraries. Leland was engaged for about twelve years on the project and, among other things, saved a raft of late-seventh and eighth century Latin epigrams.
A full translation has defeated at least one of my Latin specialists!
55 St Deicola is venerated by the Catholic Church on the day of his death – 18 January 625 – and is best known as the founder in 611 of Lure Abbey in the Vosges. St Cecilia's origins were not recognised until 496 when Pope Gelasius introduced her name into the papal sacramentary. No church was known to have been dedicated to her until the discovery of an old basilica in Rome during the early ninth century. Her feast day is 22 November. (See *Catholic Encyclopaedia* Vol 4 (1908) Appleton, New York and Baring-Gould: *Lives of the Saints* (1914) Edinburgh).
56 Malmesbury Abbey library was well-stocked during William's life there, so there is little doubt about the accuracy of his quotation.
57 Another Leland discovery.
58 Florence of Worcester (died 1118): *Chronicon ex chronicis* which concluded in 1140. While much of the compilation of the work was attributed to Florence, his younger colleague, John, is now thought to have written the work we know; it is in a single hand.
59 *Oxford Dictionary of Saints*.

Daniel – Counsellor and Scholar

60 Britwald, or Beorhtwald, Archbishop of Canterbury 693–731. According to Edward Carpenter in his survey of the archbishops (*Cantuar*: Mowbray 1971 p22), he concentrated on the organisation of his province. It is too early to talk of influence in the North, where York was elevated to an archbishopric in 735.
61 Bede (Book V Chapter 18), but later (see V: 23) the bishopric fell vacant

and pastoral care returned "for some years" to Bishop Daniel. A major obstacle to Christian expansion was the adherence of the South Saxons to their traditional pagan way of life, a situation not dissimilar to the uncertain early days of the diocese of London.

62　Ibid p217: Miss Deanesly records that the synodical decision to set up Sherborne permitted Aldhelm to retain the abbacies of Malmesbury, Frome and Bradford-on-Avon, probably to help finance the new bishopric. If so, this is an early example of pluralism to be repeated constantly in future centuries and warped into the greedy acquisition of benefices during the High Middle Ages. Aldhelm may have had his doubts about the morality; he may also have felt physically challenged by the growing secular responsibilities of a bishop. He died only four years after his translation.

63　Dictionary of National Biography based on Faris *Life of St Aldhelm* iii.

64　Ibid p8: how monastic the 'Old Minster' had become is difficult to say. It seems likely that both Daniel and Aldhelm wore the tonsure and observed the Benedictine Rule, but that is not to say that the Winchester or Sherborne communities followed their example.

65　Not for the last time, however, a Winchester bishop informs others about events, but says little about himself (cf., Swithun below).

66　By tradition born in 675 at Crediton, Boniface – named Wynfrith at birth – became a monk at Nursling, according to Bede, the earliest Benedictine foundation in Wessex and dated to 686. It owed much to its proximity to a ford across the lower Test through which the old Roman road had once passed on its way between Poole harbour and other towns along the south coast and inland. It was vulnerable to the existence of Viking pirates who burnt it down in the ninth century. The fourteenth century church of St Boniface in a quiet cul-de-sac, just to the north of the M27 blighted area west of Southampton, now stands where the abbey would have been. Domesday records the existence of a Saxon church, probably tenth century, whose dedication is lost.

67　Edward Kylie: *The English Correspondence of St Boniface* (Chatto and Windus 1911) p6.

68　Kylie dates this letter to 718.

69　Kylie: p16. Boniface first made for Rome where he is thought to have begged forgiveness at the tombs of the Apostles, St Peter and St Paul during the autumn of 718.

70 Ibid: letter dated to 720–22.
71 Paul the Deacon (died 799): *Historia Langobardorum* – Book 1 Ch 9 (written post 787).
72 Ibid: letter dated to 723–5. Daniel's sentiments are reflected in Charles Oakley's once often sung hymnal words: "Hills of the North rejoice… though absent long, your Lord is nigh". Oakley (1832–65) wrote the words some years before its first publication in 1870. In the 1981 *Revised Hymns Ancient and Modern*, it is number 269 and set to the well-known tune *Little Cornard* attributed to Martin Fallas Shaw (1858–1958). Shaw was also known for his work with the 'freestyle' dancer Isadora Duncan. Paul the Deacon (see note lxxi) would have disagreed with Daniel; in the preface to his history of the Lombards, he extolls the virtues of the cold and healthy northern climes, in contrast to the hotter and diseased south.
73 Matthew 13: 24–30.
74 Gregory II was ahead of his time and a liberal as far as marital matters were concerned. In 726, he wrote to Boniface to advise on the right course for a man to take whose wife was so seriously ill she could not live with him. Gregory considered that the man was free to re-marry, provided he maintained his first wife. A particularly humane approach that would not go down well in much of the Roman Catholic Church today.
75 Ibid: letter dated to 723–5.
76 Corinthians II 12:7.
77 Florenti Wigorniensis: *Monachi Chronicon ex Chronicis* (edit Benjamin Thorpe 1848) – Vol I, p55.
78 Kylie: letter dated to 742–44.

Over One Hundred Years of Obscurity

79 I am indebted to Deborah Harmeling's work on Tetta (Abbess of Wimborne) for its insight into the major contribution made by women in the conversion of Germany.
80 The term convent today suggests a nunnery, often a place of education. But in an age of double monasteries, it had a more generic meaning. Winchester, unlike several other pre-Conquest cathedrals, was to become a wholly 'conventual' (or monastic) institution by the end of the tenth century. But, although it was the place where the bishop's chair or throne ('cathedra') was

placed, in the eighth century, it is still too early to talk of the Old Minster as a monastery.

81 Esawyer S89, better known as the Isomere Diploma. The attribution could also be a reference back to the early title of 'Bretwalda' or overlord of various sub-kings falling under greater or lesser Mercian influence. The charter refers to a grant of ten hides at Ismere by the River Stour and woodland in Morfe Forest, Worcestershire. The purpose was the construction of a minster, another early example of the secular power determining where centres of worship should be.

82 Offa (c725–796 and King of Mercia from 757 until his death). His success in subduing his many neighbours belies the inherent vulnerability of the far-flung Mercian geo-political position. His fame as the creator of 'Offa's Dyke' overshadows the fact that this was a defensive measure to keep the belligerent Welsh out while he dealt with sub-kingdoms in Kent, Sussex, East Anglia and Wessex.

83 St Cuthbert of Canterbury, archbishop from about 740 to 760. The pressure for reform was sparked by Boniface, who complained to the papacy of low standards amongst the clergy in Germania and of inebriated bishops. Cuthbert's feast day is 26 October, the date of his death. See also Peter de Rosa: *Vicars of Christ* (Poolbeg 2000) p 404.

84 Stenton: *Anglo-Saxon England*, p174. Both Cyneheard and his archbishop were involved in the correspondence, but Winchester's proximity to Hamtun would have continued to provide an important point of dispatch for clerical couriers to Paris and Strasbourg.

85 Text F (Canterbury M/S) of the *Anglo-Saxon Chronicle* for 790 (792) records that an Abbot Aethelheard from Louth – and thus a Mercian – was chosen as archbishop at about this time. He was consecrated on 21 July 763 (Hunt: *History of the English Church 597–1066*).

86 See Rudburne (late Medieval Winchester monk and annalist) and Cassan.

87 Esawyer S135 of 793. Cassan claims, quoting the Croyland annalist Ingulphus, that Egbald is mentioned in the charter. If, indeed, it is the correct identity, he would no longer have been Bishop of Winchester.

88 For fuller text of Leo's assurance, see Carpenter: *Cantuar*, p28.

89 Text E (Peterborough M/S) *Anglo-Saxon Chronicle* 799/801.

90 Edward Carpenter, in his history of the archbishops of Canterbury (*Cantuar*), makes no mention of Wigthegn and states that Archbishop Wulfred was accompanied by Wighbert, Bishop of Sherborne. Hunt, in his

comprehensive *History of the Early English Church* insists, however, that the Bishop of Winchester went with his archbishop, which is more logical. The Winchester fund of knowledge about Canterbury's cause would have been far deeper than that of Sherborne.

91 Stenton: *Anglo-Saxon History*, p231.
92 Esawyer S255: 10 April 739. King Aethelheard granted twenty hides to Forthere, Bishop of Sherborne (709 to c736), who was apparently later translated to Crediton. The town's historic church is thought to stand on the land.
93 Esawyer: S281. The vulnerability of the Isle of Wight became very much a Bishop of Winchester's concern during the continuing confrontations with the French during the post-Conquest period.
94 Cassan based on Richardson quoting Vigilantius (M/S Barlow).
95 Stenton cites a document of 838, apparently drafted at Canterbury, not Winchester. It records some of the proceedings at the Kingston Council, but "is so illiterate that it cannot be translated". Stenton confirms, however, that it shows king and archbishop dealing with each other on equal terms. (*Anglo-Saxon England*, p234n2).
96 See Kitchin's history of Winchester, p12: Dean Kitchin, writing at the end of the nineteenth century, considered that the earliest episcopal residence was previously a royal palace. The name 'Wolvesey' is said to be derived from the site known as Wulf's Isle on which the Norman cathedral was built. Wolvesey Palace, however, has been situated since the twelfth century to the south-east of the cathedral within an outer wall that still shows "long and short" masonry, herringbone flint-work and many Roman bricks.
97 Esawyer: S1263.
98 Esawyer: S284.
99 Esawyer: S272–6.
100 It is likely that the 'congregation' of Winchester had formally approved the choice of their bishop and spiritual leader for many years. It was to become, however, a jealously guarded privilege in centuries to come.
101 Ibid. p56.
102 Esawyer S294a and b.

St Swithun – The People's Saint

103 See Barbara Yorke: *The Bishops of Winchester, the Kings of Wessex and the Development of Winchester in the ninth and tenth centuries* – The Hampshire Field Club and Archaeological Society Vol 40 (August 1984) pp61–70.

104 The entry appears in both the Winchester and Peterborough texts. See also Stenton: *Anglo-Saxon England* – Oxford 1971 P244 n.3.

105 Goscelin of Saint-Bertin, eleventh century Flemish hagiographer who collected stories of saints during his stay in England. Hardy (Rolls Series 1862) considered him not to be authoritative.

106 *Domesday (Hampshire)*: Edit. J Morris (Phillimore 1982) 6:17. When Swithun was born, the land would likely have been in royal or independent ownership. By Domesday, it was firmly in the hands of St Peter's Abbey (New Minster) which was not founded until the beginning of the tenth century.

107 *Oxford Dictionary of Saints*.

108 *Gesta Regum*: 11 c 108.

109 Esawyer: S307, 309–12, 325 and 1274.

110 The combination of five sons and problems stemming from the absorption of Kent persuaded Aethelwulf to create a layer of sub-kings, which also allowed him to withdraw from government. His eldest son, Aethelstan, who predeceased him some time before 855, was made sub-king of Kent. His second son, Aethelbald, then became sub-king in the West while his third son, Aethelberht, took over Kent. This was the arrangement at Aethelwulf's death in 858. Aethelbald only lived two more years and his younger brother then ruled over a reunited kingdom.

111 Charles's uneasy relationship with his brother Louis 'the German', who ruled over the eastern half of the former Carolingian Empire, deteriorated into outright warfare when the Emperor Lothair II died in 858. Aethelwulf would have learnt of the pope's concern about the future of the Empire during his visit to Rome and may have had a papal brief.

112 There is some suggestion that a bridge existed from the early sixth century. If so, it is unlikely to have been more than a rickety pedestrian-carrying structure. St Swithun's bridge was removed in 1768, but its foundations were used for the existing two-lane span built in 1813 (see inscriptions).

113 ASC text F.

114 Florence of Worcester: *Monachi Chronicon Chronicis* (edit Thorpe) – p79.
115 Lanfrid: monk and annalist in Winchester towards the end of the tenth century.
116 A Franco-Belgian adage has the same import: "Quand il pleut a la Saint Gervais (19 July), il pleut quarante jours après".
117 *Gesta Pontificum* – p168.
118 Aelfwine (1032–1043): See below.
119   a) *Vita Sancti Swithuni Episcopi Wintoniae at Confessoris* attributed to Goscelin: it includes few facts other than that Swithun was born about 800 to noble parents.

    b) *Miracula Sancti Swithuni, Wintoniensis Episcopi per Lanfredum Wintoniensum Monachum* attributed as a copy of the work of one of Bishop Aethelwold's monks in the late tenth century; it is considered to be written in an obscure style.

    c) *Historia Translationis et Miraculorum Sancti Swithuni ex Antiquissimo*, anonymous but attributed to Lanfrid. It claims to record the events surrounding the translation of Swithun's earthly remains and miracle based on an eyewitness account.

    d) *Miracula Sancti Swithuni ex Antiquissimus Membranis Reginae Sueciae* – also anonymous but claiming to be an eyewitness.
120 The Westgate, used for many years as a museum, also stands, but it was closed to vehicular traffic decades before Kingsgate was pedestrianised.

Alfred's Bishops

121 The Winchester text of the ASC uses the word "destroyed". Florence of Worcester (edit Thorpe p79) describes the town as "depopulated". In his biography of King Alfred, Asser (chapter 18) claimed that the raiders returned to their base at the mouth of the Somme. See translation by S Keynes and M Lapidge in *Alfred the Great: Asser's Life and Other Contemporary Sources* (Harmondsworth 1983) p65–110. Compare also *The Ninth Century Annals of St Bertin*: J L Nelson (Manchester 1991) p92.
122 His colleague, Heahmund, Bishop of Sherborne, had been killed in battle only months before, a further loss to scholarship. He and/or Ealfrith would have conducted the prayers before Ashdown on King Aethelred's insistence (cf Stenton p279).

123 *Victoria County History of Somerset Vol 3* (1974) and local folklore. There is also speculation that Tunbeorht was a former Abbot of Glastonbury from 837 to before 854, but the dates do not quite tally with elevation to Winchester.

124 *Asser's Life of Alfred*: Trans A S Cook (Ginn 1905) para 53.

125 *F of W Monachi Chronicon ex Chronicis*: edit Thorpe, 1848, p97. There is no reference to Denewulf's humble origins before this account, probably written early in the twelfth century.

126 Asser's *Life*: para 54.

127 Asser became Bishop of Sherborne in c890 and wrote his biography of Alfred in the last years of the reign. Asser died in c909.

128 In 868, at the age of nineteen, Alfred married Ealhswith of Mercia (852–905), the year after he and his brother, Aethelred, joined forces with King Burgred to fight the Danes before Nottingham.

129 Peter's Pence: Also known in Saxon times as *Romefeoh* (the fee due to Rome), it was a tribute first offered by King Ine during his 725 pilgrimage. Thus, it first originates during Bishop Daniel's episcopate. Initially, it was meant to fund an English school in Rome. At the beginning of the tenth century the term was probably not yet in use, since it was not formalised until the reign of King Edgar. In due course, the levy was named after the date of its collection – 1 August – the feast of St Peter Ad Vincula. Delay in payment and misappropriation were to become a persistent sore in relations between Rome and the English Church down to the Reformation when it was abolished by the 1534 Act of Parliament. It returned briefly under Mary I, only to be finally repealed by the 1559 Act of Supremacy under Elizabeth I. (See *Jacob's Law Dictionary* first published in 1729).

130 *Charters of the New Minster (Anglo-Saxon Charters IX)*: Edit Miller British Academy (2001). Alfred set up a small monastery (*monasteriolum*) for his scholastic import, Grimbald of St Bertins.

131 Esawyer: S352.

132 Esawyer: S354.

133 Esawyer: S343. Athelney retained the land until its dissolution in 1539.

134 ODNB 2004.

135 The mancus was a gold coin weighing 4.25 grams and based on the Islamic dinar. Coins struck by King Offa of Mercia in the eighth century were copies and included Arabic script. They were worth ten times the value of silver and were often melted down for transport as bullion. See *Medieval European*

Coinage – Grierson and Blackburn (Cambridge University Press 1986) p328.
136 Esawyer: S1444, a letter from Denewulf to Edward the Elder concerning sixty hides at Beddington.
137 Liber de Hyda: British Library – Additional MS 82931.

The Bishops of Expansionary Wessex

138 A narrow strip of cloth traditionally worn on a priest's left arm during Mass. It has been described as originally a handkerchief to wipe away a celebrant's tears of penance during the early centuries (St Alphonius Liguori 1696–1787). Anglicans prefer to see the maniple as symbolic of a servant to the servants of God, not to be confused with the origins of the stole which is related to Christ's washing of his disciples' feet (John Ch. 13).

139 The laying of the foundation stone and intent is usually attributed to Alfred, but the building of the convent was progressed by his queen, Ealhswith, who died in December 902 long before its completion. According to Osbert of Clare in his life of St Edburga, the house was not, in fact, completed until the episcopate of Aelfheah I (934–51). The latter dedicated the Nunnaminster to the Blessed Virgin Mary, but after the Conquest it was always known as St Mary's Abbey. It was situated between the present-day High Street and Colebrook Street and extended into what is now an ornamental park behind the mayor's parlour with water courses (for drainage) feeding into the Itchen. The abbey was suppressed in 1539.

140 Esawyer: S370 records grants of land at Micheldever (100 hides), the Strattons (9), Burcot (3.5), Popham (8.5), Woodmancott (10), the Candovers (10), Cranbourne (10), Barton Stacey (4), Swarraton (3), Northington (6), adjacent to Selborne (3), Copythorne (1.5), Abbotts Ann near Andover (15), Collinbourne (50) and Durley & Chisledon (40).

141 Esawyer: S372 issued from Bickleigh in Devon. The exchange of land at Portchester was possibly connected with naval purposes and construction. The impressive ruins are now in the hands of English Heritage.

142 Esawyer: S373 also issued from Bickleigh and comprising a further consolidation of episcopal estate at Taunton.

143 Esawyer: S385 suggesting a smallholding within a larger tract of 20 hides in the Old Minster's hands.

144 Esawyer: S375 (Alresford); S376 (further confirmation of rights over

Chilcomb in exchange for a lease to the king at Downton); S377 (Overton, Tadley, North Waltham and Bradley); S381 (the now 'chocolate box' village of Crawley to the west of Winchester); S382 (confirmation of holdings at Farnham and Bentley); S383 (the first record of the bishop holding Highclere, another popular future medieval retreat) and S384 (confirmation of holdings at Hurstbourne Priors and at Stoke Charity.

145 The Danes had fallen back on strong fortifications they had prepared at Tempsford from which they had hoped to launch a counter-attack. The combined force of West Saxons and Mercians stormed the defences and effectively destroyed military cohesion in the Danelaw.

146 British Library MS Stowe 944 c 1031 records that Frithstan was buried, as one might expect, at the Old Minster.

147 Abbot of Cluny from 927, St Odo is credited with raising the monastery of Cluny in Burgundy (founded 909) to the influential position it held over other religious houses on the Continent. Odo was brought in to reinvigorate Fleury, which had fallen away from its previously high standards after suffering much during Danish incursions.

148 Archbishop of Canterbury 960–988 and Bishop of Winchester 963–984, respectively.

149 The entry is to be found in the Winchester version of the *Chronicle* and can only refer to Pope Gregory the Great (c540–604), the inspiration for the Augustinian conversion of Kent. Pope Gregory's death is publicised in the Vatican guide *I Sommi Pontefici Romani*.

150 *The English Church from its Foundation to the Norman Conquest 597–1066*: Hunt (MacMillan 1899) p330.

St Aethelwold – Monastic Reformer and Liturgist

151 Hunt (p339) records the story of Dunstan, as the newly appointed Abbot of Glastonbury, seeing what he took to be an evil spirit on three occasions, including on the day of Eadmund's death. Eadmund was enjoying the feast day with some of his nobles at Pucklechurch in Gloucester when robbers broke into another part of the building. It is a mark of the king's character that he led from the front in tackling the intruders.

152 Esawyer: S461 in 940 (30 hides at Waltham, probably near Basingstoke) and S486 in 943 (20 hides) at Moredon near Swindon).

153 Esawyer: S522 in 947 (five hides at Ebbesborne in Wiltshire) and S533 in 948 (three hides at Ailsworth, near Peterborough).

154 Esawyer: S561 in 953 (33 hides at 'Aesceburh'). The area is best known for the Iron Age white horse carved into the chalk hillside.

155 Current Forestry commission blurb defines the etymology correctly. Sadly, Wikipedia blurs the issue by giving the wrong date – 984, which would refer to Aelfheah II's accession.

156 *Charters of the New Minster (A/S Charters IX)*: Edit Miller (2001) British Academy Oxford p81–4.

157 ASC: Text D (Mercian).

158 ASC: Text A.

159 Deanesly p346. But see also ibid (Miller p81–4).

160 Esawyer: S614–6 (grants of land at Kennington in Berkshire; Selsey and Church Stowe in Northants) all dated to 956. A year later Bishop Beorhthelm exchanged Kennington for Curbridge in Oxfordshire held by Abbot Aethelwold of Abingdon. Confusingly, the bishop's name appears in two charters for Eadgar's reign as Brithelm, but there is little doubt that they are one and the same. S683 for 960 describes him as "kinsman" which compares favourably with the Eadwig charter of 956 (S616) and adds the condition that the land (at Bishopstoke in Hampshire) should revert to the Old Minster on Brithelm's death.

161 Hunt p322.

162 See Esawyer S567: Eadred's grant to Abbot Aethelwold of 100 hides in Oxfordshire and Berkshire.

163 Aelfric: *Vita Sancti Aethelwoldi*. Aelfric was pupil abbot to Aethelwold.

164 Aelfric: *Abingdon Chronicle* (Rolls Series) i 345.

165 *Abingdon Chronicle* i 347; ii 313.

166 *Vita Sancti Oswaldi* (Rolls Series) i 427, 446.

167 Ely was founded by King Anna's daughter, St Etheldreda, as a double monastery and refounded in 970; Medeshamstede dates from c655 and was refounded in 966 with the erection of a stone basilica; and Thorney started as a mid-seventh century hermitage and was refounded in 972. All three were destroyed by the Vikings in the late ninth century.

168 See Esawyer: Abingdon (15 charters); Glastonbury (4); Ely (3); Peterborough (2); Romsey (2); Thorney (2); and Chertsey (1). Aethelwold would also have taken an interest in the further endowment of Athelney (Muchelney); Bath; Crowland; Malmesbury; Pershore; Ramsey; Sherborne; Wilton and Worcester.

169 The charter is not identified by Esawyer. Rather we have to rely on local tradition fuelled by early fifteenth century hagiography. John Capgrave (1393–1464), born at Bishop's Lynn, Norfolk, considered in his *Abbreviacion of Cronicles* that Aethelwold was granted the land in c970 and used it for the reburial of saints' bones disinterred by the Danes at several religious houses in the vicinity. Capgrave is thought to have drawn on Thomas Walsingham's *St Alban's Chronicle*.

170 Not to be confused with the much later Hailes Abbey close to the Cotswolds' town. All trace of Winchcombe Abbey has been lost.

171 King Edward 'the Martyr' (975–978), famously murdered at Corfe in Dorset, allegedly by his rival's mother, the dowager Queen Aethelthryth.

172 Born c940. Archbishop of Reims from 991 and elected as Pope Sylvester in 999. He died in 1003.

173 *Music in the Middle Ages*: Gustave Reese (Dent 1941) p123, based on 'Cantor' Wulfstan. Reese considered the Old Minster organ to have been erected c950, but also puts Wulfstan's death at 963, which is far too early. One might imagine that Bishop Aelfheah the Bald would have had an incentive to develop music in Winchester – but not the necessary skills for doing so. Wulstan, in fact, could not have been born before 960 and was still alive at the end of the century when he completed his near contemporaneous life of Aethelwold.

174 *A History of the Pilgrims' School*: Crook (Phillimore 1981) pp1–3.

175 The compositions comprise plainchant melody (*organum*) with at least one additional voice. One singer performed a notated melody (*vox principalis*); another – singing by ear – produced a second melody (*vox organalis*), in effect a two-part harmony.

176 CD produced by Herald AV Publications label HAVPCD151.

St Aelfheah – Martyr

177 Ibid. F of W i 165–6.

178 Esawyer: S777 and 785. Neither charter was overly generous and for some years after the refoundation, the abbey's monks declined to accept a more rigid Benedictine discipline.

179 Aelfric's *Lives of the Saints*: Edit and trans. Walter W Skeat (reprinted in two vols 1966 based on late nineteenth scholarship).

180 *Anglo-Saxon England*: Stenton p374.
181 The death of Edward 'the Martyr' in 978 at Corfe Castle remains a mystery. His three-year reign after the death of his father, King Eadgar, was racked with internecine strife between his supporters and those of his younger (and confirmed legitimate) brother, Aethelred. This provided an opportunity for those who had lost land to the Church under Eadgar to claw back their former property from the monastic profession for which they often had contempt. There is some suggestion that the more rigid Bishop Aethelwold adhered to Aethelred; indeed, it was Dunstan, supported by St Oswald, who crowned Edward at Kingston in 975. Aethelwold, as diocesan and aware of the shadowy circumstances of Edward's conception, does not get a mention.
182 Esawyer: S942 and 944 of the year 990 granted ten hides at South Stoneham in the lower Itchen Valley.
183 Esawyer: S894 in 998 documents a major endowment of Westminster "Abbey".
184 After the battle, the new archbishop, Sigeric (990–994), pressed by defeated Saxon leaders, is thought to have urged the king to buy off the victors. The saga – *The Battle of Maldon* – was probably transcribed at Worcester Abbey from the oral accounts of eyewitnesses.
185 Archbishop of Canterbury (995–1005). He was the son of a Kentish earl but entered Abingdon Abbey as a monk. He became, successively, bishop of St Albans and Ramsbury. His family background seems to have given him an inkling of military necessities: his will left ships fitted out for the defence of the Kent and Dorset coasts.
186 Eadmer of Canterbury's *Lives of St Oda, St Dunstan and St Oswald*: edit and trans Muir and Turner (Oxford Medieval Texts – Oxford 2006) p xli.
187 *Anglo-Saxon England*: Stenton p384fn.
188 John 15:13.

The Bishops on the Eve of the Conquest

189 Emma, only daughter of Duke Richard I of Normandy (942–96), was born in about 985 and married Aethelred II in 1002 as his second wife. It is arguable that the Norman influence and presence in England stems from her arrival at the Anglo-Saxon court.

190 Robert, Abbot of Jumièges in Normandy, was appointed Bishop of London in 1044, two years after Edward 'the Confessor's' accession. Seven years later, he was elevated to Canterbury. As Emma's son, Edward encouraged the second wave of Norman immigrants.

191 Peterborough Abbey, formerly known as Medeshamstede, was first founded in the late seventh century under the Mercian ruler, Cenwulf. It was dedicated to St Peter.

192 Hugh Candidus: *Coenobii Burgensis Historia* – edit Joseph Sparke (Bowyer 1723) p31. Sparke (1683–1740) was a Peterborough antiquarian.

193 Aelfric (qv) was trained at Peterborough and the Old Minster under Bishop Aethelwold and wrote some forty biographical homilies during the last decade of the tenth century. He also wrote a Latin grammar; hence, his nickname.

194 Simony is the purchase of a benefice or other clerical office. It derives from Acts 8:18–24 which related how Simon the magician offered money for the power the disciples possessed from the laying on of hands. The allegation against Cenwulf is included in the ODNB entry.

195 The will was preserved in the archives of Christ Church, Canterbury and, at one time, at the Old Minster. In his biography of Edward the Confessor (University of California Press 1970), Frank Barlow considers that Athelstan died in 1012.

196 I am indebted to Robert Grimley, former Dean of Bristol, for pointing out that the first known public burning in England took place in 1022. Society had sunk very low.

197 *Life in Anglo-Saxon England*: R L Page p165.

198 *Dictionary of National Biography*.

199 Esawyer: S994 granted the bishop a hide in the Meon Valley and was one of only five identified charters issued during the reign.

200 There are two brief references in the *Anglo-Saxon Chronicle*, one of which confirms the date of Aelfwine's death. There is nothing about him in the *Vita Edwardi*.

201 *Edward the Confessor's return to England in 1041*: J L Maddicott (*EHR* Vol 119 (2004) No 482) pp650–666 quoting from the *Quadripartitus* written during Henry I's reign and first edited by F Liebermann in *Die Gesetze der Angelsachsen* (Halle 1903–16).

202 The nearest was Duduc, Bishop of Wells, with sixteen signatures.
203 Esawyer: S1001.
204 *Annales de Wintonia in Annales Monastici*: edit H R Luard (Rolls Series 1864–69) Vol ii p21.
205 Esawyer: S904 which granted land to the abbess.
206 Ridyard: p29.
207 On Pope John XIX's death in 1032, he was succeeded by an eleven-year-old boy, Theophylactua, whose father, Count Alberic III, bought the holy office for him. As Benedict IX, he was best known for his extravagance and licentiousness. One of the murkier periods of papal history.
208 Stigand would have watched with interest the arrival from the Continent of Leofric of Crediton, educated in the Low Countries and chaplain to Edward the Confessor during his exile. Leofric (probably born in Cornwall sometime before 1016) was preferred as Bishop of Cornwall and Crediton in 1047 and was then appointed the first Bishop of Exeter in 1050, thus uniting the Cornish and Devon Sees. There he concentrated on diocesan administration and took little or no part in national politics, despite the king's favour towards him. After the Conquest, he was left, exceptionally, in situ until his death in 1072. A total contrast to the ever political and highly placed Stigand.
209 Edward's brother-in-law through marriage with the Confessor's sister, Godgifu.
210 *The Last Anglo-Saxon King*: Ian W Walker p34.
211 In contrast, the Canterbury manuscript (text F) is definitive: "Bishop Stigand succeeded to the archbishopric of Canterbury".
212 His father, Earl Godwine, died suddenly on Easter Monday 1053.
213 This was the third church built on the site, first hallowed in the seventh century. The land had recently come into the king's gift, which Edward had then granted to Harold Godwinson. The latter rebuilt the existing edifice and had it re-dedicated out of thanks for an allegedly miraculous cure he had received as a child. Interestingly, the church was administered by a dean and twelve married priests, another example of the English Church following its own course and behind developments on the Continent. The Normans replaced the minster in 1090 and Henry II refounded it as an abbey in 1177 as part of his penance for the murder of Archbishop Thomas Becket.

214 Gerhard, count of Calw, Tollenstein and Hirschberg, born circa 1018. He was elected pope in 1055 and supported the papal campaign against clerical marriage and simony. He died in 1057.

215 Ealdred (died 11 September 1069) was a monk at Winchester until his appointment as Abbot of Tavistock Abbey in about 1027. It seems likely that he was consecrated (as a mitred abbot) to lead this most prominent Benedictine foundation in the West of England; he is described as *episcopus* in 1043, three years before he was made bishop of Worcester. His appointment was part of a deliberate policy to send southern prelates north to help preserve law and order. Apart from his involvement in bringing back Eadgar the Aetheling to England, he was the first English bishop to go on pilgrimage to Jerusalem (1058). After his elevation to York in 1060, he faced difficulties with the Roman Curia over accusations that he was seeking to hold on to Worcester. York was an impoverished See at the time and the additional revenues from Worcester would have been a telling argument, another possible factor in Stigand's retention of Winchester.

216 The Very Reverend Dr George William Kitchin (1827–1912), Dean of Winchester from 1883 to 1894 when he became Dean of Durham. Apart from his supervision of many refurbishments at Winchester Cathedral, he published in 1890 a volume on the city's history and its leading personalities over the ages.

217 Richard of Devizes was a late-twelfth century monk at Winchester and chronicler. He is thought to have written the *Annales de Wintonia* (see Henry Richards Luard's *Annales Monastici* Vol II – Rolls Series London 1864–9).

218 See *Book of Common Prayer*: Collect for fourth Sunday after Trinity.

INDEX

Winchester bishops are shown in bold. The suffix 'n' refers to an endnote.

A

Abbot's Worthy 68, 169n
Abingdon Abbey 13, 106–107, 120, 176n
Abingdon Chronicle 106–107, 113
Adelard of Ghent, biographer 121
Aelfflaed, wife of Edward the Elder 89
Aelfgifu, Queen, wife of Aethelred II 127, 129
Aelfgifu of Northampton, wife of Cnut 138
Aelfheah I (934–951) 97–99
   appearance 97
   contribution to monastic renewal 97–98, 175n
   instruction of Aethelwold 104–105
   death and commemoration 99
St Aelfheah (984–1005) 116–124
   early life 116–117
   as Abbot of Bath Abbey 117
   appointment to Winchester 117–118, 119
   relations with Aethelred II 119, 120, 121
   translation of Aethelwold's remains 113
   Viking diplomacy 120
   election to Canterbury 76, 121
   visit to Rome 121, 126
   capture and martyrdom 116, 122–123, 123–124
   resting place 122, 123, 130
   canonisation 123

Aelfmaer, Archdeacon of Canterbury 122
Aelfric, Archbishop of Canterbury 120, 121, 176n
Aelfric of Eynsham, chronicler xv, 104, 106, 109, 118, 126, 177n
Aelfsige, Abbot of Peterborough 128
Aelfsige I (951–958) 101–103
   origins and early career 101–102
   installation at Winchester 101
   land grants 101–102
   promotion to Canterbury 103
   death 100
Aelfsige II (c1014–1032) 127–131
   appointment to Winchester 127
   loyalties and influence 129, 130–131
   death 131
Aelfstan, Bishop of London 120–121
Aelfweard, son of Edward the Elder 93
Aelfwine (1032–1043) 131–135
   early career 131
   influence and power 131–133, 134
   relationship with Emma 75, 125, 133 135, 142
   remains 149
Aelfwynn, daughter of Aethelflaed 92–93
Aelgifu, Queen, wife of Eadwig 102–103
Aescwig, Bishop of Dorchester 120–121
Aescwine, West Saxon sub-king 36
Aethelbald, King of Mercia 55, 56, 167n
Aethelbald, King of Wessex 70, 71–72, 79, 169n
Aethelberht, King of Wessex 71, 72, 79, 169n

Aethelbert, Kentish sub-king 3, 7, 20

Aethelflaed, Queen of the Mercians 92

Aethelgar, Abbot of New Minster, later Archbishop of Canterbury 108

Aethelheard (c770–c778) 57

Aethelheard, Archbishop of Canterbury 57, 58, 167n

Aethelheard, King of Wessex 168n

Aethelmaer, Bishop of Elmham, brother of Stigand 136, 143, 149

Aethelnoth, Archbishop of Canterbury 130, 139–140

Aethelred, Archbishop of Canterbury 82

Aethelred, son of Eadgar 112

Aethelred I, King of Wessex 81, 112, 170n

Aethelred II (the Unready), King of Wessex 117, 118–121, 122, 127–129, 134, 141, 176n

Aethelstan, Kentish sub-king 169n

Aethelthryth, Abbess of Winchester 108

Aethelthryth, Queen, wife of Eadgar 110, 175n

Aethelweard, Wessex ealdorman 120

St Aethelwold (963–984) 104–115
- as chronicler 74–75, 95, 99
- education and ordination 97–98, 104–105
- friendship with Dunstan 105–106
- at Glastonbury Abbey 105–106
- at Abingdon Abbey 106–107, 120, 174n
- royal patronage and influence 106, 107, 108, 118, 131, 176n
- consecration as bishop 104, 107
- monastic reforms 107–109, 110–112
- management of church estate 109–110
- reconstruction of New Minster 112
- transfer of Berin's body 12
- promotion of Swithun and Edburga xiv–xv, 112, 135
- devotion to arts and sciences 113–114
- later years 112–113
- death and resting place 113
- lasting influence 115

Aethelwold, son of Aethelred I 91–92

Aethelwold II (c1006–c1014) 127

Aethelwulf, King of Wessex 61, 62–65, 65–66, 67, 70, 71–72, 74, 169n

St Agilbert 15–24
- origins 16
- time in Ireland 17
- arrival at West Saxon court 17–18
- as diplomat on behalf of Rome 19–20
- at Synod of Whitby 15, 16, 20, 20–22
- departure from Wessex 22–23
- time in Paris 23, 31, 32
- death and resting place 23–24
- recognition and achievements 24

Alberic III, Count of Tusculum 178n

Albinus, monk 3, 46

Aldhelm, Abbot of Malmesbury, later Bishop of Sherborne 33–34, 36, 40–41, 43, 45–46, 47, 165n

Alexander II, Pope 144, 146

Alfred, brother of Edward the Confessor 132

Alfred, son of Aethelred II 139

Alfred the Great, King of Wessex 71, 80, 81, 81–88, 171n

Alhfrith, Deiran sub-king 16, 19–20, 22–23

Allen, Gerald Burton, Bishop of Dorchester 13

Alphege (984–1005) *see* **St Aelfheah**

Alresford 63, 86–87, 172n

Angles 2, 7, 9

Anglo-Saxon Chronicle (ASC) xv, 12, 17, 29, 43, 53, 67, 73, 79, 84, 103, 117, 127, 128, 131, 135, 140, 143, 147, 159n, 160n, 161n, 167n, 170n, 177n

Anna, King of East Anglia 11

St Anselm, Archbishop of Canterbury 123

Ashingdon 138
Ashingdon, Battle of 129–130, 130
Asser, Bishop of Sherborne 72, 82–83, 84, 85, 92, 113–114, 170n, 171n
Asterius, Archbishop of Milan 3
Athelney Abbey 86, 171n
Athelstan, King of Wessex 93–94, 94, 95, 96, 98, 105, 162n
Athelstan, son of Aethelred II 127, 131, 177n
St Audoin, Bishop of Rouen 16, 17
St Augustine 3, 3–4, 6, 7

B

Baden-Powell, Robert 51
baptisms 8, 10, 16, 41, 83, 160n
Barlow, Frank 177n
Bath Abbey 117, 121, 175n
Bayeux Tapestry 136, 145, 146
Becket, Thomas, Archbishop of Canterbury 123, 178n
Beddington 87
Bede, *Ecclesiastical History of the English People* xv, 3, 6, 9, 17, 19, 20, 21, 22, 27, 28–30, 31, 37, 43, 46, 47, 159n, 161n, 162n, 163–164n, 164–165n, 165n
St Benedict 163n
Benedict VIII, Pope 131, 143
Benedict IX, Pope 178n
Benedict X, Pope 144
Benedictine *Concordia Regularis* 110
Benedictine Rule 106, 109, 110, 117
Beorhthelm (960–c963) 104, 174n
Beorhtric, King of Wessex 59
Beornstan (931–934) 93–96
    consecration as bishop 93
    piety 94–95
    death 94–95
    charitable bequest 95
    commemoration 95
Beornwulf, possible King of Mercia 59
St Berin (Birinus) 1–14

    journey from Rome 1–2, 5, 6, 159n
    evangelising mission 2, 5, 159n, 160n
    as counsellor and diplomat 7, 8
    base in Dorchester 8–10
    dedication of Old Minster 11
    death and final resting place 12–13
    achievements and legacy 9–11, 13–14
Berinsfield 9
Berry, Mary 114
Bishop's Waltham 91
St Boniface 47–49, 50, 51, 53–54, 56, 60, 165n
Britwald, Archbishop of Canterbury 42, 45, 164n
Bruyères-le-Châtel, Abbey of 23
Bryhtwhine, Bishop of London 130
Bugga (Edburga of Minster-in-Thanet) 49
Burchard, Bishop of Wurzburg 54
Burgred, King of Mercia 81, 82
Bury St Edmunds Abbey 81, 144
Byrhthelm, Archbishop of Canterbury 103–104

C

Caedwalla, West Saxon sub-king 38, 41
Canterbury 46, 122
Canterbury, Christ Church 111, 121, 123, 144
Canterbury See xvi, 31, 45, 58, 109
Capgrave, John, chronicler 175n
Carpenter, Edward 167n
Carpenter, Harry, Bishop of Oxford 13
St Cecilia 39, 164n
Cedd, Bishop to the East Saxons 20
celibacy 69, 131
Centwine, Saxon sub-king 36, 37, 38
Cenwealh, West Saxon sub-king 10–12, 18, 19, 22, 25, 26, 28, 31, 32, 36
Cenwulf (1006) 126, 177n
Ceolnoth, Archbishop of Canterbury 61, 65, 70, 82

Ceolwulf, King of Mercia 59
Cerdic, King of Wessex 7–8
St Chad 28, 162n
Chalcedon, Council of 160n
Champart, Robert *see* Robert of Jumièges
Charlemagne, King of the Franks 59
Charles Martel, Mayor of Paris 48
Charles the Bald, King of West Francia 71, 169n
Chelsea, Synod of 103
Chertsey Abbey 22
Chilcomb 70, 172n
choral singing 113–114
Clofesho, Council of 56, 58
Clotaire I, King of Merovingia 32
Cnut, King of England 12, 116, 123, 128, 129–131, 137, 138–139, 145
Coenwulf, King of Mercia 57–58, 58, 59
Cointrid, son of Ine 33
Colmán, Bishop of Lindisfarne 16, 20–21, 21
St Columbanus 16, 18–19, 39, 163n
Communion 42
Confirmation 42
Conrad II, Holy Roman Emperor 139
Crediton 60, 168n
Crook, John 113
Crowland Abbey 44, 57, 167n
St Cuthbert of Canterbury 56, 167n
St Cuthbert of Lindisfarne 21–22, 89, 162n
Cuthred, Kentish sub-king 58–59
Cuthred, King of Wessex 56–57
Cutred, son of Cynegils 10
Cwichelm, son of Cynegils 10
Cynebert (c785–c802) 58
Cyneburga, daughter of Cynegils 8
Cynegils, Saxon sub-king 2, 6, 7, 8, 9, 10, 159n, 160n
Cyneheard (c754–c770) 57, 167n
Cynewulf, kinsman of Ine 50

D
Dagobert I, ruler of Neustria 4–5, 16
Danegeld 119–120, 127, 128, 136
Danes *see* Vikings
Daniel (705–745) 45–52
  origins 46
  asceticism 46
  friendship and partnership with Aldhelm 45–46, 47
  administrative, pastoral and scholarly abilities 46–47, 51–52
  pastoral care of Selsey 164–165n
  role in legend of Haeddi 43
  mentorship of St Boniface 47–49, 50
  counsel to King Ine 49–50
  visit to Pope Gregory II 50
  physical suffering 50–51
St David of Wales 46, 51
Deanesly, Margaret 165n
Deerhurst 116, 130, 137
St Deicola 39, 164n
Dempsey, G T 163n
Denewulf (c878–908) 84–87
  origins and education 84–85
  appointment to Winchester 84, 85–86
  land grants 86–87, 91
Deusdedit, Archbishop of Canterbury 19, 20, 27, 28, 162n
Dissolution of the Monasteries 76
Dorchester Abbey 8, 12–13
Dorchester-on-Thames 7–9, 12–13, 19, 22, 34, 36
Dudd (c780–785) 57
Duncan, Isadora 166n
Dunstan, Abbot of Glastonbury, later Archbishop of Canterbury 97–98, 98, 102, 104, 110, 111, 111–112, 112, 113, 114, 117, 117–118, 121, 173n, 176n
Dunwich See 31
Durham, Bishops of 156

E

Eadgar, King of Wessex 103, 104, 107, 108, 109, 110, 117, 119, 131

Eadgar II (the Atheling), uncrowned King of England 145, 146, 147, 148

Eadgifu, Queen, wife of Edward the Elder 106

Eadgyth, daughter of Eadgar of Wessex 111

Eadhun (838–839) 61–62

Eadmer, chronicler 143–144

Eadmund (836–837) 61–62

Eadmund, King of Wessex 101, 173n

Eadred, King of Wessex 101, 102, 106

Eadric, Mercian ealdorman 129

Eadsige, Archbishop of Canterbury 133, 140, 141

Eadsige of Winchcombe, clerk 75

Eadwig, King of Wessex 102–104, 106, 108

Eahlmund (c802–811) 58, 63

Ealdred, Bishop of Worcester, later Archbishop of York 144, 145, 146, 147, 148, 179n

Ealdwulf, Archbishop of York 126

Ealfrith (c862–c871) 79–80, 81, 170n

Ealhswith, Queen, wife of Alfred the Great 87, 89, 108, 172n

Ealstan, Bishop of Sherborne 64–65, 65–66, 70, 72

Eanfled, Queen, wife of Oswiu 20

Earconwold, Bishop of London 22, 29, 41, 162n

East Meon 149

Easter, dating of 17, 19, 20

St Ebregisel 23

Ebroin, mayor of Francian palace 23

Ecgbert, King of Wessex 59–61, 62, 62–64, 69

Edburga of Minster-in-Thanet *see* Bugga

St Edburga of Winchester 135

Edgar, King of Wessex 75

Edith, Queen, wife of Edward the Confessor 134–135, 141, 147, 149

Edmund, King of England 81, 101–102

Edmund Ironside, King of Wessex 116, 129–130, 137

Edred, King of England 44

Edward III, King of England 134

Edward the Atheling, son of Edmund Ironside 145

Edward the Confessor, King of England 125, 128, 132–133, 134, 140, 141–143, 144–146, 153, 177n

Edward the Elder, King of Wessex 85, 87, 91, 91–93, 93, 95, 96

Edward the Martyr, King of Wessex 111–112, 118, 175n, 176n

Edwin, Earl of Mercia 147, 148

Edwin, King of Northumbria 7, 20

Egbald (778–780) 57, 167n

Electronic Sawyer 163n

Ellendun, Battle of 59–60, 66

Ely 137, 148

Ely Abbey 108, 110–111, 143, 144, 174n

Emma, Queen of England 75–76, 125, 128, 133, 133–135, 138, 139, 140, 141, 142, 149, 176n

Eric Bloodaxe, former King of Norway 101, 102

Ermenfrid, Bishop of Sion 149

Ethelred, King of Mercia 37, 42–43

Ethendun, Battle of 83

Eustace II, Count of Boulogne 142, 178n

Evreux Cathedral 76

F

Faris, *Life of St Aldhelm* 47

Farnham 63, 70

Felix, Bishop 6–7

feudal system 154–155

Fleury Abbey 97, 106

Florence of Worcester, chronicler 43, 51, 74, 117, 127, 164n, 170n

Fontmell Magna 33
Forthere, Bishop of Sherborne 168n
Fox, Richard (1501–1529) 29, 43, 162n
Frisia, missionary work in 48–49, 53–54
Frithstan (909–931) 89–94
   education 89–90
   as mainstay to King Edward 91, 93
   scholarship 94
   burial 94, 173n
   commemoration 94
   vestments 89, 94, 162n

G
St Gallus 39
Gelasius, Pope 164n
Gerbert of Aurillac, mathematician 113
Germania, missionary work in 48–49, 53–54, 56, 57
Gewisse, Anglo-Saxon tribe 6, 7, 8, 34, 160n
Gildas, chronicler 40
Glastonbury Abbey 39–40, 105–106, 117
Godgifu, sister of Edward the Confessor 178n
Godwine, Earl of Wessex 132, 133, 134, 139, 141–142, 178n
Godwines of Sussex 138, 139, 141, 142
Goscelin of Saint-Bertin, biographer 13, 79, 169n, 170n
Gregory I (the Great), Pope 3, 6, 99, 173n
Gregory II, Pope 50, 166n
Gregory VII, Pope 123
Grimbald, Benedictine scholar 90, 94
Grimkettel, Bishop of Elmham, later Selsey 140
Grimley, Robert 177n
Guthrum, Viking leader 82, 83

H
St Haeddi (Hedda) (676–c705) 36–44
   origins 36–37
   monastic training 37
   installation at Winchester 37–38
   Latin epigram 39
   transfer of Berin's body 12
   consolidation in the west 39–41
   administrative ability 38, 40
   influence on secular law 41–42, 131
   opposition to division of diocese 42–43
   death and burial 43
   miracles and canonisation 43–44
   legacy 44
Haemgills, Abbot of Glastonbury 40
Harald III (Hardrada), King of Norway 146
Harmeling, Deborah 166n
Harold I (Harefoot), King of England 138, 139–140
Harold II (Godwinson), King of England 144, 145–147, 178n
Harthacnut, King of England 132, 139, 140
Hastings, Battle of 147
Hatfield Chase, Battle of 7
Headbourne Worthy 70
Heahmund, Bishop of Sherborne 170n
Helmstan (c839–c852) 61, 64–66, 69, 70
Henry de Blois (1129–1174) 12
Henry II, King of England 178n
Henry III, German Emperor 145
Henry IV, German Emperor 145
Herefrith, suffragan bishop 60, 61
Hereward the Wake 148
Hersfeld Abbey 54
Hertford, Synod of 31, 56
Higebert, Archbishop of Lichfield 55
Highclere 173n
St Hilda of Whitby 21, 37
Hitler, Adolph 152–153, 154
Honorius I, Pope 3, 4, 5, 14, 159n, 160n
Honorius II, antipope 146

Honorius III, Pope 12
Hugh Candidus, chronicler 126
Hunfrith (745–754) 55–56
Hunt, William 99, 167-168n, 173n

I

Importunus, Bishop of Paris 23
Ine, King of Wessex 34, 41–42, 49–50, 131
Ine, Laws of 41–42
Ingulphus, Abbot of Croyland 167n
Ireland 17, 19
Isle of Wight 1, 38, 45, 62, 62–63, 168n
Isomere Diploma 55, 167n
Itchen, River 7–8, 64, 96
   bridges over 67, 68, 73, 169n

J

Jaenbert, Archbishop of Canterbury 55
Jerusalem, pilgrimage to 179n
John XV, Pope 121
John XVIII, Pope 121
John XIX, Pope 139
John of Worcester, chronicler 146, 164n
Jouarre Abbey 16, 23
Judith, Queen, wife of Aethelwulf 71, 72
Jutes 1, 20, 38, 45

K

King's Worthy 96, 152
Kingston 93
Kingston Council 61–62, 72, 168n
Kirby, D P 159n
Kitchin, George W, Dean of Winchester 148, 149, 168n, 179n

L

Lanfranc, Archbishop of Canterbury 123, 150
Langton, Stephen, Archbishop of Canterbury 12
Leland, John, antiquarian 39, 164n

Leo III, Pope 58
Leofric, Bishop of Cornwall and Crediton, later Exeter 178n
Leofric, Earl of Mercia 142
Leofsige, Abbott of Ely 136
Lichfield See 31, 55, 57–58
Lindisfarne Gospels 161n
Lioba, Abbess of Tauberbischofsheim 54–55
London See 4, 28–29, 31, 38, 42–43, 58, 65
Lothair (670–676) 31–35
   early life 31–32
   installation at Winchester 31, 32–33
   at Synod of Hertford 31
   founding of West Country abbeys 33–34
   expansion of diocese 35
Lull of Malmesbury, Bishop of Mainz 54, 57

M

Maddicott, J L 132–133
Maeldulph, Irish monk 33, 40–41, 45–46
Magna Carta 131
Magnus (the Good), King of Norway 134, 140
Malcolm II, King of Scotland 139
Maldon, Battle of 120, 176n
Malmesbury 66
Malmesbury Abbey 33–34, 40–41, 46, 57, 86, 163n, 164n, 165n
mancuses 87
maniple 89, 172n
Maserfelth, Battle of 18
Medeshamstede Abbey 108, 112, 126, 174n, 177n
Mercians 4, 6–7, 18, 22, 27–28, 36, 42–43, 55–58, 58–60, 92, 103
missionary work overseas 48–49, 53–54, 56, 57, 156
Montacute 82–83

Morcar, Earl of Northumbria 147, 148
Morcar, thegn of northern Danelaw 128–129, 140

N
New Forest 10
New Minster, Winchester *see under* Winchester
New Model Army 13, 29
Nicholas II, Pope 144
Normanisation of England 141–142, 147–149
Northumbrians 7, 18, 80, 81, 103
Norwich 136
Nursling Abbey 46, 48, 165n

O
Oakley 67–68
Oakley, Charles 166n
Oda, Archbishop of Canterbury 97, 101, 103, 104, 107–108
St Odo, Abbot of Cluny 97, 173n
Offa, King of Mercia 57, 59, 117, 167n
Olaf Tryggvason 120
Old Minster, Winchester *see under* Winchester
Old Sarum Calendar 13
Orleton, Adam (1333–1345) 134
Osbern, biographer 123
Osbert of Clare, biographer 135, 172n
Osburg, wife of Aethelwulf 71
Osgar, clerk, later Abbot of Abingdon 106, 108, 110
St Oswald, Bishop of St Albans 99
St Oswald, Bishop of Worcester, later Archbishop of York 111, 176n
Oswald, headmaster of Winchester School 107–108
Oswald, King of Northumbria 7, 9, 128, 159n
Oswiu, King of Northumbria 16, 18, 20, 20–21

P
Paul the Deacon, chronicler 166n
Paulinus, Bishop of York 7, 16
Peada, Mercian sub-king 28
Pecthelm, monk, later Bishop of Whithorn 43, 163–164n
Pelagianism 14, 160n
Penda, Mercian sub-king 7, 9, 10, 18, 28
Peterborough 126
Peterborough Abbey (Medeshamstede) 108, 112, 126, 174n, 177n
Peter's Pence 85, 171n
pilgrimage 179n
Plegmund, Archbishop of Canterbury 85, 90, 92
pluralism 143
Portchester 26, 91, 172n
primogeniture 61, 72
public burning 177n

R
Rathbod, King of the Frisians 48, 49
Reese, Gustave 175n
Remigius, Bishop of Dorchester 147, 148
Richard I, Duke of Normandy 121
Richard II, Duke of Normandy 128, 141
Richard of Devizes, chronicler 134, 149–150, 179n
Robert of Jumièges (Robert Champart), Archbishop of Canterbury 125, 141–142, 142, 143, 144, 177n
Rochester See 31
Roger Bigod of Norfolk 148
Rouen 16, 17

S
St John's Almshouses, Winchester 95–96
St Médard, Abbey of 32
Schola Gregoriana 114
Seaxburh, Saxon sub-queen 36
secular clergy 107–108, 111, 121, 126
Selsey See 45, 164–165n

Sergius I, Eastern Patriarch 4
Shaw, Martin Fallas 166n
Sherborne 80
Sherborne See 45, 72, 90, 92
Siferth, thegn of northern Danelaw 128–129
Siferth, wife of Edmund Ironside 145
Sigeric, Archbishop of Canterbury 120–121, 176n
simony 30, 103, 126, 143, 177n
Siward, Earl of Northumbria 142
slave ownership 103
Southampton (Hamtun) 1–2
Southwark Palace 155
St Denys (Hampshire) 118
St Paul's (London) 118, 122
Stavanger Cathedral 76
Stenton, Sir Frank 10, 60, 65, 168n
Stigand (1047–1070) 135–151
 early life 136
 character 135–136, 140, 143, 149–150, 150
 recruitment by Cnut 137
 diplomatic skills 137, 139, 142
 early clerical appointments 137, 138
 possible trips to Scotland 139, 148
 transfers of allegiances 139–140
 appointment to Elmham 140
 appointment to Winchester 140–141
 as king's chancellor 140, 146, 146–147
 promotion to Canterbury xvi, 142–144
 relationship with Rome 144
 search for successor to Edward the Confessor 145–146
 survival post-Conquest 147–149, 150
 death and burial 149
Sudbourne Manor (Suffolk) 110–111
Swein Forkbeard, King of Denmark 120, 127–128, 136
St Swithun (852–c861) 67–77
 origins 68–69

education and training 69
counsellor to Ecgbert 69–71, 71
consecration as bishop 70
stature and reputation 68, 72–74
legends and miracles xiv–xv, 67, 74–76, 79, 125, 135
death and remains 74–75, 76, 112, 121
commemorations 76–77
Synod of Chelsea 103
Synod of Hertford 31, 56
Synod of Whitby 15–16, 20, 20–22, 37

T
Taunton 71, 86, 91, 172n
Tempsford, Battle of 92
Theodechild, Abbess of St Jouarre-sur-Seine 16, 23
Theodore of Tarsus, Archbishop of Canterbury 23, 31, 32, 38, 42, 163n
Thietmar of Merseburg, chronicler 123
Thorney Abbey 108, 174n
Thrum (Viking) 116, 122
Thurkill (Viking) 122
Tichborne 91
tithes 41–42, 74
Tostig, Earl of Northumbria 146
Tunbeorht (872–878) 79–80, 82–84, 171n

V
Venta see Winchester
Victor II, Pope 145, 179n
Vikings 44, 60–61, 67–68, 69, 72–73, 78–79, 80–83, 92–93, 101, 116, 119–121, 122–123, 127, 129–131, 136, 165n, 173n, 174n
St Vitalian 23

W
Waldhere, Bishop of London 42–43
Walkelin (1070–1107) 76

Waltham Abbey Church 144, 178n
Wantage 80
Warnford church 20
Wessex, derivation of name 25
Westminster Abbey 109, 118, 153
Wherwell Priory 134–135
Whitby, St Hilda's Abbey 15, 37
Whitby, Synod of 15–16, 20, 20–22, 37
St Wigbert, Abbot of Ohrdruf 54
Wighbert, Bishop of Sherborne 167–168n
Wigthegn (811–825) 58, 60, 61, 63, 167–168n
Wilfrid, Abbot of Ripon, later Bishop of York 16, 20, 21–22, 22, 22–23, 28
William of Malmesbury, chronicler 33–34, 37, 40, 70, 74, 75, 149, 163n, 164n
William of Poitiers, scribe 144, 145, 146
William the Conqueror 143, 144, 145, 146–149, 150–151, 153, 154
Willibald, Bishop of Eichstaett 54
Wimborne 54, 80
Winchcombe Abbey 111, 175n
Winchester
  derivation of name 26
  as episcopal seat 34, 36
  growth as settlement 12, 25–26
  Hitler's plans for 152–153
  in mid tenth century 95–97
  Viking raid in 860 78–79
Winchester, Hyde Abbey 96
Winchester, New Minster
  as centre of legal drafting 131–132
  estates and endowments *see under* Winchester See
  founding and construction 85, 112
  secular clergy 107–108, 126
  shrine to Berin 12
  Swithun's grave 75–76
Winchester, Nunnaminster (St Mary's Abbey) 89, 108, 135, 172n
Winchester, Old Minster
  building of 11–12, 160n
  destruction in 860 78–79
  estates and endowments *see under* Winchester See
  gift from Stigand 150
  music 113–114, 121, 175n
  as religious community 32–33, 55, 165n, 166-167n
  scholastic activity 47, 53–54, 57, 73, 78, 85, 89–90, 90–91, 96–97, 107–108, 113–114, 114, 115
Winchester Annals 134, 149–150
Winchester Calendar 13
Winchester Cathedral
  Cartulary xv, 103
  coronation of Edward the Confessor 133
  mortuary chests 29, 43, 149, 162n
  St Swithun's shrine 76
Winchester See
  estates and endowments 32, 55, 57, 63, 70–71, 86, 87, 90, 91, 98, 109, 118, 133, 154, 172n, 173-174n
  expansion to east 38, 42–43
  expansion to west 34–35, 39–40, 60, 163n
  extent post-Conquest 154–155
  importance of xiii–xv, xvi, 31, 131–132, 153–154
  jurisdiction over Isle of Wight 38, 45, 62, 62–63, 168n
  mercantile role post-Conquest 155–156
  overseas missions 156
  reduction in size by Britwald 42–43, 45
  reorganisation by Plegmund 90–91, 92
  role of post-Conquest bishops 155–156
  royal chancellery and treasury xvi, 132, 140, 147, 153

in seventh century 14
Winchester Troper 114, 175n
Wine (c660–666) 27–30
    installation at Winchester 27–28
    consecration of Chad 28, 162n
    move to London 28–29, 30
    death and interment 29–30
Wing, All Saints' Church 9–10
Winnebald, Abbot of Heidenheim 54
Wintancaster *see* Winchester
Witney Manor (Oxfordshire) 133
Wolsey, Thomas 110
Wolvesey Castle, Winchester (medieval bishop's palace) 62, 168n
Wulfhere, Mercian sub-king 18, 22, 26, 27, 28, 30
Wulfred, Archbishop of Canterbury 58, 61, 167–168n
St Wulfsige, Bishop of Sherborne 118, 121
Wulfstan, Archbishop of York 101, 122
Wulfstan, Bishop of Worcester 144, 146, 150
Wulfstan, Precentor at New Minster 104, 114, 175n
Wulfstan, thegn to King Eadgar 108
Wulftrud, nun at Wilton Abbey, later Abbess 111

Y
York See 31, 179n
Yorke, Barbara 68, 86, 160n

Z
St Zachary, Pope 56

For writing and publishing news, or recommendations of new titles to read, sign up to the Book Guild newsletter: